friends of mine

PUNK IN MANCHESTER 1976-78

Martin Ryan

EMPIRE
PUBLICATIONS

First published in 2018

EMPIRE PUBLICATIONS
1 Newton Street, Manchester M1 1HW
© Martin Ryan 2018

ISBN: 978-1-909360-60-0
Cover image by Kevin Cummins

contents

about the author

MARTIN RYAN was born in 1955 in Stockport where he still lives with his wife Kate. They have 3 grown up children. In 1976 as a 20 year-old rock music fan he regularly checked out local bands on the Manchester pub rock circuit.

1977 would prove a defining year as he began the short-lived Manchester punk fanzine *Ghast Up* alongside fellow punk convert Mick Middles – thus beginning an involvement with the fabled Manchester scene that revolved around several bands and local luminaries such as Paul Morley and Kevin Cummins who frequented the mythical Sunday nights at the Electric Circus.

Martin has written for the *NME* as well as contributing to several Mancunian publications, including the legendary *City Fun* fanzine that ran from 1978 through to the mid-eighties.

He has been called on to provide his knowledge of the Manchester music scene to authors, film researchers and university students.

foreword

I AM NOT ONE TO NAME-DROP – ask Genesis P-Orridge – but in the spring of 2011 I found myself sitting in the semi-rural Belgian home of the late Annik Honore, flicking through a lavish German tome dedicated to the lost upsurge of 'punk art'. As I sipped the Raspberry beer that Annik served me, in the misguided belief that we British adore it, my heart almost stopped as I came across a beautifully reproduced plate featuring Martin Ryan's cover of *Ghast Up 3*, the lowly fanzine that Martin and I had produced in 1977. My mind tripped back to the genesis of that cover – a 'Polaroid' – I think– photograph of Ashton-under-Lyne's deadening precinct; a hollow place, patrolled by latter-day skinheads on the look-out for punkish prey. It was Martin's aesthetic awareness plus some random effects produced by our lo-tech printing machine that teased a punkish glisten from the stark image. And why not see it celebrated in some elevated Euro-tome, three and a half decades later?

Martin and I met as twelve-year-olds aloof in the kind of school featured in Morrissey's 'Headmaster Ritual'. He seemed artistic, bookish and quiet. I gravitated towards that. These were not attributes generally celebrated in those fevered playgrounds. The school was 'secondary' - a massive psychological slam down, designed to suppress talent or creative thought. We sat in our darkened vortex, discussing the *NME*, United, City and Stockport County and, a little later, *Sounds* magazine. These were our only avenues of escape.

Punk happened weirdly for us. In 1976 I was estranged, lost in a beautiful village – Silverdale – while Martin, closer to the action, lived and worked in Stockport. When I returned to Mancunia in December '76, the local scene had shifted a little, rather than exploding with the cultural violence that repeatedly fuels the Manchester myth.

Manchester punk had certainly been triggered. The bullet

could never return to the barrel, but it still appeared to be tentatively dressed in flares. A jagged little gathering, holed up in the Ranch Bar or Band on the Wall... or the Phoenix on Oxford Road. This is the point, really. For many months, this new Mancunian activity dragged a foot in the pre-punk alleyways. Hairy hoary places where the curious would stride that divide between rock and a hard place. The crumbling venues of pre-punk – the Electric Circus, the Mayflower – edgy before edgy became the point. This is where Martin's extraordinary book begins. While so much has been written about this Mancunian era, little resonates with such an honest 'path-into-punk' with the author admitting to missing out on key moments, while slowly aligning himself with this Zeitgeist bubble. Think of this book as, to steal a phrase, 'a necessary corrective' – a rise from the dourest estuaries of the North. And never before has Manchester punk been explored with such piercing accuracy.

Martin remembers. Most of us see a fug.

Never forget that, from the dingy and disagreeable, the fantastical habitually looms. It loomed for Mancunians, thrillingly, in '76 and '77. Arguably the greatest era of one of the greatest musical cities on Earth.

Despite Tony Wilson's claims to the contrary, it isn't always better to go with the myth. A real Manchester exists right here.

Read it and watch it unfold. Punk at the heart but with greying edges drifting into pub rock, wayward metal and survivors of mid-seventies flotsam and jetsam. The devil resides happily in these vivid details. I read it twice on the bounce and constantly found myself hurtled back to memories that had long since languished in a thick gluey mist.

For myself, there is a bearable downside. I am only a bit player in these jerky tales. Nevertheless, I seem to gently haunt these pages as an ungainly illiterate lost to juvenile idiocy. The reproduction of the pages of *Ghast Up* duly enforce this. But, embarrassing as this is - the poem, the poem - it needs to remain untouched. For that is how it was and how it should always be. Thankfully, there are weightier and more meaningful hauntings. You will meet them soon.

One more thing. More often than not, it is forgotten, but the punk era was powered by lost aspects of genuine possibility. The music press – *NME, Melody Maker, Sounds* and *Record Mirror* – could parade relatively obscure bands before gargantuan circulations. In the shadows hovered record companies armed with chunks of money that now appear absurd. Even in the uncommercial undertone, in the fabulous area of growing awareness, musical prowess and aesthetic innovation later known as 'post-punk', lasting careers could be forged. Ambition was the heartbeat of punk. Oh that and a truly volatile arena of street-level politics.

I was hugely fortunate to stumble into and share such times with Martin. I feel enlivened here, now, to re-engage with these memories through the hugely evocative visions of 'Friends of Mine'. Never did a 'corrective' seem so necessary.

Mick Middles

1976

then one day...

Friday 4th June 1976

APPARENTLY ANY ACCOUNT of this period in the history of Manchester music has to begin on this date at the event that took place. An event that, courtesy of those in attendance, is said to have altered the city's musical landscape for good thereafter and has even been credited by some sources with altering the city of Manchester itself from a dilapidated state of post-industrial Dickensian squalor to a bustling metropolis complete with a Metrolink System, two world class Universities and the splendid Beetham Tower.

Of all places it was the Lesser Free Trade Hall on Peter Street that provided the venue. This was the smaller upstairs theatre within the main Free Trade Hall, home to Manchester's famous Hallé Orchestra but, equally important, the city's main music venue.

The Free Trade Hall had been built over one hundred years previously to commemorate the repeal of the Corn Laws in 1846 on the site of St Peter's Fields where the Peterloo Massacre occurred. The hall suffered extensive damage in the Manchester Blitz of 1940 and a new hall was constructed behind the original front walls, opening as a concert hall in 1951 and even being designated a Grade II listed building in 1963. Although its relevance to live music would start to wane in the coming years, the hall retained the title of Manchester's premier concert venue until the Bridgewater Hall opened in 1996 taking the Hallé Orchestra with it.

A few bands had begun to expand their set to fill the more cavernous confines of the Kings Hall situated in the Belle Vue Amusement Park to the east of the city on Hyde Road, Gorton. Such was the attraction of this park that boasted a zoo and a fairground as well as the Kings Hall and Elizabethan Ballroom, that the immediate area containing the park became known as

Belle Vue with the local railway station on the Manchester to Sheffield line also bearing the name.

Other musical acts opted for the more theatrical ambience of the Palace Theatre on Oxford Road. I would witness a chemically inspired Sci-Fi show at the Palace towards the end of the long hot summer of 1976 as Hawkwind – following the dismissal of Ian Kilmister (who was in the throes of re-emerging with the soon to be legendary Motörhead) brought their "Astounding Sounds Amazing Music Tour" to the theatre.

The Who, serious contenders for the accolade of 'greatest live band', had also trodden the boards at The Palace in 1971 on the tour that followed the release of "Who's Next". When they returned in 1973 they upped the ante playing Quadrophenia, complete with taped seagulls and crashing wave sound effects, on two separate nights to a Kings Hall packed to its 5000 capacity with Ian Dury's Kilburn and the High Roads in support.

The Hardrock in Stretford also made a short but spirited challenge to the home of the Hallé, hosting glam contenders Roxy Music, Slade, Bowie and Steve Harley's Cockney Rebel in the first half of the seventies as well as providing the stage for Chuck Berry to deliver a late and very truncated set following his return to the UK charts with the novelty hit, "My Ding-A-Ling". And, lest we forget, rock superstars Led Zeppelin would grace the future B&Q store years before they opted to play for the masses at Earls Court.

But in those days it was invariably Manchester's Free Trade Hall where you would discover the life-altering joys of live music. Dylan appeared twice in the sixties. First on 7th May 1965 as part of a UK tour by the acoustic folk singing Dylan featured in the cinéma vérité documentary "Don't Look Back", then again on 17th May 1966 when an electrified Dylan and band returned for the second set prompting an audience backlash that culminated in the noted "Judas" heckle, now credited to one John Cordwell.

John Fogerty had delivered his Creedence Clearwater Revival trio minus his older brother in 1971 and Bowie introduced his androgynous persona to the young Mancunians in the same venue, a few years after his glam forerunner, Marc

Bolan had offered his by then commercial T-Rex for a bargain 60p a ticket.

On the Friday night in question two bands would play the Free Trade Hall's lesser venue. The first, a thinking man's "prog rock" outfit from nearby Bolton who had chosen the name Solstice, possibly to reflect their musical leanings and perchance as a nod to one day playing the Glastonbury Festival (even then a major event on the musical calendar before Robbie or Kylie were given space).

According to the most common version of the story, the call to Solstice came because the two students from Bolton Institute of Technology who had arranged this critical event had done so with the intention of forming a band to play support but had been unable to rehearse sufficiently. Or more specifically they had come together in embryonic form at their college in Bolton on 1st April and played a couple of numbers before the organisers pulled the plug.

Solstice, on the other hand, were already plying their trade at various pubs and small venues and were proficient enough to deliver a lengthy interpretation of Mountain's "Nantucket Sleighride", a memorable contribution to what would become a legendary evening. There is a further suggestion that Solstice got the gig thanks to providing their own lighting and PA system for use on the night.

Had I been aware of Solstice's support appearance I may have been persuaded to be there. Their fledgling career had earned them a local reputation as one of the better live bands playing on what listings magazine *New Manchester Review* called the "Pub Rock" circuit.

However the honest if slightly pretentious Solstice were not the main reason people were in town that night. I was also not conveniently in the city centre to witness the Fagin-like figure of Malcolm McClaren reportedly diving in and out of neighbouring drinking dens, in either a tartan suit or dressed head to toe in black leather (depending on which recounting of events you prefer) proffering tickets to see his band who were the headliners. In short I was *not* there when the Sex Pistols first played the Lesser Free Trade Hall.

Bolton Institute of Technology, now the University of Bolton, was actually said to be the original choice of venue for that night's show but the notoriety that the Sex Pistols had already engendered forced a rethink, with the educational establishment being unwilling to accommodate them. A decision that, no doubt, altered history with the gig now gaining a city centre location.

As for those who made it... the numbers involved have been quoted as anywhere between a few dozen and many hundreds. According to the archives, 28 tickets were sold at a cost of 50p. The size of the venue would have precluded numbers from exceeding 425 according to the stated venue capacity.

One factor that must surely confirm a paltry attendance has to be the support act. For the first 20 years following the date in question, the accolade was repeatedly given to The Mandalaband, some of whose membership resurfaced as "one of the finest conventional bands to emerge" – an accolade Tony Wilson would later ascribe to Manchester's Sad Café.

Solstice were not spoken of for twenty years following the event. This may in part be a reflection of their modest wish to maintain a dignified silence but it does question the statistical probability that the facts could have remained concealed had there been as many witnesses to the event as was later claimed, particularly given the bands complete lack of affinity with the Sex Pistols. It was not until Jon the Postman mentioned the Bolton outfit and their twenty minute reading of "Nantucket Sleighride" as the forgotten support at a 1996 reunion at the same venue arranged for television (complete with twentieth birthday cake) that the picture was complete.

Whatever people's memory of the occasion, at least part of the Sex Pistols set was captured for posterity on a bootleg release "The Good Time Music of the Sex Pistols" that would appear in the Manchester area the following year. The generally poor quality recording offered a gratingly discordant vocal from Johnny Rotten, most noticeable when tackling The Who's "Substitute" or their own "Pretty Vacant", the bootleg's availability to purchase outside venues coincided with the following year's single release.

In fact the recording contained a high ratio of covers; besides "Substitute" and The Small Faces' "Watcha Gonna Do About It", with the lyrics crassly altered to, "I want you to know that I hate you baby", the choices of Dave Berry's "Don't Gimme No Lip Child", The Monkees' "Stepping Stone" and The Stooges "No Fun" were evidently felt obscure and unique enough to allow Rotten to sneeringly dismiss cover specialists Eddie and the Hot Rods as "our imitators".

Salford-born broadcaster Tony Wilson, who swore he was there at the first Lesser Free Trade Hall, recounted the boiler suit clad Pistols' guitarist Steve Jones' penchant for mimicking The Who's Pete Townshend, twirling his arm windmill style. Wilson apparently raised the concern with Malcolm McLaren who pre-empted the observation with an instant "I know" response.

Whatever the numbers involved, in what Morrissey would describe as a "front parlour affair", one near certainty is that few of the audience resembled what would come to be termed punks. The fashion, like the accompanying pogo dance purportedly invented by Sid Vicious as, "a beastly way of knocking the Bromley Contingent around the 100 Club" was largely unknown, except to the handful who arrived in the Sex Pistols' company such as Jordan (Pamela Rooke).

Journalist and social commentator Paul Morley would recount a less than animated audience behaving much like any other rock concert of the time, motionlessly watching the band on stage with arms folded.

Tuesday 20th July 1976

On the second occasion the Pistols graced the small stage of the Lesser Free Trade Hall, I recall being at least aware of the event. It marked the debut of Manchester's Buzzcocks, the band whose founder members had arranged that first gig for the Sex Pistols but it was the other Mancunian support act that would draw the gig to my attention.

Slaughter and the Dogs, who hailed from the south

Manchester area of Wythenshawe, had been together and gigging since the previous year. I am not sure when I would come to regard this local band as 'punk' but I suspect it stems from sighting a poster somewhere in Manchester announcing that Slaughter and the Dogs and the Sex Pistols were to appear at the Lesser Free Trade Hall. If the font size was indicative, they would share equal billing. Unsurprisingly the Dogs' management were behind the posters in an act that, in all fairness, mirrored the self-confident swagger that would become the Pistols' trademark.

A far more respectable audience greeted the Sex Pistols' second coming in Manchester, said to be a sell-out. The local following accrued by Slaughter and the Dogs in their frenetic existence to that date must have played a part, although the rise in stock of the Sex Pistols that had warranted a full page live review in *Sounds* has to be the principal factor.

As several accounts, including Jonh Ingham's *Sounds* review, observed, a sizeable delegation had followed the Pistols from the capital. Thus many more could later claim to have been there, even if many of those hailed from beyond Manchester and its satellite towns. Indeed, attendance on this second night is considered by many to qualify as having "been there". Furthermore the support bands have never been victims of mistaken identity.

Unsurprisingly it was debutants Buzzcocks who opened proceedings, sharing their vision of how a band influenced by Captain Beefheart, Velvet Underground, The Stooges and now the Sex Pistols should sound. Accounts of their set have varied with the passage of time and the benefit of hindsight but reports around the time suggest a loose musical presentation that culminated in one member fleeing into the night "like a scared rabbit". Sixteen year-old drummer John Maher is on record as being the absconding musician although Mark Smith, who is confirmed as being in attendance, averred that the escapee was guitarist Pete Shelley.

Slaughter and the Dogs claimed the second spot, probably on account of their having experienced live performing before tonight. Sex Pistols' bassist Glen Matlock remembered Slaughter and the Dogs' performance favourably, although he struggled to class them as belonging to any new movement. Others recall being more perplexed by their amateur glam threads and their eagerness to deliver an encore that was not requested by anyone outside their local following. Mark Smith was to describe much of their set as Bowie out-takes with "Suffragette City" being the inaugural point of reference.

As for the Sex Pistols; their set, like their followers, had grown to include their signature "Anarchy in the UK" that would become their first single later in the year. In fact, if you allow for a few tracks yet to be written and one or two covers that continued to bolster their self-penned numbers, the Pistols virtually premièred their one and only studio album. The pogo was still yet to make an appearance although the southern tourists exhibited some novel dance moves to accompany the music.

play me old King Cole!

AS FOR WHERE I WAS on either night the Sex Pistols laid down their marker in Manchester… if I had ventured into Manchester it is highly probable that I would have been checking out some rock music at the Phoenix pub on Oxford Road, Manchester. That would be via the DJ's vinyl, as the Phoenix offered live music on a Thursday with a rock disco on other nights. In fact, according to the listings in the *New Manchester Review*, the only live competition the Pistols faced on their 4th June visit was either from the band Menace, who appeared 9½ miles away at the Commercial Hotel in Stalybridge, or from one of the resident bands who played each Friday at the Grey Horse (The Kicker) in Romiley, Stockport.

Situated up the elevator on the first floor of the University Precinct, the Phoenix was just another pub with a bar and plenty of seats and tables. The clues that it offered slightly more than beer and crisps, cans of Breaker being a preferred tipple, was the dance floor in the centre that doubled as a stage. There was also a permanent poster on the wall advising of the live bands to be seen each Thursday.

To clarify, the term of choice at this place was "rock music". Not "rock and roll music" and never "heavy metal" a term that would fall into extensive use in the coming years and rarely "prog rock". Presumably by the loose definition where artists such as ELP could fall into the rock and roll category, it was all the same thing but to the ears of those within, it was the more select "rock music".

For most of its denizens, rock music was a way of life. The purchase of an album was a major event that you would feel obliged to share with fellow fans. One conversation might begin, "I got 'The Welsh Connection' by Man. You have to listen to it a few times but it's brilliant when you get into it." Caring about your music extended to the careful handling of a vinyl record by its edges and regular use of an Emitex Record Cleaning Cloth.

I always struggled with the concept of all current music being deemed rock and roll. Surely the genre referred more specifically to the sounds created by Bill Haley, Little Richard, Chuck Berry et al. There were others you could offer to the cause such as Creedence Clearwater Revival's "Travelin' Band", a point reinforced when the John Fogerty composition attracted a law suit from the publishers of Little Richard's "Good Golly Miss Molly" – but was "Roundabout" by Yes or "Musical Box" by Genesis rock and roll?

Although rock music was chiefly my music of choice at the time, the roll call offered by the Phoenix DJ was actually quite repetitive week to week, mainly harking back to previous years. If I discovered anything new musically during my Phoenix nights it was the existence of Graham Parker and the Rumour although inevitably it was the one track "Don't Ask Me Questions" that was played on weekly repeat, despite the artist having two albums worth of material to choose from by the close of the year.

Presumably the view in such circles was that you could not have too much of a good thing with Rainbow's "Stargazer", Ted Nugent's "Stranglehold", Led Zeppelin's "Kashmir", Joe Walsh's "Rocky Mountain Way" and, most pointedly, Lynyrd Skynyrd's "Freebird" blasting out on a regular basis alongside artists such as Rick Derringer, Genesis or Lone Star.

Lone Star were, I presumed, from the same vast state of Texas as bearded rockers ZZ Top. As for their music, they did a thunderous cover of The Beatles' "She Said" with the emphasis on the line, "She's making me feel like I've never been born". The Beatles were too passé and far too lightweight for the self-indulgent Phoenix crowd but the track passed the "rock" test despite the DJ's willingness to divulge the song's origins. Lone Star presumably generated a sufficiently raucous sound through their guitar amps to invalidate the fab four origins.

In fact, far from being Texan neighbours of Frank Beard and co, Lone Star were a Welsh band hailing from Cardiff and featuring Paul "Tonka" Chapman in their line up between two separate stints as a member of UFO. Their debut album had penetrated the UK top fifty earlier in the year and to confirm their rock credentials they had supported CBS label mate Ted Nugent on a UK tour, who would coin the phrase, "If it's too loud, you're too old!"

To remind the audience that they were a more exclusive set than the general music fan, the week before the Knebworth Festival the Phoenix DJ helpfully informed that the only artist we would be going to see were not headliners the Rolling Stones but Todd Rundgren, before proceeding to play a track by the man's Utopia.

As the year wore on, the playing of Manfred Mann's Earth Band's rare foray into the singles chart with their interpretation of Springsteen's "Blinded by the Light" would cause many a wild mane of hair to be swirled through an ecstatic facial grimace on the dance floor. Ironically, away from the garish floorshow of the Phoenix, it was the Stravinsky inspired "Starbird" on the B side that was the jukebox choice of many a serious rock fan, who appreciated the flash moog-laden instrumental section that followed the operatic prelude.

Not that the playing of a current hit was evidence of a lack of musical snobbery. In what, with hindsight, was obviously a crassly staged routine, a request for Bowie's "Suffragette City" was followed by a declaration that, "If you're going to play that you may as well go the whole hog and play this", before unleashing the Bay City Rollers' current hit "I Only Want To Be With You" to a smug reception. The likes of Bowie or Roxy Music were far too glam (or maybe too popular) to be credible artists within these circles, although curiously Queen's "Now I'm Here" merited needle time. Presumably Freddie Mercury's soaring vocal range or Brian May's inventively layered guitar work delivered solid interludes when required.

The audience were something of a mystery at this place. For the uninitiated the stretch of Manchester's Oxford Road from beyond the BBC building down towards the Whitworth Art Gallery and Park is home to the thriving student community. In 1976 you would pass the city's main Victorian University frontage on Oxford Road with the Polytechnic nestled behind and the renowned University of Manchester Institute of Science and Technology (UMIST) on nearby Sackville Street.

The Cavendish Street part of the Polytechnic had seen L.S. Lowry study under Pierre Adolphe Valette in the faculty that was then the Manchester School Of Art in the early twentieth century before later railing against the establishment, turning down no fewer than five honours before his death in 1976, the jewel in his flat cap surely being his refusal of a knighthood in 1968. In 1976 Manchester Polytechnic included Pete Saville, Malcolm Garrett and Linder Sterling among its students. Mick Hucknall, who some would swear was there at the first Pistols' gig at the Lesser Free Trade Hall, although not Hucknall himself, would later study fine art at the same institute.

Despite its location, I was never convinced that the Phoenix audience contained many students, despite the offering of an NUS discount on the 30p admission price to see a band. That was just my observation as I never conducted a survey, although of the few regulars I got to know not one claimed to be studying further or higher education in or around Manchester. The attendees were predominantly male with any females in attendance seemingly there on the arm of a male rock aficionado rather than of their own choosing. The playing of a "floor filler" such as Led Zeppelin's "Kashmir" was the cue for a horde of male denim clad individuals to invade the dance floor and swirl their luxuriant locks whilst practicing air guitar riffs.

Indeed, rock music in Manchester was very much a male oriented audience. A live gig was usually a night of male bonding, unless in a more settled relationship where the lady might support the man's indulgence of seeing Genesis at the Free Trade Hall. You would see a smattering of females at gigs but the general impression in Manchester was very much that live music was a men-only pursuit.

★

It was always the Thursday live nights at the Phoenix that drew the biggest crowd. Or to put it into perspective, the majority of bands attracted more of a crowd than the actual number who bothered to check out the Sex Pistols on 4th June 1976, which in turn suggests that Solstice were used to bigger audiences on their own. If the Phoenix's appeal was mirrored across the other live music venues around Manchester, it is highly likely that more people saw Menace play in Stalybridge than made the trip to the Lesser Free Trade Hall. *New Manchester Review* would describe Menace as "Very Strong" and "Very loud" with the volume sometimes masking musical deficiencies but ultimately "Still, worth a listen".

The one band whose listing I recall drew a larger than usual gathering was Rudy and the Zipps. Led by an ex-member of Be-Bop Deluxe, whose "Ships In The Night" had penetrated the lower reaches of the charts earlier that year, it has since been claimed that Rudy and the Zipps was the considered band name before Bill Nelson settled on the jazz referenced Be-Bop Deluxe. Robert Bryan, who played bass on Be-Bop Deluxe's debut album Axe Victim, as well as contributing the track "Rocket Cathedrals", was the main man in question who now led his own band.

The acceptance of a musician with Be-Bop Deluxe connections was perhaps curious given the glam leanings of said band. True, they were on the Harvest label, EMI's famous home of Pink Floyd, Syd Barrett, Pete Brown and Piblokto, Kevin Ayers and the Whole World – anything labelled "progressive" really, as well as a shop window for the great Hipgnosis LP sleeves. I suspect more people were familiar with the shot of New Scotland Yard on the Quatermass album cover than they were with its musical content. It was definitely cool in the early seventies to be seen carrying an LP with a Hipgnosis sleeve, although the same would somehow apply to the crass fantasy art of Roger Dean.

On the other hand, frontman Bill Nelson was not averse to sporting eye shadow or composing titles like "Jet Silver and the Dolls of Venus". Perhaps Be-Bop Deluxe's modest chart success compared to their glam contemporaries helped retain their credibility alongside Nelson's not inconsiderable prowess with his "Axe". Either way the Phoenix crowd, who displayed a high level of tolerance for one or two abysmal outfits, were happy to put Rudy and the Zipps on a pedestal and cite their Be-Bop Deluxe connection as a plus factor.

Although my memory of most Phoenix bands' sets has blurred into one over the years, I do have a more distinct recollection of Rudy and the Zipps. They had a number called "Rudy" and their tour de force "Peter Pan" was catchy enough to recall the tune on the drive home. In fact, unlike most bands, whose sets only came to life when their bland and usually derivative original compositions gave way to one of several rock covers, with the final cover often being "Johnny B Goode" as an encore, Rudy and the Zipps had an identity shaped by their own material. To emphasise my point Johnny Rotten is recorded on "The Good Time Music Of the Sex Pistols", the bootleg of the first Lesser Free Trade Hall gig, announcing, "not Johnny B Goode" to an encore request.

A highpoint of the year should have been an appearance by Nirvana who had been booked to play a Thursday night benefit gig for the RNIB, an event that attracted the rare sight of a queue down the escalator. The Nirvana in question, who had played the Phoenix earlier in the year were, I assumed, the London-based band who had released several critically acclaimed albums in the sixties and early seventies, most notably for Chris Blackwell's Island Records and whose members were later to take Kurt Cobain to court over the use of the band name.

Whether the scheduled line-up would feature the original singers and songwriters: Irish-born Patrick Campbell-Lyons and Greek composer Alex Spyropolous, or any of the various session musicians who had been recruited to accompany the vocal duo for album recording and live shows, was not revealed on this occasion due to the apparent unwillingness of their guitarist to fulfil the booking despite, as the DJ repeatedly reminded us, the guitarist in question being "the blind guy".

The dilemma was partly explained when Richard Boon, writing in the *New Manchester Review* "Pub Rock" listing, advised that Nirvana, described by Boon as a "Post-Hendrix power band" had split up on the eve of the benefit gig suggesting the band had been, "Struggling in vain for too long" before turning his attention to Slaughter and the Dogs and Buzzcocks imminent studio activity. Prior to Richard Boon's stint, the "Pub Rock" listing in *New Manchester Review* had been compiled by one Howard Trafford (Devoto) with a former UMIST chemistry graduate called Martin Hannett also contributing to the fortnightly magazine.

The Nirvana mystery was resolved in subsequent years when it emerged that the guitarist in question was Rochdale born multi-instrumentalist Tony Crabtree, who lost his sight at 18 months and whose virtuosity with the guitar, described as being able to reproduce the sounds Jimi Hendrix produced from an electric guitar, was widely acknowledged by rival bands on the circuit. Crabtree and his band had taken the unusual step of choosing a previously-used band name for their Rochdale based trio.

Thankfully for their multitude of admirers, Nirvana's reported split was only a brief interlude with them reforming the following year and playing their comeback at the Seven Stars on Tower Street, Heywood, a pub that reappeared on the live music circuit having hosted bands since the sixties including early appearances by Be-Bop Deluxe and Supertramp.

Tony Crabtree sadly passed away in 2005 having also played keyboards with Rochdale's Tractor at venues around Manchester, Tractor having the distinction, alongside Timperley's Stack Waddy of having recorded an album for John Peel's Dandelion label.

A band who every long-haired denim-clad rock fan seemed to endorse were Son of a Bitch. I was prompted to check them out by a stranger at a pub rock gig on Morecambe Pier back in the days when the Lancashire resort still had some nightlife and two piers. When I finally gained a Phoenix audience with the South Yorkshire outfit, their bland mixture of standard heavy rock fayre contained few clues that, of all the rock hopefuls plying their trade at the Phoenix, these were the ones with a future.

Several years later, when *Sounds* writer Geoff Barton penned an article foretelling the "New wave of British heavy metal", Son of a Bitch, having condensed their name to the less hackneyed and slightly more HM friendly Saxon, took their place alongside fellow South Yorkshiremen Def Leppard in selling vast quantities of albums.

★

The Phoenix was not the only place you could go for a fix of rock music thanks in some part to brewers Bass Charrington who operated many of the pubs in and around Manchester showcasing live rock bands. The El Patio in Stretford's Arndale Centre delivered similar fayre and, like the Phoenix, featured in *New Manchester Review's* "Pub Rock" listing, along with such venues as the Cavalcade on Wilmslow Road in Didsbury.

In the surrounding towns significant venues were the Streetbridge Inn in Hollinwood, the Spread Eagle in Ashton-Under-Lyne, the Victoria Hotel in Heywood and probably the most active of the local venues, the Commercial Hotel in Stalybridge. The Commercial even featured gigs by Wild Ram and, more significantly, Buzzcocks – the latter arranged due to Howard Devoto's acquaintance with the pub's landlady during his time compiling the "pub rock" listings for the *New Manchester Review*. So curiously Buzzcocks would join Son of a Bitch as the two successful graduates of the Greater Manchester pub rock circuit.

Despite the use of the term "pub rock" the circuit in and around Manchester bore little resemblance to the r'n'b flavoured pub rock scene south of Hatfield (and the North). As well as Solstice, Nirvana, Son of a Bitch and the minor legends that were Rudy and the Zipps, these venues would also feature bands with such names as Slack Alice, S.F.W., Swede Larsen, Grendel, Spacers, Leo, Dead Fingers Talk, Captain Zap, Azel, and, surely the most outrageously overblown group name of them all, Caterpillars Don't Believe in Butterflies. A name that observers shrewdly abbreviated to "Caterpillars and Butterflies" or "Caterpillars etc" as *New Manchester Review* once listed them.

Their handle aside, Caterpillars Don't Believe in Butterflies' were regarded as one of the better bands who played the Phoenix, even drawing modest approval from *New Manchester Review's* Richard Boon who implored readers to support their gigs, describing them as "A band that have attracted record company interest". Boon suggested their own compositions verged on the predictable but their use of rhythm and lead guitars displayed, "an assured, original interpretation of country rock styles". The last word fell to lead guitarist and vocalist Alan Shore who, possibly echoing the sentiment of those who would turn their adoration to the punk cause, indicated that the local scene must change from the, "thousands of three-piece heavy bands" doing the rounds.

★

The self-indulgent Phoenix crowd, not unlike the curiosity seekers who had checked out the Sex Pistols, doubtless possessed a condescending view of the mainstream pop music that populated the charts of 1976 that once more delivered an unacceptable proportion of novelty hits.

Another indication that the music industry may have run out of ideas was the decision to reissue singles from The Beatles' back catalogue. A move that finally saw The Beatles' "Yesterday" become a hit single as well as "Back in the USSR".

On the other side of the coin soul legends Candi Staton and The Isley Brothers enjoyed time on the UK charts and there was another significant breakthrough in Liverpool's The Real Thing, whose years of persistence were finally rewarded with chart action. Even the Sensational Alex Harvey Band returned to the charts with a genuine contender this time in "Boston Tea Party", having scored a novelty hit themselves the previous summer with "Delilah".

Of equal interest to some was the singles success finally granted to Aberdeen born brothers Gavin and Iain Sutherland who had, perhaps like Dylan, forsaken their folk roots to join forces with rock band Quiver with the union finally seeing the collective dent the UK top ten.

Whether ABBA's inevitable fate as a major musical force was a cause for alarm or veneration was a matter of personal judgement but by the close of 1976 it became futile to continue to disregard the Swedish former Eurovision winners. Equally impossible to ignore was the sudden chart rise of Peter Frampton who seemed to be a radio fixture throughout the summer of 1976 and any scrutiny of the music of that year would be incomplete without mention of Donna Summer's "Love to Love You Baby".

Saturday 4th September 1976

A chance for everyone in Manchester and beyond to sample the Sex Pistols as the band made their television debut on the final show in the first series of Granada TV's "So It Goes".

Hosted by Tony Wilson and featuring broadcaster and sometime poet and lyricist Clive James, who apparently did not hit it off with the Sex Pistols, the "So It Goes" series had earned itself a reputation as a slick unconventional format coupled with a bold choice of music that saw Alberto Y Los Trios Paranoias and Tom Waits perform.

The series had also showcased a surprisingly memorable early TV appearance from Eddie and the Hot Rods, whose selection suggested Wilson did not buy into Johnny Rotten's "our imitators" jibe. If he did, the band's performance of their current single, a no frills cover of Sam the Sham and the Pharaohs "Wooly Bully" complete with Roxy Music's Andy Mackay on saxophone, meant that they were at least worthy imitators.

At the thirtieth anniversary of the Pistols Lesser Free Trade Hall gig, Glen Matlock described Johnny Rotten as having "made mincemeat" of Clive James in their confrontation. James had written of the experience later in 1976 in *The Observer* where he suggested the Pistols' singer had a name like "Kenny Frightful".

The Sex Pistols played one number, closing the show with an acceptable performance of "Anarchy in the UK" despite the distinctively dissonant Johnny Rotten vocal that seemed to resonate long after the fade out, with punk icon Jordan in close attendance at the front of the stage.

Friday 10th September 1976

If I was to make the cultural leap from "rock" to "punk rock" it would have to be via the other band on *that* poster. The Wythenshawe Forum Theatre featured three bands with the headliners being local heroes Slaughter and the Dogs and yes, they were genuine headliners this time.

I only caught the end of the opening act, Wild Ram. Also Wythenshawe residents and with a name suggesting they should have stuck with the Manchester pub rock circuit, rather than attempt to convert this mainly juvenile audience of Bowie clones, singer Eddie Garrity's irreverent manner gave the band an edge that rightly drew cries for an encore. Tony Wilson, TV presenter and compère for the night, asked rhetorically, "You liked them did you?" before taking issue with one of several hollering for "The Dogs" with a barbed "Up yours an' all matey."

The wait for the main act involved another band appropriated from the local pub rock scene named on the poster as Madanza, although correctly called Mudanzas, having named themselves after an LP by the English hard rock band Stray. Wilson, clearly not familiar with this band or Stray, introduced them as "Mudantas".

Whilst not yet familiar with the type of noise a punk band might produce, I was fairly confident that Mudanzas, with their studied Hammond organ driven sound, were following a similar route to the other acts who played the Phoenix, at least those who might cite the likes of Genesis or Yes as influences. It could be questioned whether the main purpose of slipping Mudanzas in between Wild Ram and Slaughter and the Dogs was an attempt to emphasize the latter's freshness and originality – Solstice to the Dogs' Sex Pistols as it were. As it transpired Mudanzas completed their set to a general wave of approval and, like Solstice at the Lesser Free Trade Hall, would have left the stage thinking the gig had gone okay. Unlike Solstice there was to be no rude awakening following the headliners.

The anticipation that greeted the Dogs' arrival on stage was briefly rewarded in the band's opening numbers as the second title had a catchy chorus of "what you doing to me, what you saying to me" that drew approval from the South Manchester audience. Doubts crept in when the set dissolved into a couple of covers. The first was the Chuck Berry classic "Round and Round" as performed by the Rolling Stones at the 1976 Knebworth Festival. However, unlike Jagger and co, who have never tried to disguise their debt to the duck walking guitarist, one suspects the Dogs did not draw their influence directly from the man himself.

Visually Slaughter and the Dogs presented a strange hybrid of imagery, clearly not subscribing to the denim anti-fashion look so favoured by live bands. Bassist Howard Bates, with long dark hair and a top hat, would have looked at home in many of the prog rock acts who Decca indulged in their "World Of" series of budget albums, before they turned their attention to punk bands like Adam and the Ants and Slaughter and the Dogs. I recall guitarist Mike Rossi as a diminutive figure beneath a white trilby hat who certainly knew his way around a guitar. If the Dogs had star potential it was to be the dextrous skills of Rossi who would provide it but the most telling aspect of the Dogs' appearance was singer Wayne Barrett.

In white shirt, dark waistcoat and flicked blonde hair, Barrett was clearly on a Bowie trip circa Young Americans and it was surely The Thin White Duke's choice of Chuck Berry's "Round and Round" as the B-side to "Drive-In Saturday" that brought the song to Slaughter and the Dogs' attention. The Dogs had described punk as a cross between Bowie and the Rolling Stones so by their definition "Round and Round" was the definitive punk anthem.

Any doubts as to where the Dogs' stimulus lay were removed with Barrett's cry of "Bryan Ferry" before launching into "Both Ends Burning" and my cue to leave. If I was to make a judgement on the phenomena known as "punk rock" based on tonight's headliners, it would be heavily slanted in favour of glam contenders David Bowie or Bryan Ferry but without the creative edge.

Maybe a clue had been the group's moniker. Something Jonh Ingham had alluded to in his *Sounds* review of the second

Lesser Free Trade Hall date. On noting Mike Rossi's authentic Mick Ronson barnet, Ingham had suggested the name blended Ronson's "Slaughter on Tenth Avenue" with Bowie's "Diamond Dogs". Wayne Barrett would advise their fan club that he thought the name up whilst lying in bed before the first gig, although years later Ingham's version of the band's name origin would be adopted as the correct one.

Monday 20th September 1976

Just over a week after Slaughter and the Dogs commandeered the unlicensed Wythenshawe Forum, it was the turn of Buzzcocks to arrange an alcohol-free gig. North London band Eater had chosen Manchester to make their debut and the story ran that *New Manchester Review's* Martin Hannett had advised Eater's singer Andy Blade to contact Buzzcocks. Pete Shelley would later explain the running order was decreed by the flip of a coin which Shelley suggested with hindsight he "should have made best of three".

Francis Taylor, a University student on summer leave, had his first baptism of punk that night. "I was away at University till the end of July '76. When I got back my mates were all talking about the Sex Pistols gigs at the Lesser Free Trade Hall how good they were and that there had been a Manchester band called Buzzcocks on the bill at one. They were adamant that I had to see them at the earliest opportunity! A gig at Houldsworth Hall was coming up soon, so, the scene was set, the tickets bought, all systems go!

"Houldsworth Hall on Deansgate was a shed of a place; all ornate cornices and overdone Victorian Gothic, it had been used a few times for gigs but not often. No licence, so no booze, just soft drinks. We had already been to the pub to meet up and put a few pints away, Cox's Bar probably if I remember it rightly. We got inside and in among the small crowd were people scattered around the place who looked very different to anything I had ever seen. Some were pretty outrageous, even somewhat dark and intimidating. Girls with heavy eye make-up and short hair dressed in short skirts and long boots gazed around the room as if it were empty. Some of the boys were in leather, dyed hair and thousand yard stares. Here and there a safety pin or a razor blade hung from an ear, a lapel or a sleeve. People clustered in groups with their mates, eyeing others with some suspicion, sticking close with those they knew. I didn't know any of them, only my own little group, they didn't know me, there was no scene - yet.

"I don't recall there being any sort of real build-up but there might have been music playing. A girl with a Bowie-style haircut and a pale face takes the stage, goes to the mike and shouts "Buzzcocks are gonna fuck you", then the band are there plugged in and ... BLAM!!! They launch into the music!

"Music! Is it music? The sound is loud, the bass and drums underpin a scratchy, trebly guitar. The singer sounds like a cockney wide boy, who finishes every sentence with a pronounced breathy "-aah". Suddenly lots of people want to be at the front, some are jumping about, others look like they are fitting, twitching and jerking around, faces contorted. I am rooted to the spot! What the fuck is this? This is amazing; the noise is raw and bounces around the cavernous hall echoing back from the walls, not enough bodies to soak it up. The lyrics are screamed and gasped, vaguely discernible. The front man, a skinny dervish replete in shiny black trousers, tears the words out and spits them at the crowd, swearing and cursing. Singing about what? Boredom? Orgasms? Taking a line?

"The guitarist is a sight in some god-awful glittery trousers, too much mascara and butter blonde spiky hair - but he does look fuckin' cool! Suddenly they go into a tune I recognise - or do I? Is it ...the Troggs?...I can't control myself?... The guitarist pipes the Bah-bah-bahs in a reedy falsetto...yeah that's what it is ... but it isn't. It's like the tune was chewed up and those aren't the right lyrics...but...it doesn't fucking matter. This is brilliant... this is mine....they are me! Breaks between songs are filled with cursory introductions and "one, two three, four!" Then more noise. I am lost now, I'm surging with the rest of them, shaking and jumping, everything abandoned...what's that? Ya big dummmmaaae-ah, I lurve you, ya big dummmmaaae-ah, the words are drawled out, the singer's face screws up as he chews every syllable of the lyric. He looks like he is straining over a shit! All too soon it's over – did they do an encore? I can't remember, all I know is; this is it, I am in! I want to do that again!

"So they left the stage and a little later a band called Eater came on to top the bill, the bands had tossed a coin before the gig to decide the running order – Eater won. They were a bunch of kids from London making a racket, it was fun…but it wasn't what I heard just before…I wanted the other mob back…. I sometimes wonder if Eater had played first, would I even have stayed?"

The events of that night decreed that Francis' return for a second year at University was suspended indefinitely, choosing to stick around and join the soon to be burgeoning Manchester punk scene, joining Buzzcocks' road crew a few years later.

★

The Sex Pistols were booked to return to Manchester on Friday 1st October, this time to play at Didsbury College. As events would unfold a gig happened but with a more forgettable band replacing the absent Sex Pistols, who pulled out due to Johnny Rotten's voice problems. Tales persist of unhappy punters finding themselves in South Manchester and adjourning to the pub when the replacement band failed to sparkle. For obvious reasons, the number who swear they were there when the Pistols failed to show has never been fully researched.

the electric circus

A SIGNIFICANT AND LARGER VENUE appeared in the autumn of 1976. Situated in a converted cinema and later variety club formerly known as The Palladium a few miles out of town just off Rochdale Road, the Electric Circus on Collyhurst Street, Collyhurst opened its doors as a rock venue on Friday 8th October 1976.

The venue, run jointly by heavy rock fans Graham Brooks and Allan Robinson who had previously run rock nights at yet another rock venue, Waves on Dantzic Place in Manchester, was candidly described as "a proper dive" by witnesses at the time. On one of my few visits to the place I recall it as a dingy basement down some stairs, where I was approached by two revellers to request if I could supply any "dope". Although I only recall paying on the door, a ticket from 1976 has come to light that names the resident DJ as Graham Brooks.

The legend runs that Brooks and Robinson had fallen into disagreement with the management at Waves and launched the Electric Circus as a joint enterprise, describing the venue on their own flyer's logo as "Manchester's Latest & Greatest live Rock venue".

Undoubtedly some of the events that followed in the one scurried year of its existence happened more by default than design but the Electric Circus was to play a major role in the musical history of the city. At the Manchester Punk Event of 2005, held at Manchester's Urbis, Anthony Wilson would suggest the Electric Circus was, "as important as the Twisted Wheel or The Hacienda". His sparring partner on the night, Paul Morley, would describe the Circus as "an earnest attempt to supply a Manchester stopping place for bands that wouldn't generally get the chance to play there" in an early *NME* review.

Being a club it was available after the pubs flashed "last orders" at 10:30 p.m. as was the case in 1976, so you could move on and check out a proper band with record releases under their belt, rather than some pub wannabees. No doubt with licensing laws in mind the admission price, capped at 60p most nights, rose to 75p after the 10:30 curfew. The October flyer also helpfully informed that, "We are open every THURSDAY + FRIDAY & SATURDAY BAR TILL 2 AM" offering "Good Music, Good Food and TOP BANDS".

In its first month, October 1976, the Electric Circus boasted such acts as Upp, Tiger (who the flyer reminded us included notable session guitarist Big Jim Sullivan) and Richard Strange's Doctors of Madness for the 60p admission. A charge of 70p before the 10:30 p.m. hike would buy you an audience with Liverpool's Supercharge who played the opening night and who had, in case anyone was interested, scored a top three hit in Australia.

The additional 10p also entitled you to catch Phoenix, whose claim to fame on the flyer was the inclusion of one Phil Wood, credited with being an ex-member of the band Argent and Hatfield outfit Babe Ruth, who had recorded several albums for the Harvest label. What the flyer failed to tell us is that the album success enjoyed in Canada and the USA by Babe Ruth featured the distinctively forceful vocals of Janita (Jenny) Haan and the songwriting and musical arrangements of multi-instrumentalist Alan Shacklock, neither of whom remained in the band.

To balance the misinformation, the flyer also failed to elaborate that Phoenix actually contained three ex-members of Argent in guitarist John Verity, bassist Jim Rodford and drummer Bob Henrit. Future Electric Circus flyers would also become renowned for the odd spelling error with ex-Babe Ruth singer Jenny Haan's new band twice being misprinted as "Jenny Hans Lions" and Jenny Hanns Lion".

First impressions of the Electric Circus, or the "Circus" as it inevitably became known, were of a larger late night version of the other rock venues in and around Manchester. Situated in an urban landscape surrounded by blocks of flats that had entered the seventies in a state of decline, the immediate plot of land that contained the Circus had that air of dilapidation visualised by

David Bowie in the spoken prologue of his "Diamond Dogs" album. If seventies Manchester was in the downbeat state that some claim before the Sex Pistols arrival, then this part of the city did lend some credence to those theories.

You entered the place on the front right of the building via the cash desk that led through a door and down a few steps to the main room. The stage, with the iconic black and white tiled backdrop design that would always identify this particular venue on live shots, was at the far end, presumably where the cinema screen once stood, with a standing area–cum–dance floor in front. The bar was to the right as you entered the main room with some tables and chairs opposite for those punters happy to sit and drink rather than demonstrate approval of the heavy soundtrack played from the DJ booth, to the right of the stage and beyond the bar. The soundtrack remained predominately Rainbow, Nugent, Skynyrd, although an odd inclusion in late 1976 was Wild Cherry's "Play That Funky Music".

Being an old cinema there was an upstairs with a view of the stage, which was accessed to the left on entering the main hall. Although the general decor could hardly be termed salubrious, I recall the upstairs almost having an air of dereliction and thus not a regular retreat from the main room although it did provide some sanctuary in the later months when the numbers of attendees began to swell.

The most common descriptor applied to the Electric Circus was "dump" although in its defence that aptly described most venues peddling similar music at the time. In the seventies there was a straight choice. There were the traditional clubs, descended from the Twisted Wheel and its ilk that played soul and dance music and required a jacket or tie or both to gain entry. Then there were clubs like the Circus playing less dance orientated rock music but operating without the dress code. In fact the wearing of a jacket and tie would probably raise the question, "Are you sure you've come to the right place?" You could hear Tina Charles or Led Zeppelin played at a club in 1976 but never both at the same one. Well apart from the Wild Cherry anomaly at the Circus.

As if by way of justification, a club's decor in turn reflected the dress policy, perhaps thinking that denim-clad loungers would probably get cigarette ash on the carpet if they provided one. Whatever the rationale, the casually-attired rock audience were happy to play air guitar in less wholesome surroundings. As a last word in defence of the Circus's threadbare scheme, many of the slicker dance clubs of the seventies looked less so in daylight.

Wednesday 3rd November 1976

Still juggling with the dilemma of just what type of band were worthy of investigation following my underwhelming encounter with Slaughter and the Dogs, I found myself at the penultimate small venue appearance in Manchester by AC/DC.

I am not sure why I was there, having no prior knowledge of the band. I established that their members hailed from Scotland and Australia, they were signed to Atlantic, had released two albums worldwide with one more in Australia and were in town tonight at Manchester University's Students Union to promote their recently released album "Dirty Deeds Done Dirt Cheap".

The Students Union on Oxford Road was described by some as "the steps" in reference to the white stone steps that led to the front entrance. The venue itself was accessed up a flight of stairs with a stamp, visible under an ultraviolet lamp, impressed on the back of your hand. This ritual was deemed necessary as the hall in which the bands played was separate from the bar and the toilets, so an evening at the Students Union involved repeated hand checking each time you left the main hall.

I soon discovered that AC/DC were a captivating live act who delivered the basics in short sharp bursts. Singer Bon Scott seemed to borrow a few mannerisms from fellow Scot Alex Harvey but when required he could provide the piercing vocal required for their rock anthems which formed the night's set, listed elsewhere as "Live Wire", "She's Got Balls", "It's a Long Way To The Top (If You Wanna Rock'n'roll)", "Can I Sit Next To You Girl?", "The Jack", "High Voltage", "T.N.T." and culminating in their working of "Baby Please Don't Go". The latter saw the apex of the band's true visual lynchpin, guitarist Angus Young, who proceeded to remove his trademark school uniform and take a piggy back ride on the broad shoulders of singer Scott before flinging himself into the audience to writhe around the floor, all the while maintaining a firm grip on his guitar that continued to churn out riffs.

The band held a solid rhythm behind Young and Scott's more extravagant showmanship, in particular Angus's brother Malcolm whose steadily restrained rhythm guitar was often considered the bedrock of the early AC/DC sound.

★

There was an arrangement in the early days of the Electric Circus whereby you could hire the place for £70 a night, an agreement utilised on Wednesday nights from November. One such night saw the Electric Circus test the waters of the burgeoning punk scene when, on the tenth of the month, Buzzcocks booked the venue with London punk band Chelsea driving north to play support. Chelsea were by this stage in the last throws of the original line-up that featured Billy Idol, Tony James and John Towe backing Gene October, before the former threesome would leave to form the more commercial Generation X.

Given that the Circus could draw a modest number of after-hours revellers, if only to listen to the heavy rock sounds and have another drink, attendance on the night in question was remarkably sparse, as confirmed in an *NME* review, despite amateur photographic evidence appearing to confirm the presence of future legend Jon the Postman and of a professional photographer from Salford by the name of Kevin Cummins. There was also a delegation from London fanzine *Sniffin' Glue* who were in town to catch Chelsea for the first time.

Despite the lukewarm response to the Circus's venture into the punk market, a further double header was arranged for the 28th, this time on a Sunday when the other Manchester punks Slaughter and the Dogs shared the bill with yet more visitors from the south, The Damned. With a single release having merited Radio 1 play on both the John Peel Show and Alan

Freeman's Saturday Rock Show, the appearance of The Damned seemed to represent a minor coup. As things transpired there would be no The Damned with Buzzcocks stepping in to share the bill with Slaughter and the Dogs for the first time since the second Pistols' gig at the Lesser Free Trade Hall, thus bolstering the modest crowd who bothered to turn out on a late November Sunday night.

There was already a degree of enmity growing between the respective followings of the Dogs and Buzzcocks that would manifest itself that night. Jon the Postman's continued endorsement of Buzzcocks was in stark contrast to his evaluation of their Wythenshawe counterparts who were early recipients of the Postman's fabled heckling. For their part the Dogs continued to work on their theatrics, this night involving one of their travelling fans from South Manchester who mounted the stage to have Wayne Barrett cut his t-shirt with a cheap knife.

Seemingly unperturbed, the Circus listed fringe punks Eddie and the Hot Rods on a flyer. Given that the Canvey Island youths' Island Records label managed to justify showcasing the band at the Free Trade Hall that month and (unlike most early Manchester punk gigs) nobody has since laid claim to having been there, it seems doubtful that the gymnastic performance of the Hot Rods ever actually occurred at the Circus.

One band who managed to play against the odds in November were Motörhead as Chris Hewitt, manager of the band Tractor and a sound engineer who had "hussled for some P.A. work" at the Electric Circus following his return to Rochdale from London, recalls, "I saw Lemmy virtually starving and then I did the gigs at the Electric Circus on his first tour. It was winter and they didn't have enough fuel to get to the Electric Circus. I had to go out to Knutsford services and take them some money. I took Lemmy in my van and I lent him some money to get fish and chips … which he never paid back.

"When we'd rescued them off the motorway and eventually got his gear in he had two four by twelve cabinets and I was going to mike 'em up and he said, 'Be careful where you put the mike on either of the cabs because there's only actually one twelve inch speaker in that one and one twelve inch speaker in that one.'

"So he'd basically got this massive stack which should have had eight twelve inch speakers in it, four in each cab and there was only one in each cab. It must have sounded fuckin' awful from memory because it would have been so overdriven. But it was a great tour, that was with 'Philthy' Phil Taylor and 'Fast' Eddie Clarke. They were always fighting. Fast Eddie Clarke had a bandage on his hand because he'd been fighting with Philthy Phil. When we got to the next gig at Wigan Casino they were fighting in the dressing room."

Tuesday 7th December 1976

Maybe it was the easy option given that *real* punk gigs are supposed to have happened with little warning. That wasn't entirely true as we have already established that *New Manchester Review* provided a detailed fortnightly listing and having both Howard Devoto and future Buzzcocks manager Richard Boon involved in compiling the "What's On" listings punk bands, particularly Buzzcocks themselves, were not going to be overlooked.

But as my sources as a Stockport resident in 1976 were often limited to that night's *Manchester Evening News*, on the occasions that my parents decided to buy one, a gig at the Free Trade Hall by Eddie and the Hot Rods with advanced publicity via the music press and advanced ticket sales seemed impossible to ignore. And so with a seated ticket in the stalls, the only area of the hall that the promoters felt worth opening given the limited ticket sales, it was an opportunity to check out a punk(ish) band.

I had been sufficiently impressed by their appearance on So It Goes and even more so by their full frontal assault on the "Live at the Marquee" EP that earned a Top of the Pops performance of "Get Out Of Denver." True, the EP contained four cover versions but their high energy delivery coupled with astute song choices of Bob Seger's "Get Out Of Denver" and the garage rock standard "96 Tears" was as much a breath of fresh air as any of the other new breed offerings that appeared that summer. The picture sleeve may have betrayed an excessive use of flared trousers but to see the Hot Rods break onto Top of the Pops almost felt like the revolution had begun.

Tonight the driving rhythm that kicked off with the self-explanatory "Get Across To You" was derailed almost before it began with sound problems causing the band to vacate the stage early in the set to allow the technical crew to repair the glitches.

"Sorry about that, some bastard's been chewing the wires" was singer Barrie Masters' apology before resuming the night's activities that included a high dive from the speaker stack by the athletic former amateur boxer Masters.

As expected the forceful R'n'B of these juvenile pub rockers kept the audience on their feet, hitting a climax when the opening riffs of "Get Out Of Denver" forced even the most inactive members of the audience to surrender to the rhythm.

As a live band it was difficult to find real fault with the Hot Rods. The music and approach had (literally) been done before, albeit in a less direct manner although their recent debut album "Teenage Depression" and title track single suggested they may struggle to produce innovative new music within this format. That said both the "Live at the Marquee" EP and "Teenage Depression" had shaved the lower end of the charts.

I was also reliably informed by my father, who had garnered his information from a younger work colleague, apparently a fan of Irish guitarist Rory Gallagher, that Eddie and the Hot Rods were one of those "stupid bands who were doing all that carrying on and swearing."

Thursday 9th December 1976

There was only one place I should have been. The Sex Pistols' "Anarchy in the UK" tour had been savagely censored following the band's tirade at Bill Grundy on the Today programme but one of the few surviving dates took place at a venue I knew well. Moreover it was a package that included The Clash and ex-New York Dolls' Johnny Thunders in town with his new band the Heartbreakers. The Damned should have completed the line-up but the band had been dismissed from the tour, apparently for their unwillingness to audition before the upholders of the moral high ground.

However this was a Thursday and I had assented to check out a mate's older brother, who were this week's turn at the Phoenix. The sibling in question, Rick Henshaw, played keyboards behind a vocalist, who seemed surplus to requirements during the lengthy instrumental intros of most numbers but was ultimately allowed to join in for the closing minutes of each song. Word from the band was that they were undecided on what to call themselves but Stash was muted as their chosen name.

To the chagrin of some of our party who had at least acknowledged the competency of the band we had witnessed, it was onwards into the shadows of Collyhurst and the Electric Circus to see that band whose followers wore ripped t-shirts held together by safety pins, or string vests held together by chewing gum. The shock was less that such unruly clobber qualified as fashion but that a Chelsea shop was apparently charging megabucks for such gear.

Approaching the Electric Circus the usual tranquillity had been replaced by an anxious edge with Greater Manchester Police obviously viewing what remained of the tour as a likely powder keg. The line of policeman along Collyhurst Street seemed intent on questioning whoever approached the door as to why they would want to go in there. A few were swayed by the force's argument motioning to the sound emanating from within, "well just listen to 'em." What we were listening to was David Bowie singing, "It's not the side effects of the cocaine" – it was *not* the Sex Pistols and appropriately not a sound you would traditionally hear at this or similar venues, the DJ obviously still wrestling with the dilemma of what to play to a punk audience.

In fact such was the deliberation before paying on the door, the main band had already taken to the stage and were poised to launch into the opening chords of "Anarchy in the UK" under a drenching of beer thrown from the front rows. The support acts, including Buzzcocks, who had been invited to step in for the dispensed services of The Damned, had played and retired whilst I was scrutinising Stash at the Phoenix, along with the skirmishes between the punks and the rest of the crowd that had long subsided by this point.

Given the tabloid hype that preceded this event, there was an edge of confusion and bewilderment to this band and its charismatic frontman. Are they really good or really awful?

I would like to say that I was instantly converted to the cause but the Pistols' laudable and surprisingly competent musical performance left a few questions. As each number followed, an element of sameness crept in despite the band's approach rising to the hostile gauntlet thrown down by a sizeable element of doubters within the audience, whose attendance seemed to be borne more of sullen curiosity than any devotion to this group of outsiders. And they covered the Monkees of all people. Was that a stroke of genius or complete absurdity?

Either way, I could finally claim that, however belatedly, I had been there to witness the Sex Pistols in Manchester. For whatever doubts remained, particularly the playing of "Stepping Stone", their spikey hypnotic performance made Manchester's "pub rock" circuit, whose furrow I had ploughed in recent months, suddenly seem shallow and redundant.

I could at least now defend the Sex Pistols honour to any Genesis or Eagles (or Stash) fan if I felt so inclined, although I sustained a muted indifference on the drive home as I was forced to endure a spiteful tirade against the band we had just witnessed, which was perhaps unsurprising considering the evening began as a journey to check out a group of "prog rock" wannabees.

The exasperation felt by these fans of "proper" music was stated not to be due to the Pistols' ostensible inability to play but to the Pistols custom of writing songs around bawled lyrics proclaiming such gems as "I'm a lazy sod". Unlike progressive bands who, of course, sang about wizards and lawnmowers! And the final affront, echoing claims that would subsequently emanate from at least some attendees at the Lesser Free Trade Hall gigs, was the banal, "If they can get away with it, why can't we?"

★

The Electric Circus gained further ground by staging a return of the Anarchy tour on Sunday 19th December, one week before Christmas and this time minus Buzzcocks. Even if the events of 1977 had never happened at the Circus, a place in local history was guaranteed having allowed the Pistols to perform their widely banned tour twice when many towns and cities would not sanction a single appearance.

The story behind the sudden censorship would also spawn bizarre claims by locals to have seen the Today programme on which Bill Grundy confronted the Sex Pistols, despite the early evening show only being broadcast in the Thames Television area of Greater London in an era long before You Tube or satellite dishes. Indeed the claims would, to a lesser extent, mirror the claims in later decades of having been at the first Sex Pistols' gig at the Lesser Free Trade Hall.

★

My final act of 1976 was not to check out another of these punk bands but to check out the local of Bill Grundy near his Marple Bridge home. In a weak act of rebellion a few of us donned drainpipe jeans assuming Grundy would recognise such outrageous attire as symbolic of the punk movement that he had inadvertently boosted and react accordingly.

The TV presenter was in fact ensconced in the Midland Hotel savouring the Christmas holiday period, so the first part of the ruse had not gone to plan. Any hope that our presence would somehow unsettle his cosy lunch time drink was thwarted as he happily chatted with the regulars, oblivious to our outlandish appearance that actually caused more outrage among his remaining drinking buddies who still regarded flares as the acceptable norm.

1977

Considering what 1977 would deliver, the year began quietly. A heavy snowfall in January prevented what would have been a final visit to the Phoenix, now that more prestigious live offerings at the Electric Circus held sway, and a final chance to judge the merits of Solstice. For whatever reasons the Phoenix would cease to offer live music at the end of April 1977 bringing that particular chapter in Manchester's live music scene to, at least, a temporary conclusion.

Maybe the cause was not helped by, as *New Manchester Review* described it, "the infamous Electric Circus" presenting local bands on a Wednesday from March with Leo, Gags and Tractor all stepping onto their bigger stage.

Friday 21st January 1977

Word arrived via a gig listing in the *Manchester Evening News* that The Damned were to play the Electric Circus. The name on the flyer for the night had been The Enid. Not the most enigmatic name ever chosen for a band, although I was repeatedly assured that it was worth checking out the music that lurked beyond.

I have since learned that The Enid were an outfit put together by former Barclay James Harvest musical director Robert John Godfrey, Barclay James Harvest being another local outfit from the Saddleworth area close to Oldham but significantly for its residents within the county of Yorkshire. I am unsure if The Enid had any similarities to Barclay James Harvest as they never actually appeared at the Electric Circus on my watch despite frequently being listed to do so. Even without the benefit of witnessing them first hand, I can confidently guess that they bore little or no resemblance to tonight's replacement.

And so it was The Damned back in Manchester who, like the Pistols, had released a single "New Rose", described in some quarters as the first UK punk single, thus eliminating contemporaries such as the Gorillas, the 101ers or the Hot Rods from the genre.

Like the Pistols, the band were on stage when I entered the old cinema. Unlike the Pistols, the place was oddly subdued with the Friday night crowd offering little reaction to the band going through their usual motions with their dark, slightly one dimensional offerings, delivered with a greater level of competence than seemed to be acknowledged.

Visually it was only the shades worn by bassist Captain Sensible that endorsed The Damned's punk leanings, although straight leg jeans were a strictly no-go area in the Circus audience, so maybe their lack of flare in the trouser department condemned them before a note was played. Singer Dave Vanian's Dracula guise owed as much to the shock theatrics of Alice Cooper or the outrageous showmanship of Arthur Brown as it did to punk fashion.

Attempts at humour such as announcing "Stab Your Back" as "Rat Scabies Is Gonna Stab You All Over" fell as flat as their musical delivery was becoming to this audience. Even "New Rose" failed to register any familiar approval to stir the crowd's apathy.

After a brief set The Damned made the long trek through the crowd and up the stairs behind the bar to where the Circus' dressing room was located. An act that elicited the first response of the evening to a chorus of "shit, shit, shit" escalated until the DJ obligingly resumed some "proper music" that would have been Rainbow or Thin Lizzy.

Although the episode had more than a trace of humour, I did feel a level of affront that this crowd, whose inoffensive nature had previously seemed so welcoming, even if some of the dirges offered by the likes of Nugent or Rainbow had not, should deliver such a categorical rebuke. Which raised the question; what was so uninviting about The Damned's repertoire? I also wondered if the Friday night regulars understood that they were probably the reason the gig went ahead, rather than the extremely meagre number of Damned fans who bought tickets.

★

My record buying, or more specifically the purchasing of seven-inch singles, took on a renewed zest in 1977 as I began to locate more punk releases, The Stranglers having signed a deal and issuing their first single and The Damned going as far as releasing an album described, like the single "New Rose", as 'the first by a UK punk band'.

The one track from this period imprinted on my memory is by a musician whose Mancunian roots I was unaware of at the time. Roy Harper's "One of Those Days in England" seemed to be constantly on the radio at the start of 1977 with the folk singer even being pictured in the *NME* fraternising with members of The Damned. The story of Harper's hereditary condition, mischievously linked to the alleged administering of the kiss of life to a sheep, also emerged at the time, despite the condition having been diagnosed some six years earlier. The story was that the condition gave him a life expectancy of around seven years, although mercifully the Rusholme born singer is still, at the time of writing, an occasional performer at the age of 76.

Probably the most telling purchase of the time was an EP by a Manchester band who, the story went, had formed their own label and self-financed the release with a sum borrowed from the guitarist's father. The disc was harder to come by due to lack of major distribution but fortunately there was a shop on Great Underbank in Stockport that stocked it.

The shop in question was principally a book shop that also stocked various magazines including one that had a monochrome image of Bob Dylan on the cover and included a fictitious interview with the singer. The magazine went by the name of *Out There* and also included features on Ted Nugent and Aerosmith alongside smaller articles on The Stranglers and the Sex Pistols with Buzzcocks also making the cut. I was to learn that the publication in question was one of those new fanzines, despite *Sniffin' Glue* editor Mark P having written to its creator Paul Morley suggesting it more closely resembled *Vogue*. Furthermore, the fanzine's originator was employed at the shop in question, although it was a lady called Chris who sold me "Spiral Scratch" by Buzzcocks.

It took me a while to assimilate the four tracks that comprised "Spiral Scratch" having purchased the EP untested in much the same way I had previously bought albums. Thus my first encounter with Buzzcocks' music was the playing of

"Breakdown" on my record deck.

The monochrome picture sleeve contained a barely focused Polaroid snap of the band on the front with the basic information on the reverse including the number of takes required to capture the tracks and the number of guitar dubs added.

There have been varying definitions of what factors distinguish a single from an EP (Extended Play) record although the most obvious delineation seems to be 'more than a single but less than an LP'. Both were usually a seven inch vinyl record played at 45 rpm but whereas a single had usually consisted of a main track or A-side backed with a B-side, the EP contained more tracks, usually four. This was apparently achieved by the EP having narrower grooves, achieved by lowering the cutting levels and also sometimes by sound compression, enabling more music per side. A more noteworthy difference between an EP and a single was the equal magnitude afforded to each track with no particular song claiming the coveted A-side status and the EP often bearing a title that was not one of the tracks – in this case the name Spiral Scratch being the definition of the groove on a vinyl record.

Spiral Scratch was curiously split with the lead tracks on each side "Breakdown" and "Boredom" offering a more direct approach than the less accessible "Time's Up" and "Friends of Mine" that concluded the sides in a more experimental vein. Thus both faces of "Spiral Scratch" seemed to contain the equivalent of an A-side followed by the B-side. With a two note guitar solo and "B'dum b'dum" refrain, it was clear "Boredom" would become a byword for the generation alongside "Anarchy". As familiarity bred acceptance, the four songs that comprised Buzzcocks' premier outing on vinyl would each have their own unique allure.

Around the same time Mick Middlehurst lodged the question, "Why don't *we* start a fanzine?" No reason at all except we knew precious little about the process of printing and publication but, undeterred, I began making serious plans including writing to the Electric Circus for forthcoming dates to publish. Graham Brooks obligingly rang to supply details of the upcoming months that would include visits by The Clash and The Ramones and others including bands by the names of Jenny Haan's Lion and The Scorpions. At the same time Mick decided to write to the *NME* announcing our intentions and giving us the pen names Mick Middles and Martin Martyn and, for some incalculable reason, promising to sell the first issue for 10p.

Thursday 3rd March 1977

The name Iggy Pop would always be synonymous with anything punk, The Stooges often being noted as the original three chord garage band. Iggy Pop had drawn approval from such luminaries as David Bowie and Marc Bolan – it has been suggested that both "Jean Genie" and "20th Century Boy" were homages to "the world's forgotten boy", as he described himself in "Search and Destroy" off his 1973 Bowie mixed LP "Raw Power". Having again collaborated with Bowie, he was about to resurface with a solo album recorded in Berlin and as a final flourish on the tour to promote the album, Bowie was to feature as keyboard player.

Predictably with Bowie in tow, there was an impressive turnout to welcome Iggy Pop to the Manchester Apollo, my first live concert at the former ABC Cinema, Ardwick that had hosted The Beatles and Rolling Stones back in the day.

Support band The Vibrators were sufficiently professional to draw approval from the house, few of whom took issue with their scurried reading of Iggy Pop's "No Fun" or indeed their reputation as older musicians riding the punk bandwagon. The latter was probably not helped by their appearance as backing band for session guitarist and former Womble Chris Spedding at the 100 Club Punk Festival, a collaboration that would re-emerge on a joint single that carried the somewhat crass title "Pogo Dancing" and reputedly led to their appearance on Mickie Most's RAK label for their debut single "We Vibrate".

Despite The Vibrators being deemed sufficiently adept to accompany the experienced Spedding, there were rumours that early Vibrators gigs were played with consciously rehearsed minimalism, some even suggesting that their set was based around no more than two chords.

Any fair observer of the time must have conceded that both sides of the RAK single were as worthy as most other UK punk releases. Indeed the band's set peaked with their delivery of the single's B-side "Whips and Furs" which carried a sufficiently strong hook to detract from the band's odd fixation with vibrators and whips.

As for the main act, Iggy Pop was happy to proceed with minimal rapport between songs as he delivered a cross section of the new and the old to appease all corners of the house. Perhaps unsurprisingly, given the increasingly vocal patronage that the crowd bestowed on the band's keyboard player, it was the excerpts from the soon to be released "The Idiot" that drew the warmest approval from the house, although you came away with the impression that more tickets had been purchased to witness the keyboard skills of Bowie than the rhythmic dancing and deep vocals of Iggy Pop. To his eternal credit, Bowie stuck to his task, making no attempt to acknowledge the acclaim, much less to milk it for his own vanity.

★

As a taster I made several aborted attempts at writing a leader page for the fanzine, should it ever come to fruition, concentrating mainly on the live music scene in Manchester, whatever musical clique it may belong to; thus Rudy and the Zipps were still being referenced even though I had not encountered them since the previous summer and, for all I knew, they could have disbanded. Mick considered The Vibrators' support slot to Iggy worthy of reviewing and fired off a typewritten critique as well as an expletive laden review of The Damned LP.

The next step would be to request the services of a band to interview. After all, was that not the trusted format of the music press? News, features (always involving the participation of the featured band), singles reviews, album reviews and live reviews. And of course a letters page, although first we would have to find a way of publishing the thing in order to acquire some readers. The small matter of the how, did not restrain me from composing a written request to the address on the Buzzcocks' EP for an interview with the band. In an attempt to gain the band's cooperation I stressed that Buzzcocks would be the main feature of our debut publication although I probably overstated the matter of it being a Manchester fanzine and them being a Manchester band. I also got into character by signing the missive Martin Martyn.

As this was the first time I had made such a bold enquiry, I went about my business assuming that any response would arrive later rather than sooner and no doubt be a standard reply from some PR at New Hormones. Thus I was unprepared for a phone call a couple of days later not from a member of New Hormones staff but from a caller identifying himself as Pete Shelley from Buzzcocks who suggested we meet outside Manchester Library on the coming Saturday. I am not sure how I would have reacted had either of my parents answered the phone and said, "It's Pete Shelley from Buzzcocks."

I should stress that, despite having dabbled in the musical phenomenon to which I was about to give my undivided attention, I was not as yet a regular on the Manchester punk scene. A scene that took in the Ranch on Dale Street and the famous Pips Discotheque behind Manchester Cathedral, neither of which I had set foot in. Apparently had I done so mine and Pete Shelley's paths may have crossed before and the process of procuring an interview may have been a mere formality.

As events unfolded I was left somewhat dumbstruck that I had just spoken to someone whose record I had just bought. Not only that but he rang me! In 1977, rock stars lived in a different universe to the rest of us. I realised that Buzzcocks were not yet operating at the level of most of the artists whose records I owned but they were still artists who created great original music. I had never done this before but I would not expect United Artists to pass a request for Dr Feelgood's services to Wilko Johnson or Lee Brilleaux with the directive, "Can you give this lad a ring and sort things out."

In my elation at having made contact in such a personable manner, I overlooked a very basic problem that we had no firm plan how we would produce this fanzine. I had a Dansette tape recorder and a Polaroid instant camera as well as unlimited access to my parent's typewriter. An interview should be plain sailing, except that neither of us had ever conducted an interview before. We had not even caught Buzzcocks live, my sole knowledge being the 4 tracks that comprised the "Spiral Scratch" EP and the tale of how they formed their own label. To add to the dilemma Howard Devoto, who sang on the EP and co-wrote all four songs, and who was probably the most recognisable of the original quartet, had left the band. All I had to distinguish Buzzcocks from the general Manchester public was the Polaroid snap from the record sleeve and a small group shot from *Penetration* fanzine taken the previous August outside St Boniface Church that depicted Pete Shelley donning shades.

Thursday 17th March 1977

Having touched base with the Electric Circus, the other requirement of live reviews seemed more straightforward. Find bands to review and maybe get some pictures, assuming the Circus management would let us take a camera into the venue. The visit of Scottish/Aussie rockers AC/DC seemed as good an opportunity as any to test both ideas. They had never been classified as punks but then I already knew that they were a great live act who didn't meander into endless and self-indulgent instrumental solos. The band may not have been caught in punk's slipstream, as other traditional bands such as the Gorillas or the Count Bishops had, although their reputation included taking turns with Eddie and the Hot Rods to outsell the Marquee, but they seemed closer to being punks than serious rock artists. The poster for the gig proclaimed –

"The Most Outrageous Heavy Metal Group In The World"

I introduced myself to Graham Brooks who was sat by the DJ. The manager was very welcoming, although disappointed at the turnout, a point at which I had to concur, although it did at least feature one very apparent punk. AC/DC would play London's Rainbow Theatre on this particular tour, so the acquisition of their services was quite a coup for the Circus management making the modest attendance all the more staggering. As if to uphold my conviction of this band's credibility, the DJ played a sequence of the Pistols' "Anarchy in the UK", The Damned's "Neat Neat Neat" and Buzzcocks' "Boredom", before reverting to more familiar rock fodder.

Despite the meagre audience, the band was sufficiently on form for my initial foray into musical journalism to be gratifying as AC/DC left their mark on the Electric Circus. Bon Scott showed a new level of authority and once again the double act of Scott and Young supplied the expected routines. There was to be no encore but that seemed more of a rejoinder to the attendance than the lack of vocal appreciation.

Saturday 19th March 1977

As it transpired Buzzcocks recognition was a straightforward task. Even their toned down punk style set them apart from the general Manchester public. The diminutive figure of Pete Shelley, clad in straight leg black jeans and an orange cagoule, asked if we had seen their drummer to which I responded in the negative rather than confess that I was not sure if I would recognise him. The comparatively towering figure of drummer John Maher duly arrived and we adjourned to the upstairs room of the Abercrombie pub on Manchester's Bootle Street and I placed a portable Dansette tape recorder on the table.

When the interview was eventually typed up for the fanzine, we suggested the landlady had "hated us" from the moment we entered her pub. I have to confess this was probably a complete fabrication to imply some degree of punk prejudice as I can recall no level of hostility towards ourselves or the band in our company.

As fortune would have it these four likely lads, who were roughly the same age as us, apart from Maher who hesitantly conceded that he should not yet be drinking in a pub, were happy to expound upon our basic line of questioning, although there was some disquiet at our revelation that we had yet to catch them live. They ran through the new line up with Steve

Diggle now handling lead guitar to allow Pete Shelley to adopt vocal duties whilst supplying rhythm guitar.

And they had a new member, introduced simply as "just Garth" who now provided the bass. "Garth" was Garth Smith and many years later he would go by his birth name of Garth Davies. A fact emerging more recently is that it was Garth who played bass in the nascent Buzzcocks before their debut proper at the Lesser Free Trade Hall. Garth did indulge one bizarre act in asking us both for our autographs.

The one element of our inexperience that the band failed to highlight was in response to the direct "How long have you been playing?" query proffered when the early conversation drifted into general chat and Shelley urged us to "ask some more questions". Given the historical significance that has been attached to the previous year's shows by the Sex Pistols at the Lesser Free Trade Hall, one factor being that Buzzcocks had formed and debuted at the second of the gigs, it seems strange with hindsight that the band did not register some element of surprise that we were unaware of this momentous fact. Moreover, the three surviving members from that event failed to even acknowledge the "eureka" moment that the Pistols appearances had been for all present.

The dialogue shifted between Buzzcocks and other matters of modern music. Shelley referred to The Damned's long player as fitting the Phil Spector description of an LP being two singles and ten other tracks, although he conceded to liking "Fan Club" which "sounds like Alice Cooper". Garth didn't like Joey Ramone's voice. Shelley liked "Anarchy in the UK" although he had reservations about its use of eight guitar overdubs.

On politics Shelley elucidated, "I live therefore I'm political" explaining Buzzcocks' politics were more personal. Diggle expanded that, "Some of the politics are rubbish. I mean Generation X!"

Subway Sect came in for criticism although Shelley did qualify that, "Subway Sect might be okay, I mean we've only seen 'em once." The once being a support slot along with Buzzcocks at the Harlseden Coliseum to headliners The Clash who the band collectively extolled. All girl group The Slits, who had also featured that night, were described as "really good."

The *NME* review of the Harlseden gig had been less than kind to Buzzcocks. Shelley suggested that the review's author, Nick Kent, may be resentful of many within the punk scene because he had been the singer with the three musicians who became The Damned before, "they kicked him out and got Dave Vanian – or so rumour has it."

As for their contemporaries, the Pistols were great lads as were Johnny Thunders and the Heartbreakers, their manager Leee Black Childers having admired Shelley's sawn off Audition guitar. Shelley gave our photographic equipment a reassuring nod of approval describing Polaroid cameras as "fantastic."

Shelley thought Iggy Pop had been "great" at the recent Apollo gig and confirmed the recent claims in an *NME* advert that he liked German technos Can. In fact he liked all music that provoked the feeling "Wow that's good".

Steve Diggle liked almost everything Bowie had done. Of the recent appearance by The Stranglers at the Electric Circus, Diggle did utter a surprised "Was there?" when we mentioned reports of trouble at the gig. Garth liked Tiger Feet by Mud that was reviewed in the current issue of Glasgow-based fanzine *Ripped and Torn.*

No doubt recognising our inexperience, they were happy to plug the gaps in our knowledge of the Manchester scene. Slaughter and the Dogs had recently opened the Oaks in Chorlton-cum-Hardy as a live punk venue with Buzzcocks attending to lend support. As well as another local outfit, The Drones, there was a newly formed band, yet to debut, who called themselves Stiff Kittens. At the time Shelley made no reference to Stiff Kittens' choice of appellation although subsequent stories have suggested that it was either Shelley himself or Buzzcocks' manager Richard Boon who suggested the name.

Pete Shelley suggested Slaughter and the Dogs' practice of including "Jumping Jack Flash" in their set was not really "progressive", which Shelley conceded was "a terrible word". When pushed they conceded the Dogs were, "okay" even "good musicians". Shelley proffered Paul Morley's description of The Drones as "Music For Pleasure Iggy Pop" after informing that their guitarist had let off a fire extinguisher at nearby Houldsworth Hall.

For the record, Music For Pleasure was a budget label of the sixties and seventies. Being partly owned by EMI, the label was able to access original artists such as the Beach Boys or Pink Floyd for their budget reissues but the label's notoriety that inspired Morley's analogy was their series of albums that carried titles such as "Hot Hits" and featured recordings of current chart hits by session musicians who attempted to replicate the original and bore the legend, "Can you tell the difference between these and the original sounds?" The chance to purchase a compilation of the hits of the day at less than half the price of an album proved too good an offer to refuse before labels such as K-Tel or Ronco began issuing similar fayre but with the noteworthy difference that their albums contained the original artists.

And there was already a fanzine in Manchester called *Shy Talk* started by a guy called Steve from Moss Side.

Saturday 26th March 1977

Another Saturday night in Collyhurst where the advertised act were again bill regulars The Enid who regularly failed to appear, tonight being another such occasion.

So it was that the band making their way to the stage via the audience were in fact Ultravox! a band instantly recognisable from the cover of their recent debut album sleeve, looking like a Rock Follies interpretation of a punk band with carefully placed zips and PVC. It was hard not to be aware of Ultravox! their LP sleeve glared at you amid The Damned and Ramones and the re-released first two Stooges albums that was almost the lot of most record stores' newly created punk section. Even Racing Cars would be slipped in to make up the numbers.

The band had landed a deal with Island Records and secured the services of Brian Eno to produce them. In fact their art school affectations were very much in the Roxy Music vein, although surprisingly singer John Foxx (Denis Leigh) was closer in age to members of Roxy Music than most of the current punk crop.

As for what Ultravox! sounded like; I was about to discover for the first time, having never been tempted to swell my meagre punk collection with the purchase of an album by a band with such a blatantly manufactured image.

Perhaps it was their stagecraft or maybe their grasp of song writing but from the opening number singer John Foxx led the band through a tempting mixture of the rough and the avant garde in a set that contained many compositional gems. With an image that might have alienated both sides of the audience, Ultravox! charmed their way to a richly deserved encore with a chant of "John Foxx, Ultravox!" echoing around the room. For some reason, Foxx modestly described "Fear in the Western World" as a Velvet Underground number when in fact it was another sturdy example of the quality of Ultravox!'s own material.

The night also introduced me to the curious art of heckling. For reasons unknown a call of, "Where's Timothy Leary?" was echoed by a response of "Where's Paul Morley?" Whether it was Morley who delivered either or both of the catcalls remains an unanswered mystery (although it was a distinct probability given that he was in attendance and would garner a reputation for verbal jousting and self-publicity).

Although the Circus had been a port of call on the Sex Pistols and AC/DC tours, tonight was the first time a chance encounter would deliver on such a level and with such force that a hasty rethink involved the purchase of the LP, assuming that no one had already been tempted by the one copy in the punk section of my local record shop.

running around
new york city
so high

Tuesday 29th March 1977

If I was to have a proper induction in punk then the appearance of Johnny Thunders and the Heartbreakers at the Oaks on Barlow Moor Road, Chorlton-cum-Hardy would prove a worthy baptism. The New York band arrived having played to a star-studded audience the previous night at London's Marquee – the audience had included Rod Stewart, presumably in recognition of the New York Dolls having opened for The Faces at a Wembley concert some five years previously.

I had visited this place several years before when the main room was a soul disco that echoed to such sounds as Stevie Wonder's "He's Misstra Know It All" or The Chi-Lites' "Stoned Out Of My Mind". the Oaks was a large pub situated opposite Manchester's Southern Cemetery. Entrance was through the front door where tickets were shown or, more usually, an admission charge was collected. This led to a large main room with a fairly central stage situated within a cage type set and, being a pub, there was a large bar to the right.

Tonight the Oaks had a complete other-worldliness with more punks than I had ever realised existed in the entirety of Greater Manchester crammed into one small venue. Although I recognised tracks by The Damned and The Stranglers, much of the dark and heavy sounds emanating from the DJ's turntable were unfamiliar to my ears, although names like the Flamin' Groovies or Richard Hell along with the complete New York Dolls back catalogue would enter my musical vocabulary with a vengeance in the coming months. In fact the only respite from the shady soundtrack was the playing of "Jump" from Peter Cook and Dudley Moore's "Derek and Clive Live".

The night's proceedings had an air of edginess triggered by the presence of some extremely tall leather clad individuals with Sid Vicious-style Vaseline spiked hair, who seemed to be monitoring proceedings, combined with an overheard conversation describing all the blood in the toilets. By contrast the band's concern was whether the audience had any rhythm, as Johnny Thunders enquired, "Don't you dance?".

What ensued was the gig that changed my life. Deep Purple could lodge a modest plea, having been the first live concert that I ever attended some six years prior, but none of the current crop, Sex Pistols included, could claim to have altered my entire musical perception in the way that Johnny Thunders, Walter Lure, Billy Rath and Jerry Nolan did that night. The band, containing two former New York Dolls in Thunders and drummer Nolan, gave a slick but colourful performance that this new sub-culture were more than happy to grasp.

Any doubts about the worth of this musical phenomenon were removed overnight by a band that delivered on every level. Their musicianship was tight, their songs strong and memorable with hints of American bubblegum delivered through sharp guitar chords and their live performance blew away any feelings of apprehension that the clientele, aided in no small way by the gangling individuals, had created within the venue.

The Pistols may have proffered the "anyone can do it" argument but the Heartbreakers reminded us what the end product should sound like. Johnny Thunders himself would later cite Iggy Pop and the MC5 along with Eddie Cochran and Gene Vincent as influences on his music that had tonight been so complete.

As Pete Townshend apparently said to his father when his dad took a young Pete to see The Blackboard Jungle – "What *is* this amazing music?"

★

The next act was to pen two further reviews for the fanzine.

Ultravox! was routine enough, although I bizarrely suggested in an editorial that the gig suffered due to Ultravox! being a late replacement. In fact Ultravox! had been booked in time to make the "Rock" list in the *New Manchester Review* and I am guessing the band were blown away by the reception afforded by what appeared to be a predominantly heavy metal audience who displayed an inexplicable familiarity with the band's only album release.

As for the Heartbreakers, I doubt my review came even close to creating the atmosphere that band and audience had fashioned on that Tuesday night in South Manchester. Maybe I did not wish to give a potential audience of punks the notion that I was a comparative newcomer to this game, so I played it straight, running through the numbers played, having jotted them down on the night, with a few added descriptions of the songs and the band's artistry, harshly mocking their American accents and Johnny Thunders querying why the audience were not dancing. Maybe I inadvertently engineered a response to Pete Shelley's descriptor of playing cover versions as "recycling" by defending the Heartbreakers' playing of Berry Gordy's "Do You Love Me".

A few albums and singles reviews and we were away except for the minor matter of how we are to print the thing... The decision to include AC/DC was always going be a gamble, although we should maybe have quit after the live review as both of us took a swipe at the band for the lack of musical force in their recorded work. I even proffered the view that any band signed to Atlantic Records and headlining at the Rainbow Theatre "deserve to make it"!

Still we had a name, although I cannot recall the precise origins of the title *Ghast Up*. The word "ghast" was derived from "ghastly" and the two words seemed to fit together. Unbeknownst to me at the time, the word had been utilised as a noun rather than an adjective. The Ghasts were a race in H P Lovecraft's "Dream Cycle" series of short stories from 1926. The DC Universe series of comics from 1962 also featured a character called Ghast and The Ghast was a creature that appeared at some point during 1977 in the "Dungeons and Dragons" board game.

I even managed to procure some local news concerning Manchester bands. The DJ at the Oaks, whilst advising of Slaughter and the Dogs' next appearance, announced the band's upcoming single release. Following my instinctive obligation to glean further information, the DJ was more than happy to furnish full particulars of both sides and the label, as well as apprising me how good the single was. Whatever truculent reputation he would later acquire, on my first encounter Rob Gretton could not have been more helpful.

I also gleaned that The Drones were to play an unlisted gig at the Electric Circus and were to release an EP thanks to a handwritten flyer in the window of "Paul Morley's shop" as Pete Shelley had referred to the book shop in Stockport where the creator of *Out There* was employed.

A factor I failed to clarify during the execution of *Ghast Up* was the name of our featured band, who were referred to as "The Buzzcocks" in the first issue, having failed to notice the band were, and always would be known simply as "Buzzcocks". We also shrank from using the term "punk" to define the music, staying with the less committed "new wave".

Good Friday 8th April

A working day if you had a ten-page fanzine to staple. I had discovered three methods of printing a fanzine; the most obvious being to entrust the work to a printing company who would deliver the best results but at the greatest cost. A cheaper way was to copy the pages on an office photocopier – a cheap method if you had free access and use of such a machine but still expensive if you had to pay for the work. *48 Thrills* fanzine was a prime example of a fanzine produced in this way. *Sniffin' Glue* also began life via the office photocopier, courtesy of Mark P's girlfriend who was able to use a machine at her place of work.

For *Ghast Up* we discovered that the most readily available form of cheap printing was with a stencil duplicating machine as invented by Hungarian David Gestetner following his move to North London in the nineteenth century. Before the days of workplace computers and emails, stencil duplicators as manufactured by Gestetner's company and Roneo were a valuable business tool in offices for the reproduction of multiple typed documents such as memos or copies of minutes and, in particular, contracts or agreements where each copy would otherwise require proof reading.

The process involved typing without the typewriter ribbon, which in turn cut the stencil. The stencil was placed around an ink filled revolving drum that rotated against a lower drum, the paper being fed between both drums and the ink forced through the cut stencil onto the paper. There was a pink liquid correction fluid that sealed the cut stencil, so errors could be overtyped.

We were able to produce *Ghast Up* in this way thanks in no small part to my sister who had access to her company's machine. It was necessary to pay for a few electronically cut stencils so photographs could be featured and the one real indulgence was paying for the cover to be cut and printed professionally so at least the fanzine had a veneer of acceptable quality.

The Easter weekend saw snatched visits to "Paul Morley's shop" in Stockport, and the Virgin Records store on Lever Street, Manchester, both of whom were more than happy to stock our primitive publication, albeit on a sale or return basis. I even recall a resounding, "Oh yeah" from John Webster, the manager of the Virgin store, a self-confessed Clapton fanatic who would subsequently welcome the burgeoning punk community into his sound booths.

The only obstacle proved to be Grass Roots bookshop who, without perusing our fanzine, deemed it, "right wing and sexist". Whether some of the subject within the AC/DC review could be construed as sexism, such as the band describing a woman with venereal disease as having "The Jack" is open to debate, but I have never grasped the right-wing accusation (unless it was Grass Roots' viewpoint that the mere willingness to afford space to a band such as AC/DC was considered chauvinist in the extreme).

If the publication of a fanzine was a labour intensive business, the distribution and selling was equally fraught. Alongside the customary requests for local record shops to stock our goods and the direct approach of selling at gigs, there were two other outlets that produced different results.

Weekly music paper *Sounds* offered classified ads together with the use of a box number for a modest fee. Although the *NME* was still regarded by many as the flagship of the UK music press, *Sounds* had extended a more sympathetic ear to the punk scene. Whilst the *NME* had granted space to punk bands, there remained a sense within its pages that the whole movement was a mere sideshow to the proper music of Pink Floyd, Genesis and the like. Not that *Sounds* had given up on the old guard, who still dominated the album charts and the news pages, but its writers and editors seemed to adopt a less pompous approach to the new breed.

So it was in the classified section of *Sounds* that we advertised our fanzine for sale together with a modest postage cost. While the ad drew an acceptable response from the length and breadth of the country from characters such as Venom Vindictive and a punkette named Maureen from Newcastle who went by the name of Maur Vanian, most customers presumed that we were a proper business with a bank account in the fanzine's name. Cheques and even Postal Orders that could simply be exchanged for cash if left blank, were invariably made payable to *Ghast Up* meaning countless copies were issued without reclaiming the cost.

Maur Vanian became a regular correspondent following receipt of the ordered publication, despite being one of several readers who accused *Ghast Up* of containing too few expletives for a punk publication. Her choice of moniker was unsurprisingly due to an obsession with The Damned's lead singer although later correspondence showed a change to the slightly more imaginative Maur Bid. Maur also alerted us to the fanzine *Deviation Street* that hailed from the north east.

Another route was to write to Rough Trade Records in London, who famously stocked and distributed fanzines such as *Sniffin' Glue* who in turn acknowledged Rough Trade as, "The friendliest shop in town." How the London shop would react to being asked to stock an unproven fanzine from up north was swiftly answered with a handwritten reply from shop owner Geoff Travis whose correspondence clearly showed he had taken the time to read our publication. Furthermore Travis requested twenty-five copies for the Notting Hill shop.

Tuesday 12th April 1977

A night on which to slay two birds with one stone; having yet to connect with the management at the Oaks, I was unsure of our reception as we carried a bagful of fanzines into the venue. Although they could have been returned to the car, the other unfinished business had to take precedence as it was the turn, and return, of Buzzcocks.

My first live encounter with the band, whose acquaintance we had made away from the stage, was fortunately a positive experience. Given that Howard Devoto was no longer at the mike, I could have found the Pete Shelley led edition not worthy of the hue and cry of being a main feature in *Ghast Up* and their opening reading of Breakdown from Spiral Scratch did present a certain trepidation that Shelley's vocals would not proffer a seamless transition. However a battery of other Shelley/Devoto compositions, that had yet to see the light of day in recorded form, allowed the new line up to kick on from there with rhythm guitarist Steve Diggle offering more than a back seat performance to Shelley and his sawn off guitar's centre stage role.

A smaller but no less animated crowd than had greeted the Heartbreakers at this venue were happy to overlook the dissimilar voice on the Spiral Scratch tracks and the final seal of approval arrived towards the end when Shelley identified a heckler's affable intrusion as Paul Morley.

Wednesday 13th April 1977

The second of the week's gatherings of the Mancunian fraternity happened the following day with a return to the familiar haunt of the Electric Circus and the matter of assessing another bunch of locals with The Drones appearing for a bargain fifty pence on the door. For the first time I found the Circus devoid of heavy metal devotees or their ear-splitting music with even the DJ possessing short hair and playing equally raucous but less drawn out tracks than the Circus norm.

On familiar territory, a bag of fanzines was no obstacle on the door and so the hands-on task of fanzine selling began. The dubious accolade of being the first face-to-face customer was a lad who informed me that his mates were from Preston but had adopted the yet to be thriving Manchester scene as a regular haunt, driving down in a battered van. He didn't part with the readies as he had already bought one in Virgin but he did offer an appraisal that, "It's alright!" His name was Woody and his mates from Preston were Ian and Allan. The trio would evolve into another local band, so I had just met the future bassist with The Worst.

I also met The Worst's future manager after successfully offloading a copy of *Ghast Up* to the DJ in exchange for a green covered fanzine that depicted a two tone picture of The Drones' singer Mike Howells, who I recognised as the pinstripe clad punk at the Ultravox! gig. The fanzine was the second issue of *Shy Talk* and somehow I found myself discussing the politics of fanzine production with its co-creator Steve Shy (Burke) who would take on management responsibilities for The Worst.

Having somehow offloaded a few copies, I noticed a tall individual in a pinstriped jacket and jeans asking Steve Shy if one of my victims holding a purchased copy was from *Ghast Up,* at which the affable fanzine writer glanced round and pointed me out. The individual offered his hand and introduced himself enquiring, "Can I write something for you?"

The aspirant in question was Paul Morley, whose initial forays into writing via the Stockport magazine *Penetration* and his own *Out There* had earned him the position of Manchester correspondent for the *New Musical Express*. If tonight's events were to make the next week's publication it would be via the scribblings of Morley, just as the recent visit by The Stranglers had been. So basically having him on board was a fairly big deal.

Pete Shelley, also present, accused our publication of offending his friends by reducing his negative assessment of Subway Sect to a blanket group dismissal, although he generously augmented that "For a first issue it's very good".

One set of locals for whom the night offered little salvation was the support band who were faring little better than The Damned had done on this stage despite playing to a home crowd. Wild Ram had reinvented themselves since that night in September (when they were warmly acknowledged by the Wythenshawe Forum crowd) and were now Ed Banger and the Nosebleeds. The origins of this new identity apparently stemmed from an occurrence during the second Sex Pistols show at the Lesser Free Trade Hall, although given that the event pre-dates their usage of the name Wild Ram, perhaps the story is best left untold.

As with Buzzcocks the previous night, they encountered a heckler, although the same intruder was in a less flattering mood, Paul Morley sprinting half the length of the venue to advise Eddie Garrity that he and his band were "boring." After a minor scuffle forced the writer's hasty retreat, the singer responded, "So Paul Morley writes for the *NME*, so what, shit shit shit?" Whilst still dishing out advice Morley told me that I should "give them a bad review, look at that" showing me his torn jacket whilst appearing dumbfounded that the singer should take violent exception to a critic offering an opinion.

And so, after a series of firsts, it was the turn of The Drones to convince. Early sound issues prompted the singer's hasty retreat pursued with equal haste by Paul Morley, who was about to confront his third singer in two nights.

I am not sure what words of encouragement Morley bestowed on the front man but, whatever the flavour of the exchange, the band retook the stage to elicit the most animated of receptions, culminating in chunks of the audience, including Morley, clearly sold on the worth of this Manchester band just as he had been with Buzzcocks the previous evening, joining them on stage and "going mad" as Mike Drone (Howells) would later describe it, "even geeks with long hair!"

I had not even contemplated the next issue of *Ghast Up* but it seemed the inherent choice to seek out this band for an interview. In the first of many acts of fanzine co-operation it was Steve Shy who gave me the phone number of Drones bassist Steve "Whispa" Cundall which I carefully wrote down on the reverse of the yellow Circus flyer for May.

★

And so it was that contact was made with The Drones. My initial call was greeted somewhat curtly by the query, "What exactly is it you want?" having found Mr Cundall not at home. Surely the tonic of last night had not raised the bar that much. As it transpired the bass player could not have been more gracious on returning my call, even apologising for having missed me earlier.

Saturday 23rd April 1977

The afternoon involved a meet up with Mike Drone at the Smithfield Arms on Swan Street, bumping into Steve Shy on the way, who came along to share views on our fanzine purchases. The publications I recall discussing were *Situation 3* that was, like ours, produced on a Roneo stencil machine, although they managed to achieve a superior photo quality and Glasgow's *Ripped and Torn*. As well as a joyous cheer when news came via the television that Manchester United were beating Leeds United in the FA Cup semi-final, Mike concurred with *Ripped and Torn*'s description of Ultravox! as "a product". The Drones singer apologised for the unavailability of his bandmates but promised to assemble his troops for the following day.

That evening at the Electric Circus the visitors were American band Roogalator. Their sole release to date was a 33 rpm EP on Stiff Records entitled "All Aboard". The release pre-dated The Damned's "New Rose" so I suspect the powers that be at Stiff didn't consider Roogalator to be a punk band, although they grew out of the same London pub rock circuit that produced the likes of the Hammersmith Gorillas (later just The Gorillas), the Count Bishops, The 101'ers and of course Eddie and the Hot Rods. While the punk credentials of all those bands was questionable, with the possible exception of Joe Strummer's 101'ers, their regular gigs coupled with their early vinyl releases provided an early alternative to the old order before The Damned and the Sex Pistols started to make records.

The Circus management were equally unmoved by Roogalator's appearance on Stiff Records as the regular DJ worked through his collection of Rainbow and Lizzy and (what would be the last time I was forced to hear) Ted Nugent.

In contrast to the air guitar friendliness of the night's sounds, Roogalator's laid back jazz-blues, described by guitarist and singer Danny Adler as 'the "Gusha-gusha" sound' was a strange fit for a Saturday night Circus crowd.

In between the lush sounds created on stage, Adler regaled the appreciative crowd with the refrain, "We can't see ya, but we can feel ya." Their songs were mostly in the feel good format of their Stiff release "All Aboard" and "Cincinnati Fatback" sometimes boasting lengthy titles like "(If You Don't Like Smelling It, You'd Better) Stop Selling It.". They even had what seemed a sure-fire hit with "Love and the Single Girl" although it never took off despite Creation boss Allan McGhee being among the purchasers of the subsequent one-off Virgin release.

I overheard someone remark that it would be good to catch Roogalator on home territory. Whether that referred to the club circuit in Adler's native Cincinnati or the London pub circuit where their unique take on blues had built an appreciative following, was unclear. Either way the Electric Circus, with the exception of Mike Drone who would dismiss the band with a one word adjective, warmed to the sounds created by Danny Adler and Roogalator.

Sunday 24th April 1977

Which brings me to the date when my involvement in this thing called punk suddenly seemed to be the prevailing factor in my life. Even the first rung bands at the Phoenix seemed to have an artistic distance from the audience and here I was swapping notes at a kind of after-show party.

Sunday punk nights at the Electric Circus had yet to happen and even a night with the fabulous Oldham Tinkers at Poynton Folk Club couldn't tempt me from a face-to-face encounter with a current punk band. The Smithfield Arms on Swan Street, Manchester was the site chosen by The Drones singer, now calling himself M J Drone and then strictly teetotal but nevertheless averring a preference for this particular drinking den.

We were joined by bassist Steve, whose acquaintance I had already made by phone and guitarist Gus Gangrene (Gary Callender). Pete Howells, the drummer and Mike's younger brother was absent (jamming with Bad Company or Led Zeppelin according to two explanations) unlike their new manager. Having joined most of the audience in gushing over their performance at the Electric Circus and mounting the stage to rhythmically demonstrate his approval during the encore, Paul Morley was now proclaiming himself The Drones' manager and calling himself Modest Young. The pseudonym and later pen-name Modest Young apparently arose following a review in the *NME* of Morley's fanzine *Out There* where Julie Burchill described the fanzine's creator as a "modest young man".

Before the task of interviewing The Drones got underway, there was a brief discussion of Paul Morley's recent elevation within the *NME* having been dispatched to Munich to review Status Quo at the Great Easter Rock 'n' Blues Express festival. The published edit of the original piece apparently gave the impression that the writer was a keen fan, which Morley stressed he really was not.

In true management style Paul/Modest discreetly coxswained his team, interjecting at chosen moments with themes designed to convince us of The Drones' worth in comparison to the remaining bands riding the "New Wave" or "'77 Pop" as Morley/Young delineated the likes of Buzzcocks, Clash, Chelsea etc.

In an act of mutual admiration Mike Drone attributed a put down of the band that Paul Morley had written in the *NME* as the catalyst to their progress (or progression), "When Morley ripped us off we thought, 'let's do it right!'" The review in question, although largely dismissive of The Drones' set list, did offer redemption in their one track "City Drones" that Morley likened to a Sweet B-side.

Mike Drone conceded that the comparison had initially been lost on the band who presumed that the flip side of the Chinn and Chapman penned A-sides contained more or less the same packaged glam pop. In fact it was the B-sides where Sweet were allowed to indulge their serious rock aspirations with self-penned solid workouts built around convincing guitar riffs that perplexed and irritated serious music fans in equal measure.

The gig in question had been the band's debut as The Drones at Manchester's Houldsworth Hall on Friday 17th December 1976 when they were supported by Generation X who had only debuted themselves the previous Friday, before squeezing in the opening two nights of London's Roxy Club earlier in the week with Slaughter and the Dogs appearing with them on the second of the two nights. The gig in question had been agreed with Generation X and Roxy Club manager Andy Czezowski in return for Czezowski's promise to put The Drones on at the Roxy. Whichever band *NME* had tasked Morley to appraise, it is fair to say they were both on a sharp learning curve.

Unlike our encounter with Buzzcocks, which had nevertheless been a noble initiation into the process, this was a more laid back dialogue between parties with the manager's awareness of the journalistic side of the music business affording suitable reference points to convince us that whichever punk bands lacked talent or commitment to the cause, The Drones were not among them. Morley even likened The Drones to the innovative free jazz of Ornette Coleman, a musical style to which he would later compare the loose but somehow tight musicianship of Siouxsie and the Banshees and The Slits.

Morley conceded the interview process could be "painful" when I humbly asked how long The Drones had been playing, although the simple enquiry prompted Steve Cundall to reveal that the band had been playing "new wave" for about eight of their twelve month existence. What that actually meant was they had existed in a previous incarnation as a teeny bop outfit in the Slik mould who had issued stickers and released a single entitled "Rollercoaster" backed with "Jump Jump Boogaloo" but that detail was not disclosed on the night. Nor was the fact that The

Drones, like so many of the current breed, had taken the Sex Pistols' appearance at the Lesser Free Trade Hall (in this case the second one) as the catalyst to switch musical direction.

Smack (later The Unwanted) and The Models were summarily dismissed in a rounded volley against all bands and audience members for whom the current scene was little more than a fashion quest or, as M J Drone put it, "They're just poseurs". On the subject of rock'n'roll style, absent drummer Pete Howells was commended by his brother for his vision in wearing a string vest on stage long before Bristol band The Cortinas adopted the garments.

Slaughter and the Dogs' less than slick approach to stagecraft attracted derision, although Morley did offer in their defence that, "I like Slaughter and the Dogs but they're not a new wave band". Morley suggested the Dogs were, "too eager to be accepted by the new wave clique" with the coterie of new wave repelled by such eagerness.

M J Drone shared Pete Shelley's declared approval of The Vibrators and cited The Only Ones, with their Velvet Underground image, as credible. Although he did point out that the restrained approach of Peter Perrett and co had caused them to struggle to follow The Drones more animated set when sharing the bill.

Illustrious neighbours Buzzcocks were spared any derision from the band or management, Morley even conceding that Spiral Scratch was his favourite EP, although he appended the assessment with the warning that the forthcoming Drones EP "jumps out at you".

Miles Copeland Junior, the financial whizzkid brother of Police drummer Stewart and later to work with Buzzcocks in America, took the biggest hit. Apparently Copeland was beginning to show an interest in the new music and Morley accused him of putting bands in situations where they were not in control of their own destiny.

In a round-up of the respective sub-categories on the punk family tree, Morley cajoled in us the view that The Drones belonged with The Boys, Generation X and The Vibrators, whereas Buzzcocks belonged more with The Clash as a band who were, "saying something". M J Drone's opinion that the Clash LP was, "a bit more poppy" was courteously but brusquely overruled with the album being, "too heavy to be pop". The term "punk" was barely used with band and manager preferring, "new wave". When Mick referred to followers as "punks" Morley jokily added the descriptor, "individually dressed personages".

Morley was to further endorse The Drones suggesting that they, like The Boys, The Vibrators and Buzzcocks, had taken Johnny Rotten's call to see more bands like the Sex Pistols at face value and now provided a worthy alternative to the staid rock scene of the previous year that had been based around such places as the Phoenix.

For such vision, Rotten was described by Morley as "a poet" although he expressed sympathy for Rotten who was, according to Morley's sources, spending six nights a week with his mother. Rotten had recently made the news for threatening behaviour with a broken glass involving DJ Bob Harris at London's Speakeasy Club which Morley was content to explain away with a dismissive, "well we've all done that in our time, let's be honest".

One aspect of The Drones business model that struck a chord was their readiness to ply their trade in the less modish environments of Carlisle, Doncaster or Morecambe where they had appeared at the nearby Inn on the Bay, although Gangrene suggested there was a lack of youth culture in the provinces with people going straight from childhood to middle age. Morley also included the cities of Liverpool and Sheffield on the roll call of unfashionable places on the punk itinerary, a curious observation with hindsight. And did someone mention Leeds Fforde Grene?

Their live set included two cover versions interspersed within the band's compositions. "Search and Destroy" ran closely to The Stooges arrangement, while the frenetic reading of "My Generation" borrowed the pace of Patti Smith's cover. "Highly definitive" was Morley's interjection although it was unclear whether he was referring to The Drones' cover or, more likely, Patti Smith as having alighted on the definitive interpretation of

Townshend's standard.

Maybe we should have queried the position of a manager about to contribute to our fanzine offering pointers as to why we should back his charges. I suspect Morley would have used such a conflict of interest to spice up proceedings if faced with a similar scenario in his *NME* role.

In defence of both parties, the band members were amiable enough in their own right and I doubt their first time responses would have caused us to question their significance at that moment. If we were not firmly onside at this point, Morley went on to describe our fanzine as "really cute" and observed that everyone was "doing something" be it writing or performing. He then mentioned that there was a photographer called Kevin who would supply photos. Kevin Cummins had taken several Drones shots, including a stroll through Manchester's King Street, that would grace the forthcoming EP sleeve and came highly recommended.

The Drones' convivial nature would remain thereafter, unlike Morley's overseeing of The Drones which seemed to quickly fade, particularly once he had included them in a double page *NME* spread entitled, "They Mean It M-a-a-a-nchester" that also appraised fanzines *Ghast Up* and *Shy Talk* and the rest of Manchester's current musical crop, curiously including a tentative nod to The Nosebleeds.

★

True to his word a letter from Paul Morley arrived by post, the envelope bearing the legend, "A communication from Modest Young". Contained within was a handwritten article over three sides of exercise book paper entitled "On the fringe of new wave!!! (huh!) by Modest Young." The fourth side of paper contained a friendly directive.

"hey martin,

remembering that your magazine is a pop magazine here's some pop writing for you about things that aren't new wave but must be worth mentioning, huh?

don't forget keep it fun!!!!

but be impolite!!! too!
Don't spare blushes!!!
But ya gotta entertain too!!!!!
MODESTx"

What Morley/Young had contributed spanned such diverse musical subjects as Three Dog Night, Judas Priest, Brian Eno and Gary Glitter, the then glam rocker being credited with delivering the definitive "Baby Please Don't Go" and cited as an influence on The Ramones.

It also referenced Pete Shelley suggesting that his composition "Sixteen" "strains with realism" compared to American contemporaries Jonathan Richman and the Tuff Darts and curiously, in what seemed a response to the live review of Ultravox! at the Electric Circus from our first issue, a critical elaboration of one of their performed songs "The City Doesn't Care" which he urged must be a single. Presumably neither band nor management were aware of our generosity to their cause as the song remains unrecorded.

The article concluded with a roll call of possible candidates to occupy the stated fringes of new wave that included the more obvious choices of Tom Verlaine, Velvet Underground, Iggy Pop and Patti Smith to the more obscure Henry Cow or Lol Coxhill, throwing the doors further open and inviting the reader to suggest their own contender, with the inclusion of Burt Bacharach and Beethoven. At the 2005 punk event at the Urbis in Manchester, which Paul Morley and Anthony Wilson co-hosted, Morley likened bands such as the early Siouxsie and the Banshees to free form jazz, which may explain his choice of Lol Coxhill within the list as well as jazz artists Keith Jarrett and Duke Ellington.

Tuesday 26th April 1977

Another journey along Barlow Moor Road to witness Slaughter and the Dogs return to the Oaks and a second chance for the band to impress. Having found Buzzcocks and The Drones in such fine form recently, I felt a duty to probe this band's worth, even if the general assessment so far was that they were a capable outfit but in a purely traditional sense.

They kicked off proceedings well previewing both sides of their forthcoming single, before the one with the catchy, "What you doing to me" chorus. Maybe I had been wrong to leave Wythenshawe Forum early back in September. My escape was less urgent this time around, in fact I stayed for the encore. True, there was a bar at the Oaks and then there was the matter of selling enough fanzines to fund a future issue.

The Dogs validated most of the opinions levelled at them. They were good musicians, particularly the enigmatic Mike Rossi, whose playing and performance more than compensated for their less than subtle theatrics. The twin rhythm section of Brian "Muppet" Grantham and Howard "Zip" Bates gave a solid basis for the gifted Rossi to force his art home and their current look owed more to the Hammer Horror genre than to any dated glam threads. Like a less slick Dave Vanian, singer Wayne "The Count" Barratt donned a cloak and pallid make up and appeared amidst a cloud of smoke or more specifically talcum powder.

It was even apparent that they had hurdled the middle men of Ferry and Bowie, preferring to cover acts revered by those elder statesmen and, more pertinently, by current punk pretenders. So it was the Velvet Underground and New York Dolls who supplemented the Dogs own creations.

So I had gone the distance with Slaughter and the Dogs, although I am not sure I would have guarded their honour if I had caught this performance before encountering Buzzcocks or The Drones. In fact their repertoire fell short of any of the bands I had analysed in recent weeks, albeit their delivery was near note perfect.

On the plus side we encountered Kevin Cummins who, I was informed, was wearing a brown leather jacket. A bigger clue would have been the professional looking Zenith camera with which he was photographing the Dogs. I was ushered to a quiet corner and, true to The Drones' endorsement, he was more than happy to supply some Drones pictures. "Yeh just write down the address for me."

Thursday 28th April 1977

Of all the affable exchanges that took place in the cosy confines of the Oaks it was possibly the ramshackle visit of all girl group The Slits that struck the greatest chord. Despite the impious approach of Ari Up, the singer crafted an air of intrigue that demanded further interrogation.

Steve Shy bluntly observed, "She's only fifteen but she's fucking amazing." Kevin Cummins obtained a series of snaps to accompany Steve's *Shy Talk* feature. Paul Morley's beleaguered attempts to persuade the *NME* to grant him space for an interview were apparently rebuffed prompting an approach to ourselves to let him, "do an interview with Ari Up".

Whether Morley was met with similar resistance by the band and its singer or whether he felt he had enough in the locker without the participation of The Slits' front person, a piece that grew out of tonight's events found its way to us and appeared in issue 3 of *Ghast Up*. Decades later Morley would recall The Slits appearance at the Oaks and the close proximity of the stage putting artists within touching distance as being, "so glamorous".

Saturday 30th April 1977
The Roxy, Neal Street, London WC2

"The palace of untold legend and hidden promise" was how *Ripped and Torn* fanzine described the Roxy on Neal Street in London's Covent Garden. My one visit to the theatre of punk was to establish whether The Drones could affect a London audience the way they recently had in Manchester.

Although London was hardly awash with punks, my first encounter with a couple on the tube left me somewhat embarrassed by my lack of sartorial adventure. Although I could not now recall the precise articles that made up their punk attire, it was fair to say I suddenly felt timid and conservative in comparison.

Like any tourist I checked out all the predictable haunts the big city had to offer. The Kings Road was always a stopover, although I never got as far as Seditionaries, the then name of McLaren and Westwood's shop, having gained previous notoriety as Sex. I also somehow missed any skirmishes between teds and punks, despite events later being described as a near civil war.

The one essential punk hot spot was the Rough Trade shop. It actually took some finding as I assumed, despite its punk HQ reputation, that it was in the upmarket Borough of Kensington, rather than the then more modest neighbourhood of Notting Hill. Having located the shop in the vicinity of Portobello Road rather than the Victoria and Albert Museum, the hosts were as genial as the London based fanzines had advised. Geoff Travis thanked us for sending *Ghast Up* down and made an unforced offer to pay us from the till. The one artefact that stuck in my mind in this museum of modern culture was an original photograph of Lou Reed as used on the Transformer sleeve.

The Roxy was easier to locate and provided possibly the most confusing fashion conflict of the visit. Another punk looking couple clad in what appeared to be designer gear and looking every inch the Roxy regular approached to enquire, "what sort of people go in there, are they a leather lot?" The question was later qualified with, "are they punk?"

Downstairs the Roxy was pretty much as expected, including the exorbitant prices or, to put it in a 1977 perspective, one pound fifty admission and over fifty pence a pint for draught beer with cans offering a slightly cheaper alternative! A murky basement club with limited décor – the ambience being provided by music and modish punters.

Dee Generate, the ex-drummer with Eater, was present and someone mentioned Glen Matlock the ex-Pistol but the famed roll call of punk royalty that was said to frequent the Roxy was conspicuously absent. A young woman sat scribbling was identified for me as journalist Jane Suck and *NME* writer Tony Parsons admits to having been present, although he has repeatedly denied the accusation that he was the disgruntled patron who smashed a table towards the end of the night.

There were a smattering of Mancunian characters with Steve Shy and Paul Doyle. The latter was another punk regular who somehow managed to hitch a ride to many English towns despite his punk attire having a limited semblance to actual clothing. In attendance alongside The Drones entourage of girlfriends and manager, we were quickly acknowledged by Drones' singer Mike who was genuinely grateful for our making the journey south.

In true music journalist style, Paul Morley's initial greeting was to recount the events of the previous night, having caught The Jam at The Royal College of Art in Kensington, West London. The Jam drew few if any plaudits from the band's manager, unlike the support band, UK based reggae outfit The Cimarons who, "blew them off stage".

The Roxy's original management of Andy Czezowski, Susan Carrington and Barry Jones, who had built the club's not inconsiderable reputation as a punk nucleus, had recently vacated the premises which was now under new management. Paul Morley was particularly unimpressed with the new management's suggestion that he should pay to get in. Don Letts had retained his post as resident DJ and it was the rattle of dub reggae that reverberated around the club, in between the growing punk releases. The Clash had a whole album to choose from with Paul Doyle declaring he was going to ask Letts to play "Janie Jones". Another loud guitar-driven track was identified to me by Steve Shy as The Adverts new single "One Chord Wonders". Paul Morley, true to his description of the music as "'77 Pop" or "music that you can dance to" performed a jig to DJ Letts' playing of Buzzcocks' "Breakdown".

The Drones' performance ran smoothly this time as the band gave a rehearsed delivery of their original set supplemented by The Stooges "Search and Destroy" and their take on Patti Smith's take on "My Generation". The Mancunian exuberance that would give way to dancing and spitting was clearly absent from the London punk persona that demanded an icy cool lack of emotion. The level of applause suggested modest approval but there was no evidence that this crowd had been enlivened by a set that petered out to an indifferent finale. Perhaps I was placing myself in the role of away supporter as was Morley who was flummoxed by the tepid response to his lads who asked in bewilderment "What exactly do they want?"

In fairness the XTC set that followed included a cover of

Bob Dylan's "All Along the Watchtower" which surely lessened any punk credibility, elicited only a little more reaction, although their less forced delivery and disjointed rhythm perhaps demanded a less frenetic response than The Drones.

year zero

Sunday 1st May 1977

Back on territory both familiar and affordable, the chance to catch New York legend Wayne County was scuppered, not just by the non-appearance of The Electric Chairs but also the failure of the Electric Circus to secure a replacement. Thus the legendary month of Sunday nights at the Circus, that would culminate in the debut of artists subsequently to be known as Joy Division, began with a "New Wave Disco" that included playing the self-proclaimed "Godfather of Punk" Marc Bolan's "Laser Love".

Monday 2nd May 1977

The first Monday in May would not be designated a bank holiday in England until the following year, so the Buzzcocks appearance at Manchester's Band On The Wall on Swan Street happened on just another working day. The venue is a large pub formerly known as the George and Dragon that had been turned into a jazz club a few years earlier by local jazz musician Steve Morris.

The name Band on the Wall was apparently chosen in a conversation with Mancunian music legend Johnny Roadhouse and was a former nickname from the 1930s when the landlord of the time placed a stage high on the wall on which bands would play. The stage remained connected to the back wall but at a more conventional height and, being a jazz club, there was plenty of seating, although when required there was space for over 300 to stand around the 150 seats. The striped wallpaper and monochrome photographs complemented the jazz venue aura as did the efficient bar staff and a blind eye being turned to the odd joint being shared.

Curiously splitting the show into two sets, Buzzcocks' continued endeavour to forge a life after Devoto was slightly derailed towards the end of the second set when the former singer chose the moment to leave the audience and re-join the band onstage to the collective approval of all present.

As was becoming my habit whenever an historic event befell this city, I conspired not to be there. Or more accurately I had underestimated the growing appeal of a Buzzcocks appearance and arrived too late to be shoehorned into the small jazz club. I caught some of the first set, along with other disenchanted followers, through a side window, the observed revellers within causing a level of resentment as it was suggested that many were more Band on the Wall regulars than *bona fide* Buzzcocks fans.

Mike Drone's arrival with his girlfriend Maggie added fuel to the bitterness by his suggestion that the venue was "full of pseuds" before proceeding to the front of the queue where his status quickly gained access. There was a fleeting discourse regarding The Drones' upcoming release, with one member of the queue innocuously advising the EP featured a track called "Puppy Crap".

As fortune would have it Paul Morley, who had unsurprisingly procured entry, would gushingly articulate that we had to cover such an occurrence before turning his ebullience into a review of the night. Presumably the *NME* did not deem the Shelley/ Devoto reunion worthy of a live review in the "On the Town" section, even though the event made their news pages, although I like to think the decision to entrust such a passionate account to our humble fanzine rather than London-based editorial staff was the wiser choice. In a slightly self-defeating action, I only found a spare half page so the printed review was limited to an account of the second set.

Along with the Buzzcocks' review Morley also dispatched short articles on all girl group The Slits and X-Ray Spex, whose original line-up also contained two female members, together with "fax on the negatives".

The Negatives were Morley's latest effort at shaping the Manchester skyline. The facts provided included the band members who, along with Morley (using the Modest Young alias) also featured Steve Shy, Kevin Cummins (who chose the name Kevin Snap for band purposes) and Dave Bentley, who was decreed by some to be The Drones' manager and who adopted the title Dave Bent. For some quirky reason we were told the combined age of The Negatives was eighty-five and they had "brought fiction back into music". An emotion not expressed until the Urbis event of 2005 was that The Negatives were formed because Morley and his bandmates, "decided that we wanted to take part in this exciting thing that was happening".

In what seemed like an interminable desire to play the music media like the proverbial fiddle, Morley also began his own fanzine *Girl Trouble*, a single page weekly produced on a photocopier in a limited run of 50 with each copy hand numbered. One side would feature a Kevin Cummins photo of, among others, Pete Shelley and Wayne Barrett, while the reverse contained Morley's regular musings on events and personal viewpoints that naturally included guidance on how The Negatives should be perceived, within a mainly fictitious paragraph.

According to an article in issue 2, The Negatives had an EP entitled, "Bringing Fiction Back To Music" that featured the tracks, "Sixteen", "Sick of London", "You're a Pregnant Pole Vaulter", "When Did the Queen Lose Her Virginity", "Disabled Flab" and "Drumtardute". "Sixteen" was the Buzzcocks' track that would have pre-dated the original as the song would not appear in recorded form until the following year's "Another Music in a Different Kitchen". Not that such a point was germane as the article concluded with the note "this record is not available."

If creating a fanzine was perceived as a lesser form of involvement within the burgeoning punk scene and it's "anyone can do it" ethos, it is worth mentioning that Pete Shelley also produced such a publication in 1977. For some reason the Buzzcocks' singer felt duty bound to enquire if I had seen his fanzine, whilst cadging a cigarette, presumably off Mick Middles as I was such an occasional smoker I rarely invested in an actual packet. The title was misheard as "Placing" over the background music, although I later established the correct title to be *Plaything*. Like Paul Morley's *Girl Trouble* it consisted of a single sheet of typing that covered Shelley's personal ruminations, including revisiting the matter of politics being as much personal as party political that had been his response to our questioning Buzzcocks' politics.

This being the DIY year of 1977; together with Morley's overreaching desire to publicly recount the events of 2nd May, Part 1 of Buzzcocks review at the Band on the Wall appeared in Issue 3A of *Girl Trouble* and graciously referred the reader to "popzine ghast up number two" for Part 2 whilst inviting the reader to "make up your own part three".

★

An essential haunt of 1977 for any dedicated follower of punk fashion was the Ranch Bar on Dale Street close to the centre of Manchester on the edge of what is now Manchester's Northern Quarter. the Ranch was a small downstairs bar owned by local entertainer Frank 'Foo Foo' Lammar and located in the same building as Foo Foo's Palace where Lammar performed his drag act.

It was suggested that the Ranch Bar's place within the gay community made it a safe haven in which to don punk gear, even if the walk from Piccadilly Bus Station and it's gathering of teddy boys and whatever other factions took exception to what Paul Morley would describe as "these tentative holders of a new youth sub-culture" remained hazardous. The many tales of assaults on punks, usually on the way home after a Friday night at the Ranch, include Pete Shelley and Francis Taylor who were victims in Piccadilly Gardens whilst heading for the bus home.

There was a tale of Ranch regulars venturing en masse to Piccadilly to confront the teddy boys who, according to the story, chose the bus station as their hangout. The only account I garnered was from Steve Shy who arrived in the city centre after the conflict to discover his fellow Ranch goers out in numbers and giving various accounts of what had just taken place. Whatever form the confrontation took, it was suggested that the action brought about a ceasefire between the rival factions.

To safeguard the clientele within there was a door policy

where you were inspected through a sliding panel before being granted entry. I cannot recall my punk style being gauged or causing any overt problems accessing the Ranch on the few occasions I visited but I assume I must have gone through the ritual.

The club was in a basement decorated in a country and western theme, best exemplified by the western style lettering on the club sign. Although the Ranch had showcased live bands, including an early show by Buzzcocks that was stopped after a few numbers on the instructions of Lammar for being too loud, the club was principally a hangout for the inner circle of Manchester punks, including members of Buzzcocks and The Distractions, a Stockport band who also performed at the Ranch during 1977.

My first visit involved trying to shift some copies of issue one of *Ghast Up*. Fortunately Steve Shy was on hand to persuade his regular readers, who had in all likelihood purchased *Shy Talk* from there, to invest 20 pence in this other fanzine. On the night in question Steve was not working behind the bar from where he sold his fanzine as issue 3 of *Shy Talk* was currently "at the printers".

The legend persists regarding the Ranch DJ's musical choices that interspersed the punk soundtrack. This included the calypso hit from the forties "Rum and Coca Cola" whose controversial lyrics were no doubt lost to the ears of Ranch regulars as they had been to the Andrews Sisters when they recorded the song. The evening's revelries would be wound down with the playing of Liverpudlian art rock band Deaf School's cabaret driven "What a Way To End It All". Other inclusions were the vinyl rarity "Al Capone" by Prince Buster with its "Guns don't argue" line easily being misheard as "Punks don't argue" alongside the usual glam selection of Roxy, Bowie, Reed and Ronson.

Sunday 8th May 1977

For the first time that I could recall accessing the Electric Circus involved standing in the famous/infamous queue that stretched down the side of the venue and, depending on the draw of the band, behind the iconic building. Despite the average Mancunian punk looking far from outrageous, the queue drew the attention of a handful of the kids from the neighbouring flats who appeared each Sunday to watch the curious patrons stand in line. The term "feral youth" had yet to be coined by politicians and in fairness, on the one occasion the youths created the slightest of conflicts, the distressed minor returned in the company of his mother who remonstrated with his adversary.

The queue was more a ritual than a necessity as even the possession of a ticket would not fast-track your entry. For those who preferred a cosier wait there was a pub just around the corner on neighbouring Rochdale Road where you could wait for the queue to abate whilst being entertained by an organist whose act seemed to consist mainly of playing Opportunity Knocks winner Bernie Flint's current breakthrough "I Don't Want To Put a Hold On You". Although it was a traditional pub with family entertainment we did encounter a friendly gentleman who had presumably deduced that this particular watering hole was a stopover for fans en route to the nearby rock venue and who offered to sell us some "gear".

The visit of The Clash, who had previously appeared as part of the "Anarchy" tour, also attracted the attention of the police as they monitored the situation. The sight of uniformed police around the building was somehow fitting.

The queue tonight was at least apposite for one of the top Manchester gigs of all time. I had seen The Who in 1975 when they generously bequeathed the cream of much of their back catalogue and there was the earth shattering appearance by Johnny Thunders and the Heartbreakers earlier in the year. I was to witness the double bill of The Ramones and Talking Heads later that month and David Bowie's post-Heroes showing at Stafford the following year. Whichever of those occasions was the gig of my lifetime still varies daily but the appearance at the Electric Circus of The Clash on their White Riot tour remains an abiding memory.

For what seemed like the first time, the Circus DJ played an exclusively punk soundtrack mixed with early stirrings of the obligatory dub reggae that would become punk's brother-in-arms courtesy of Don Lett's role as DJ at London's Roxy, reinforced possibly by Mark Perry's command in punk bible *Sniffin' Glue* to "try to listen to Reggae".

The Slits short set confirmed Pete Shelley's description of the all-girl band. There was none of the restraint in which women in rock tended to engage; the solid guitar bass drum sound supplying a potent force behind Ari Up's equally uninhibited vocals. The singer roared her musical preference whilst returning via the crowd to the dressing room with a cry of "Reggae reggae reggae." Steve Shy candidly described them as "amazing."

There was a suitable congeniality to Subway Sect. Less direct than most of their contemporaries, singer Vic Godard emphasised their unpolished approach by referring to a piece of paper before announcing each number. Despite the lacklustre presentation, there was clearly a level of sophistication to this band. Like fish out of water, the exuberant response to the structured arrangements seemed almost to mystify the band and their deadpan approach.

Unlike both support bands whose sets I had to learn on the night, The Clash set had been pre-burned into my memory with the "White Riot" single, debut album and the *NME* freebie "Capital Radio" ensuring there would be no musical surprises. The question mark over their decision to spout their political dogma via the international set up of CBS was still a hot topic and their contemptuous re-reading of "London's Burning" as "Manchester's Burning" for the opener should have raised further questioning of The Clash's stance. But at this point in time The Clash seemed untouchable with the music press collectively assessing them as the only band that mattered.

Once the band hit their stride, which was almost instantaneously, it was quickly obvious that they were firmly in the driving seat of the punk revolution. The Clash had certainly benefited from the notoriety that the Sex Pistols had sown but the latter's refusal, or probably their overbearing manager's refusal, to exploit them as a live act, left the way clear for The Clash to rise to the top of the pile. The Clash's standpoint as people's champions may have been compromised by their choice of a major record label and their manager's personalised CLA5H number plate on his limousine but their willingness to deliver their music to the masses in all its power and glory, both in the flesh and via their quickly released debut album, seemed to earn them clemency from the judgemental punk audience.

Whether there was much truth in Malcolm McLaren's claims that there were insurmountable obstacles to his band playing live remains questionable given that both The Clash and Johnny Thunder's Heartbreakers had both been quarries for the kind of self-righteous indignation that had annihilated much of the Anarchy Tour. Then there was the fact that the Circus had hosted the Anarchy Tour twice and would surely throw the doors open to a further showing as would many other venues across the nation. Either way it was The Clash who fired the warning shots and sent us back to our cosy existence in a state of delirium. I am not sure I had yet come to regard any punk band as the greatest band in the world but on tonight's showing maybe it is The Clash.

Tuesday 10th May 1977

Following a large venue nationwide tour in the illustrious company of Iggy Pop and Bowie, The Vibrators returned to Manchester to the more intimate confines of the Oaks on a Tuesday night when DJ Rob Gretton had stocks of Slaughter and the Dogs' debut single "Cranked Up Really High" on sale.

Having been persuaded by notables from Buzzcocks to Paul Morley that The Vibrators were worthy, Mick Middles felt the band would be a laudable inclusion in a future *Ghast Up* on the strength of this appearance. An attempt to make contact was a simple act of writing a message on a copy of our first issue and handing it to singer and guitarist Knox (Ian Carnochan) as he left the stage, which had now been moved further back in the venue and, like the Circus, involved a walk via the audience to the dressing room.

The attempt failed, largely due to the singer being laden with guitar rather than it being a snub to our primitive publication, as the said missive cascaded to the floor. The situation was explained to Paul Morley who promptly grabbed the fanzine and fled in haste, returning minutes later in the company of drummer John (Eddie) Edwards. Far from being too eminent for the likes of us, the drummer gratefully accepted the complimentary fanzine enthusing that, "it would be really cool to do an interview."

Paul Morley's act of benevolence was rewarded with a lift home to his Heaton Moor address, during which he reassured us that The Vibrators were "nice blokes". Regarding my purchase of Slaughter and the Dogs' debut single Morley again reminded us, "They're alright if you don't look at them."

Friday 13th May 1977

American singer Cherry Vanilla failed to appear with her backing band The Police for the second time, which at least meant Manchester would now catch up with Wayne County and his Electric Chairs.

The legendary fishnetted and stilettoed sometime Patti Smith impressionist (his 'act' usually came complete with a lampooning of the New Jersey singer's poetry) had now given way to peg leg trousers, shirt and tie, later topped off backstage by a woolly hat. There was still some eye shadow on display and an indiscreet line complete with stiches on his neck. Not that the toned down stage show was to grant a reprieve from the Friday night rock audience who presumably had not come for the advertised headliner.

What ensued was reminiscent of The Damned's reception by a similarly dogmatic crowd, although unlike Vanian and co, County was happy to trade insults with the rock crowd, even telling the band to "shut the fuck up" at one point to allow the audience to express their opinions.

The crowd, in turn, seized the moment to establish a hostile rapport with the band on stage, the more polite rejoinder being, "new wave rubbish". As a straight talking New Yorker, County must surely have felt a sense of smug satisfaction to be yelling, "fuck off" repeatedly at the end of their renowned song of that title.

My first venture back stage brought me into the company of Wayne County and his band and road crew. I felt I should reassure the man and his band, who had maintained a dexterous level of musicianship in the face of such enmity, that some of us had actually enjoyed the gig. As it turned out I had been beaten to the punch by several locals including Mike Drone, who introduced us to an assembly that included his brother Peter. We were assured by a few of the locals that *Ghast Up* was good but "it's just a shame about the photos."

The assembled Americans were in fact the nicest people you could meet and it was quickly forgotten that the band we were talking to, although unequipped to formally interview, had just been hung out to dry in our neighbourhood. Their road manager was happy to share his wealth of knowledge of the music industry including an encounter with Sid Vicious who he described as, "about as vicious as a fly". Apparently the tragic figure of Sid had demanded his leather jacket to which the road manager asked, "Which side of your head do you want it on?"

Someone asked County about his conflict with "Handsome Dick" Manitoba, who had barracked County at a New York appearance at CBGBs resulting in a brawl that caused The Dictators' singer to suffer a fractured collarbone. The case had gone to a New York court but the charge was reduced to a misdemeanour due to, as County put it, "self-defence".

Wayne County was quick to explain his non-appearance a fortnight earlier with the simple explanation, "I knew nothing about it." As for his response to the night's events he wrote succinctly on the back of a *Ghast Up*, "I'm glad I didn't get killed!!! Wayne XOXO".

As well as the punk devotees there was a young lady who I presumed was a Circus regular based on her line of questioning, asking what people got out of doing the pogo, illustrating that she had tried it and it did nothing for her. When that drew a puzzled blank from the singer she honed the query with the more direct, "what is punk rock all about?" County shrugged his shoulders and explained, "I dunno, I just play rock'n'roll."

The lack of support for Wayne County from within these

walls was probably explained by a gig that took place the same evening in nearby Warrington. Parr Hall was hosting a package presented by Warrington Technical College Students Union with Johnny Thunders and the Heartbreakers headlining. But it was at least one of the support bands who hauled regulars such as Kevin Cummins and Jon the Postman away from the Circus, or as Francis Taylor put it, "most of the Ranch decamped to Warrington for the night", with both Buzzcocks and Slaughter and the Dogs supporting.

Francis recalls the Mancunian support was bolstered by a few visitors from Liverpool accompanying the other support band The Spitfire Boys who featured Paul Rutherford in their line-up and had chosen the name at the suggestion of Wayne County. Being a student union gig the attendance included, "a fair crowd of non-punks and the curious".

The main story that emerged from those returning from Warrington was of a lack of local camaraderie, with the Dogs protesting about the running order that placed them third behind Buzzcocks. Maybe this was the first real test of their relative footing on the punk ladder since the second night of the Lesser Free Trade Hall supporting the Pistols when Buzzcocks were making their debut. Both bands had subsequently ploughed separate furrows, playing similar sized venues to similar sized audiences.

Francis Taylor was unaware on the night of the back stage shenanigans between Buzzcocks and Slaughter and the Dogs that surfaced later but did have an encounter with the headliners, "we were smoking a spliff outside (I think) when Johnny Thunders walked by, smelt it and dragged us all to the Heartbreakers' dressing room, we spent the rest of the evening in and out of there."

The inclusion of The Spitfire Boys making their debut on the Warrington bill saved Slaughter and the Dogs the ignominy of being the warm up act as the Liverpool band opened proceedings with a selection of Ramones covers.

★

An unsolicited contribution mysteriously arrived in the post. Although the sender of the article was not identified in the mailshot, the handwriting was none other than Paul Morley/ Modest Young. Almost as perplexing as the dispatch itself was the subject matter. A critique on a band named Paris and the Atmospheres entitled, "The Tragedy of a Switchboard Operator".

On first impressions the article read like an abstract piece on Buzzcocks with its reference to guitarist Steve and their cute singer and second guitarist Pete. The drummer was named as Bry although he would transmute from Ringo to John Maher, leaving Dave the bass player the only ambiguity.

There was a further suggestion that this was a fabricated band and story by Morley's reference to this band recording an album but not releasing it, echoing the invented story surrounding The Negatives recording an EP and deleting it before release.

THE TRAGEDY OF A SWITCHBOARD OPERATOR

Paris and the Atmospheres: an experiment in impermanence. Unintentional evolving into studied practice – their one gig is allowing Little Bob Story to top over them as they recite various early seventies suburban surrealistic borrowed songs and odd technicolour bursting new ones that will have the record labels burstling, but they can't have them because they're splitting. The only way to avoid the success trap? Self destruct before that Earls Court gig blunders up. I asked Steve, their white collar worker guitarist, as we lay calmly on a walnut desk in an office in Stockport Town Hall. "Yes," he said staring into middle distance à la Robert Powell's Jesus, weighing his words, "our stance is more introverted than, say, Steve Stills, more extrovert than, say, Rat Scab and we're concerned with manipulating the Industry, So we're going to dangle the bait and then scarper". Oh! Where to? "America we've got a support job at Max's supporting the Ramones with the Rockettes below stairs". I don't believe you – the Ramones wouldn't tackle Max's. "Our offer was too good a temptation". Oh, I left.

In W H Smiths I nicked my weekly reading material and bumped into Dave, bass player. He was sporting a large badge. The badge said 'Paris and the Atmospheres'. He saw me look at it and ripped it off. He burned it. The ashes fell to the carpet. "We're not out for fame, we're into art. It is, let's face it, the cult of impermanence". He collapsed. I stormed out aiming to find Pete their cute singer and second guitarist. Perhaps he would cut the artistic crap and give me the duce.

I found him outside Woollies. We chatted amiably about the two gigs Limey-Yankee, and how the record companies sure we're gonna be up the shute as they scuttled chasing the no-more group. "In fact" he remarked, "we are gonna make an album 'The Cult of Impermanence' produced by Marc Bolan, but we're not going to release it". Gosh, these lads are getting to me. They've really got it sorted out.

At Bry, the drum-drums house later that evening, we talked, me, Bry and Brian Eno who came by offering his services on the follow up album. Bry was genuinely touched by all the interest, but frightened me and Eno away by soaking us with his ZZ Top records, the weak link in the group? Why no! Was Ringo! Is John Maher?

So, I thought, what to do. I needed some conclusive evidence as to the motivation behind the band and their strange 'cult of impermanence' theory.

I rang my good pale pal, ace investigative metal writer, Geoff Barton who's always good for advice in these situations. "Hey" he said tossing his fairy blond hair away from his peach cream cheeks no doubt, "have they a Manager? Ask him!" Gosh good guy Geoff!!

I rounded up a man called Syd Jerram who owned VP, a part time record label designer. We talked over a chocolate milkshake. I flung questions at him. He looked at me knowingly, answering non-commitally with soft monosyllabic grunts. I got out a dagger in sheer frustration and stabbed wildly. He grinned knowingly and blood spurted uncontrollably out of my groin. "The Bastard" I screamed, "he doesn't exist".

*The sleeve note for Paris and the Atmospheres album were written
by Philip K Dick.*

In what seemed a case of life imitating art, a band by the
name of Paris and the Atmospheres would release a single in
1979 entitled "Atmosphere" with "Deborah and Me" on the
flipside. The single in question was packaged in a hand cut and
sellotaped glossy sleeve that revealed a line-up of Pete Maine on
vocals and guitar, Steve Williams on guitar and vocals and David
Le Frais on bass guitar, with a mention for special thanks to
Bryan Boon who provided the drums. There was also a contact
address placing the band as from Hazel Grove, Stockport, to
almost complete the solution.

A Syd Jerram, or Sid Jerram as he was also referred, had been
a rugby footballer from Swansea who reportedly died in 1959
having played at both the union and league codes in the early
twentieth century.

Saturday 14th May 1977

One upshot of producing a fanzine that I could not have
predicted was the deluge of letters from readers appreciative
of the labour of love that was *Ghast Up*. One such reader was
Bernard from Failsworth, a Manchester suburb that happened to
lie en route to another suburb, Middleton. Thus Bernard's efforts
in posting a flattering dispatch our way were rewarded by a free
ride to the Middleton Civic Hall where The Damned were to
headline supported by Stiff label mates The Adverts.

With a long player under their belt and a hall full of punks,
several of whom used Dave Vanian's Dracula persona as their
particular blueprint, this was never going to be a repeat of their
Circus showing in January.

The Adverts were another tick in my list of bands seen as they
established themselves as being more than a one single wonder
and had a beautifully photogenic bass player, although the crowd
seemed to want a repeat of the familiar "One Chord Wonders"
rather than to be taught the rest of Tim Smith's compositions.

The Damned delivered a robust set that Paul Morley would
dismiss as "too slick". Either way the safety net of familiarity

their album release had afforded made sure The Damned would not have to tussle for audience approval; the mob clicked into a demonstration of the mandatory requirements of a punk audience, with the opening riff of The Stooges "I Feel Alright". One was the pogo, which had been modestly performed during The Adverts' showing and the other, less wholesome practice, was to shower the quartet with phlegm.

For the first time I was to experience a crowd bestow their approval in a shower of spit. Although it would become the norm in the months to follow, despite being a habit that was seldom received as a gesture of approval and more grudgingly accepted after failed pleas to stop, this was unquestionably the most incessant delivery I was to encounter.

The Damned's attempts to dissuade the audience fell firstly to tutu-clad Captain Sensible who delivered a patronising, "no spitting, naughty" before Rat Scabies tried the more combative approach of emerging from behind the shelter of his drum kit to gulp a swig of beer and direct it into the crowd. The only act that seemed to quell the gusto of the delivery was Brian James threatening to take on the comparatively youthful crowd.

A single act that set the grapevine buzzing was Bernard's precarious leap from the balcony to avoid missing any of The Damned's set, a stunt that made the next issue of *Shy Talk* by some alternate route.

Tuesday 17th May 1977

"Good evening, Siouxsie and the Banshees," was the singer's modest introduction to a sparsely-filled Oaks. Siouxsie Sioux was a recognisable face from her TV appearance alongside the Sex Pistols as a member of those prominent Pistols' followers the Bromley Contingent, when she was famously invited backstage by Bill Grundy. In the dressing room later she expressed some sadness to Paul Morley that she did not think her band had played particularly well.

Whatever Siouxsie and the Banshees were meant to sound like, the chopping musical arrangements behind Siouxsie's strident vocals produced an agreeable sound that threatened to disintegrate at times but ultimately flowed loosely and freely and contained several sturdy reference points in titles like "Love In A Void" and "Make Up to Break Up" that distinguished the Banshees from other aficionados of the Sex Pistols. As Paul Morley would later define the early Banshees they were, "all in their own zone… somehow it fitted and yet didn't fit."

The gig was as much a learning curve for the audience as it was for the band as the Banshees turned the venue that had been cloaked in mystique for the visit of Johnny Thunders and the Heartbreakers into an informal private viewing for those of us fortunate enough to catch these future Goth punks at an embryonic stage.

Thursday 19th May 1977

It would have been a travesty if The Adverts' fragile delivery had not been tested in the intimate surroundings of the Oaks. As it transpired the sharp pop of their songs met a mixed and at times unconvincing reception.

Their limited musicianship was questioned when guitarist Howard Pickup improvised a section of Yes's "Roundabout" between numbers that, for reasons best known to Paul Morley, prompted a shout of "Steve Howe" that, in turn, seemed to ruffle some feathers. The band's tolerance would be further tested when a youthful member of the audience chose to participate with TV Smith on stage, echoing the chorus of, "We don't give a damn" into the singer's face before being forcibly removed from his brief flirtation with provincial stardom by a dancing melee.

Sunday 22nd May 1977

Manchester seemed to have acquired a status where bands struggled to fulfil the obligation of actually appearing at an advertised gig. The Enid ritual that had seemingly been adopted by Cherry Vanilla, was now being practised by The Jam. A gig at the Oaks on 5th May had failed to transpire in the week their debut single entered the lower end of the national charts and word quickly spread that they had cancelled at the Electric Circus on Sunday 15th May 1977.

Their replacements should have been more than adequate with flyers being amended to list Johnny Thunders and the Heartbreakers for the date, but they were equally conspicuous by their absence. Although never officially confirmed, there was a rumour that the Heartbreakers behaviour on the "Anarchy" tour, that included the trashing of the dressing room on at least one of the visits, made them unwelcome guests at the Electric Circus.

And so it was a week off from the famed Sunday nights at the Circus before the appearance of The Ramones supported in no small part by Sire label mates Talking Heads.

The crowd seemingly failed to notice that Talking Heads approach to song writing was less hectic than The Ramones, despite both bands having geographically similar creative influences. Their restrained delivery drew a vehement reaction from the punk crowd who found their crafted music surprisingly danceable under the glare of the house lights that David Byrne had requested be left on "so that they can see us".

As for The Ramones, they had earned an encore before playing a note as the chant of, "Hey ho let's go" that preceded their arrival on stage served to inform them that victory was theirs whatever ensued. In fact there were several sound problems that prompted Johnny Ramone to proffer repeated "1-2-3-4s" as the chords failed several times to crackle through the PA, but this only served to reinforce The Ramones image as cartoon punks.

The limited expectations that throwaway numbers like, "Now I Wanna Sniff Some Glue" cultivated did mask a depth to The Ramones that so many of their copyists lacked. A song like "Swallow My Pride" owed more to the tortured genius of Brian Wilson's Beach Boys than the Velvets or Stooges. Strange that a band whose roots lay firmly in sixties American bubble gum should be the blue print for so many of the current crop to try and emulate, albeit falling short of the original.

Tonight The Ramones' subtle edge married to their theatrical punk persona – surely no one believed that Joey couldn't afford a new pair of Levis – ensured that the approval earned before playing a note was justified as they ripped through both their albums at pace.

The odd pairing of these two label mates was replicated the following week when Tom Verlaine and Television were supported at the Free Trade Hall by Debbie Harry's Blondie. Many people, including Paul Morley, suggested the chiselled guitar structure of Television would have sat easier with David Byrne's Talking Heads, leaving the bouncy pop of Blondie as the ideal bedfellow for "da brudders Ramone".

Tuesday 24th May 1977

Ed Banger and the Nosebleeds were back supporting The Drones and, in a curious display of Mancunian unity that seemed to bury any hatchets that had previously been wielded, the openers were The Negatives whose membership included Paul Morley (or Modest Young). Unlike The Drones, who appeared by the stage to pogo in support of their manager(s), Ed Banger wisely kept a proverbial low profile until it was time for them to supply their set.

The Negatives, who were to undergo several line-up changes of varying but mainly negligible musical ability, debuted as the standard four piece of guitar, bass, drums and vocals. Morley supplied whatever guitar riffs he could manage whilst Steve Shy's attempts at bass were rewarded with several blood stained fingers. The voice of the band belonged to Dave Bentley. And if you thought the band were solely an unmusical in-joke, photographer Kevin Cummins was actually a capable drummer who supplied some rhythmic backbeat to titles like "Sick of London" and "My Kind Of Girl Pays Four Pence on the Bus" that Bentley hollered from a sheet of paper.

As if to maintain the waggish approach of The Negatives, Ed Banger adopted a similarly tongue-in-cheek manner, at least between numbers, as their flawless sound system allowed them to gain some ground on their contemporaries with each passing support slot.

The Drones were as studied and professional as they had been at the Roxy in London but back on home soil a positive reception was never really in doubt as Mike Drone conducted the intimate gathering in a steadily moving appreciation.

★

Prior to the digital age, unreleased music was usually hawked on a C30 or C60 cassette tape before its ultimate appearance on vinyl, so any music sharing required the physical exchange of a tape. It was in the Oaks car park that the merits of The Drones 4 track EP were discussed with the manager and the sleeve photographer Kevin Cummins, who furnished a copy of the tape, which he proceeded to play on his car cassette player – a fairly high tech accessory for the time. Most drivers had a radio at most so I suppose we were operating at the cutting edge of musical technology in 1977.

And so with one listen we were asked to provide the band's manager, who had apparently produced the recording, with a measured judgement of what would be The Drones maiden outing on vinyl. As always, Morley was keen to coax approval proposing, "It's better than the Dogs... at least say it's better than the Dogs". Kevin Cummins responded to our delayed reaction with the suggestion they just leave us if we don't like it, albeit in jest.

I assured both parties I would give the cassette a proper listen but if they needed an instant response the last track "You'll Lose" sounded okay. Morley found my opinion interesting given that the track in question was not a mainstay of the live show unlike the crowd favourites that preceded it. Interestingly The Beastie Boys hit of ten years later, "(You Gotta Fight For Your Right (To Party!)" bore more than a passing resemblance to the chorus of "You'll Lose". Maybe Rick Rubin or one of The Beasties was lurking in the car park within earshot!

Sunday 29th May 1977

On what was a Mancunian night, Penetration were down from the North East to lend support and, like Birmingham's The Prefects, the Geordie band would become welcome guests in this city and venue but the night began with the band Pete

Shelley had forewarned us of...

Whether the name Stiff Kittens came at Shelley's or Richard Boon's suggestion, by the time of their debut at the Electric Circus they had alighted on the more mainstream Warsaw, after the track "Warszawa" on David Bowie's current album "Low".

As the band's name did not appear on the bill I was unaware that I was witnessing the debut of another Manchester band until Steve Shy enlightened me following their mostly forgettable set. For, whatever the good intentions the band had following their inspirational witnessing of the Sex Pistols some 12 months earlier, Warsaw trod the familiar path of most punk support bands, which is where they looked destined to remain. They held down an acceptable level of musicianship but were ultimately indistinguishable from the growing number of punk bands clamouring for a chance to play.

By contrast Penetration, who seemed to follow most of the rules befitting a band that included songs called "Destroy" and "Hate State", had a lustre to their music that would ensure these visitors from County Durham would become a fixture in this city. Penetration had evolved the previous year following trips to the capital to check out the Sex Pistols and, as if to demonstrate that their musical interests did not spontaneously occur on witnessing that particular chaos, their name was a straight lift from an Iggy Pop song.

Buzzcocks were as reliable as ever despite their appearance at the Circus not yet attracting the full houses that had greeted The Clash and The Ramones – yet it was another improved performance as the band further consolidated their line-up. And yet it would be the other two acts that would set the tone for Manchester's claim to be a happening city where original talent always got a fair crack of the whip.

Before Buzzcocks' set, it was the Electric Circus debut of poet John Cooper Clarke, billed in *New Manchester Review* as compère for the night, who seized the moment to dumbfound the punk audience. The comforting Salford accent had the crowd clapping and cheering and even moving to his rhythmic rapid-fire delivery and any self-doubt that punks could tolerate poetry were brushed aside by the obvious humour within such gems as "You'll Never See a Nipple in the *Daily Express*" or the greaser girl put down "Psycle Sluts". The latter reminding the crowd which side Cooper Clarke played for.

The reading became a performance when the poet was joined by a male stripper who acted out the main character of "Salome Malone (Queen of the Ritz)" a poem that no doubt inspired by Clarke's previous career on the Northern Club circuit. The trick of utilising the Salford poet for punk purposes had been borrowed from conventional band Sad Café, for whom Cooper Clarke had provided support back in April at the Band On The Wall.

If the response to John Cooper Clarke was one of joy laced with bewilderment, the final act would surely defy customary definition. In what looked like a totally impromptu act (but which has since been described as a "first gig proper") local legend Jon the Postman, a real life employee of Royal Mail, who Morley had referred to whilst in the manager's seat at The Drones interview and subsequently cited in writing, took to the stage to deliver (no pun intended) an accapella rendition of the garage classic "Louis Louis".

Clues that the performance was perhaps not entirely spontaneous were missed by those present, although the flawless run through of altered lyrics that referred to "having VD treatment" among other things, coupled with the convenient availability of the sound system following the departure of the main band should have betrayed the contrived nature of the act. The sustained rendition held the audience for as long as the GPO legend wished to endure and presumably until the road crew wished to finish their job.

Friday 3rd June 1977

The Squat on Devas Street was the former home of Manchester College of Music and was to play a brief but crucial role in the advancement of a few local bands. Situated close to where the much larger Manchester Academy now stands among the University buildings, the Squat was a small, basic venue described by Tony Moon in *Sounds* as "an ancient Colditz-type building". The bar and seating area were situated away from the main hall comprised of a floor space facing the stage across the back.

The night had apparently been arranged by Dave Bentley and was whispered to be a "Stuff the Jubilee" night, although the printed flyers that emerged later (and actually contain the wrong date) proclaimed "PUNK ROCK RULES!" as the header.

Warsaw again tried a run through of their material with mild applause mixed with a general indifference to their laboured fare that only sprang into life when Jon the Postman joined them for what may have been the first accompanied version of "Louie Louie".

If Warsaw were still on a laboured exercise to metamorphose into the peerless combo that would become Joy Division, the second-ever appearance of The Fall looked equally doomed. Like Warsaw, The Fall's existence would ultimately be stated to be as a consequence of last year's Lesser Free Trade Hall gig and singer Mark Smith asserted their purpose at the outset, his spoken intro to the band's set informing the audience several times that whatever you were expecting "you got The Fall". The Fall we got was seemingly just another four-piece punk combo who were, like Warsaw, being chased up the usual cul-de-sac, albeit with slightly less haste.

A further appearance by The Negatives demonstrated how the Manchester scene was morphing into a private members' club as their spontaneous set received modest acceptance from at least the punk element in attendance, all the stranger considering the opposition Ed Banger and the likes had encountered from the same people. There seemed to be a level of opposition from a crowd that I described in *Ghast Up* as made up of "mostly students" although, given the way M J Drone would later conduct the swaying masses, I suspect that this was an unproven assumption. A rumour did emerge that there was opposition from the event organisers (presumably the ones with whom Dave Bentley made the arrangements) who lodged various threats to drive them from the stage, ranging from turning the sound off to closing the bar. Apparently they ultimately complied with the request.

It was left to The Drones to whip the crowd into the usual frenzy as Paul Morley's repeated calls for "Sad So Sad" were ultimately rewarded although much of the audience were grateful for what was becoming a familiar set of tunes.

History has also decreed that tonight marked the debut of punk purists The Worst, although I cannot recall their coming into the picture on this occasion. Unlike The Fall, their name appears on the aforementioned flyer, although the story runs that the band just turned up and asked Dave Bentley if they could play. Bentley had to decline their request due to lack of space on the stage, so the trio set up in front of the stage and delivered an impromptu set.

My only outstanding recollection of the evening is of being introduced to Ian Hodge by Steve Shy. Hodge had recently featured in a Sunday tabloid after somewhat naively co-operating with a journalist writing an expose on the horrors of the punk cult sweeping the nation. The main nub of the story was Hodge turning his back on his educational qualifications to become a punk. I suggested we could print his side of the story in a future *Ghast Up* to which the odious punk king of the headline smiled and offered a heartfelt, "thanks".

Monday 6th June 1977

As well as being the year punk broke in the UK, 1977 was also the year Her Majesty Queen Elizabeth II celebrated her Silver Jubilee, to the delight of many who organised street parties decked out with flags and bunting. Someone even told me I would probably be around for Charlie's when enquiring if I had enjoyed the day. I resisted the temptation to advise him that my real achievement that long weekend had been the production of a follow up issue of *Ghast Up* that bore the legend, "Special Jubilee 'We're Too Clean' Issue". Moreover, most of the magazine had been cranked out by hand on a Roneo Stencil Machine and the pages lovingly stapled at the corner, so, in the true DIY spirit of punk, this really was all our own work – well, apart from the contributions of Morley and Cummins, who had bestowed about 25% of the twelve pages and the chart compiled from readers' votes that totalled about five letters plus our own choices. Intriguingly the votes only put "Anarchy in the UK" at number 4, with "White Riot" a clear winner.

The Roneo Stencil Machine in question was a second hand purchase from a shop in Ashton-Under-Lyne following a classified ad in a local paper, probably the *North Cheshire Herald* Bredbury and Romiley edition. The machine cost a princely £20 and arrived with a drum containing green ink, a hue that would stubbornly remain despite adding a generous measure of black ink. Richard Boon, in a round-up of the Manchester fanzines in *New Manchester Review* intriguingly entitled "Hot Poop on Punk Papers", suggested *Ghast Up* was, "more attractive" even describing the green ink as "an innovation", patently unaware that the colour chose us and refused to budge.

There are differing memories of the actual procurement of the machine, although Mick recounts that the journey into Ashton-under-Lyne had been by public transport, the machine being transported to my parents' home aboard a 330 bus, leaving an audit trail of green ink along Old Street and on the Selnec-owned bus that served as the delivery vehicle.

Thursday 9th June 1977

Having established itself as the key pub venue in Manchester, supplanting the Phoenix for some of us as a Thursday night regular haunt, the Oaks disappeared from the circuit when, on Thursday 9th June a scheduled gig by Slaughter and the Dogs was relocated to Rafters on Oxford Street, thus passing the responsibility for showcasing bands in a more intimate setting to what the club billed as "Rock Nite".

Rafters was situated downstairs below its sister club Fagins, a cabaret club run by soul singer Dougie James that had hosted many stars in its history including Scott Walker. Being in the basement, Rafters did indeed have rafters on the ceiling. The bar on the left always seemed inadequate for the number of drinkers in attendance. A vivid memory of queuing for a drink was of John Cooper Clarke also struggling to purchase an alcoholic beverage shrieking "Two bottles of Guinness please. The literary voice needs refreshment."

As a nightclub, Rafters could boast a plusher interior than the usual live venues with carpet underfoot and white walls with dark wood panelling. A curious item was a large painted cartoon picture in the comic strip style of pop artist Roy Lichtenstein containing a speech bubble proclaiming: "Relax Sister, This Is A Real Friendly Club"

The stage was situated across the back wall with a dance floor directly in front that doubled as a viewing area once a band was on stage, and as a discernible spot from which to sell fanzines if that was your desire. Given that tonight heralded the public launch of issue 2 of *Ghast Up* that's where I spent most of the evening.

True to form Paul Morley and Kevin Cummins, who tonight sported a light blue tee shirt bearing the title of Cliff Richard's recent long player "I'm Nearly Famous", were ready and waiting to evaluate our efforts. I felt a duty of care to the photographer and showed some contrition for the standard of reproduction of his photos, unlike the words of Modest Young that had appeared without modification. I didn't await his approval as I had units to shift from a plastic bag.

I was also approached by Rob Gretton who courteously asked if I remembered him before revealing his own publication *Manchester Rains*, whose pages were devoted solely to tonight's headliners Slaughter and the Dogs. As was protocol among fanzine writers, copies of our respective publications were exchanged, meaning I could learn more about the band in question while Rob could discern just what I had made of the Slaughter and the Dogs single he sold me that night at the Oaks.

Having hawked a fair few copies to the clientele, including Woody who now held the bass position in The Worst (although it was probably recognition from the earlier approach with *Ghast Up* 1 that earned him a free copy) it was time to face the music, or rather the constructive feedback of Morley and Cummins who generously proffered a round of applause on our return.

I had somewhat immodestly judged that our second issue

was a creditable product. As a main feature The Drones interview made good copy and Morley's main contribution had freed the editorial restrictions imposed by ourselves. And, of course, Kevin's live shots of The Drones had lifted some self-doubt over picture quality. Curiously Morley had previously been defensive of the cloudy reproduction of my basic snaps in Issue 1 with the appraisal, "No that's good, that's artlessness" an opinion Cummins seemed loathe to share.

With such an illustrious seal of approval, the matter of once more gauging Slaughter and the Dogs' worth was trivial by comparison. In fact they were beginning to grow on me at the third time of asking, now that the pressure to be blown away by any Manchester punk band had been lifted by The Drones looking worthy pretenders to Buzzcocks' order.

I had been genuinely impressed with their single despite its lightweight production, which they again launched into as the opener with the B-side in close proximity. Plus we had recently cornered bassist Howard Bates in the Oaks who, it transpired, was a perfectly approachable young man who happily gave his phone number and expressed a willingness to do an interview. He also helpfully informed that their song with the catchy chorus was called "You're a Bore".

So, with the reference points of the single and "You're a Bore" played alongside their growing number of originals, plus their remaining choice of covers, an evening in Slaughter and the Dogs' company was becoming tolerable, acceptable even.

Saturday 11th June 1977

For once a trip into Manchester city centre on a Saturday afternoon did not involve the delights of HMV on Market Street or Rare Records on John Dalton Street. Instead the inevitable Virgin Records on Lever Street was the meeting place for our next interview before we reconvened downstairs at the city's Portland Bars to meet The Nosebleeds and their newly appointed manager Vini Faal, having been summoned to survey their new guise, with Eddie Garrity still very much in situ but his stage name now detached from their lengthy appellation in a bid for a more serious assessment.

As with all word of mouth events, it was the dependable Steve Shy who alerted us to the gathering. There was a third fanzine in attendance, *Manchester Rains* being represented by its creator Rob Gretton, who spent much of the summit quietly observing proceedings.

The occasion also coincided with the acquisition of another new face in the ranks; the slight frame of Vini Reilly, whose schoolboy blazer masked an articulate awareness of social matters that immediately projected him as the thinking man's Nosebleed. Vini was a Wythenshawe lad just like his band mates and manager. As such Reilly felt compelled to refer to my locale Bredbury in Stockport as "middle class" although, like the South Manchester suburb that Reilly and his band called home, we did have a Manchester overspill estate built to rehouse former Mancunian residents of districts such as Hulme. I don't recall Reilly's precise response to this revelation. Perhaps my inexperience of political debating thwarted any forcing of the issue in what was, after all, a chance to discuss musical aspirations rather than local politics.

Vini Faal was keen to outline the band's new direction following the condensed name and the arrival of their new guitarist. Faal had previously booked the bands for the Oaks, the venue that had delivered so much in such a short space of time. A previous encounter saw him deliver a justified reprimand for my printed lampooning of the Heartbreakers' New York accents. There was a whisper from other sources that strategies were in place for the Oaks to resume its midweek position and in all probability the opening act would be the Pistols.

Most tellingly from our perspective, invites had been limited to the fanzines, a press conference without the real press. Vini Faal had been generous in his opinion of *Shy Talk* and advised that he was "very impressed" with our latest issue of *Ghast Up*. Apparently Paul Morley's presence had been requested and Vini Faal was somewhat miffed by his absence although, given the adulation being bestowed on our flimsy journal, it may have been Morley's weekly single sheet outing *Girl Trouble* that was the intended target rather than his freelance contributions to the

NME. Despite his non-appearance, Morley would acknowledge The Nosebleeds' part in an *NME* article about the Manchester musical uprising that also recognised Vini Faal's influential role in reshaping the band and its objectives.

Unsurprisingly the band members were far more amicable than their stage persona would intimate. Eddie was smaller than I envisaged, with a genial disposition that endured being asked about his close encounter with Paul Morley back in April. "I'd have killed him" was his jokey response although, in Morley's absence, there was to be no re-match today.

Once more Slaughter and the Dogs came in for a level of reproach although Faal intercepted any tirade with the reminder that we are here to discuss The Nosebleeds adding as a rationale, "I like the Dogs". Oddly the band members claimed scant knowledge of the movers and shakers of the current punk movement, despite their sometimes inclusion of "Stepping Stone", no doubt wishing to cement the view that here was an original band with no conscious influence. In fact the figures of Garrity and Reilly could claim a level of inimitability and the rhythm section of drummer Toby Toman (Phillip Tomanov) and bassist Peter Crookes could have justly held down positions in most current bands.

As for the purpose of today's rendezvous, apart from supplying us with copious amounts of Holsten Pils, Vini Faal suggested a double page feature might be in order. If that sounded like unfettered bribery it is because it probably was. It is also customary practice in the music industry for record companies to pay all expenses for a journalist to spend time with their band and write a lengthy feature in return for the hospitality. The practice is cheaper than a similar sized advert in the paper and, crucially, it fuels the notion that the paper deems the act worthy of coverage.

So The Nosebleeds' new manager was just playing the game in a modest way by utilising the Manchester fanzines in preference to *Sounds* or *NME* and to be fair, two pages was not a huge ask compared to the space afforded previous interviewees. As Paul Morley's observed in the *NME*, "Vini has the consciousness and fingers to work the strings wonderfully".

It was bizarre and, I suppose at the time flattering, that Vini Faal judged that two middle class lads from Stockport, as Vini Reilly had defined us, could "speak to the kids". Perhaps Faal, like Rob Gretton when he graciously furnished me with details of Slaughter and the Dogs' single, was acknowledging the potentially important role that fanzines could play. Or maybe these two men, slightly older than ourselves, saw no purpose in dismissing any potential outlet.

Sunday 12th June 1977

The city of Sheffield was cited by The Drones as one of their early conquests with the South Yorkshire crowd showing sizeable appreciation for the band's willingness to venture into an unfashionable place. Or, as Paul Morley would more succinctly put it, "Sheffield's a fucking apathetic city".

I was assured by Steve Cundall that The Drones had received a notable endorsement from The Stranglers and furthermore their bassist Jean Jacques Burnel had declared a wish to produce Gangrene's composition "Persecution Complex" as a single. Whether such a union would have altered the course of The Drones' history shall remain a moot point but the claimed association between the two bands had been given credence by the towering presence of Hugh Cornwell at a recent Drones party held at Dave Bentley's home on Tootall Road in Salford. Cornwell was spotted in conversation with the more diminutive Howard Devoto. I had boldly given the educated Stranglers' singer a copy of our fanzine that included a full page review of their debut album. I declined his offer to pay suggesting we don't charge the bands. "Aren't we the only people who read them?" was Cornwell's comeback.

Backing from The Stranglers meant landing some support dates on the "Rats On The Road" tour and a short drive through the Peak District, with Steve Shy along for the ride, presented the opportunity to catch The Stranglers for the second Sunday in succession whilst assessing The Drones credentials in this city.

The Sheffield Top Rank's security were less than

accommodating to our requests to speak to The Drones although Gus Gangrene came into view and acknowledged us. Adjourning to a nearby café, I was able to show The Drones the published results of our question and answer encounter. The extrovert M J Drone took pleasure in reading the transcript, concluding it produced a worthy article. He was also somewhat overly complimentary about my artwork that included drawings of him and guitarist Gangrene. Steve Cundall judiciously queried whether my review of the band's "Temptations of a White Collar Worker" came from the heart rather than my burgeoning acquaintance with the band. I could at least reassure the bass player that I had been adequately impressed with the tape of their vinyl debut.

Also in tow were Kevin Cummins and the inevitable Paul Morley, although a perceptible distance between manager and band was becoming evident as he was frequently addressed as "Morley". Paul presented an article on the Sex Pistols to Steve Shy for inclusion in the ill-fated issue 4 of *Shy Talk*. An impressed Shy looked up periodically from reading the hand written article to enthuse, "it's really good this." He also revealed he had an interview with the Heartbreakers that a fan from Stretford by the name of Steven Morrissey had submitted.

Queuing outside the Sheffield Top Rank presented a further chance to make acquaintance with fellow fanzine writers. Steve Shy, who seemed to be on first name terms with all fanzine creators, introduced me to Martin of the Leeds based *New Pose* fanzine, whose main mission for the night was to secure an interview with The Stranglers. It was mission accomplished for in their second issue Jean Jacques Burnel revealed that The Stranglers had been banned from Martin's home city of Leeds and the neighbouring city of Bradford, explaining why a journey to south Yorkshire was required. Also working the queue was Adi of the acclaimed Sheffield fanzine *Gun Rubber* selling his latest issue in a green folded cover that depicted the Sex Pistols' God Save the Queen logo in red ink.

Inside, The Drones opened proceedings with M J Drone utilising one of his girlfriend Maggie's plentiful talents, wearing customised Union Flag trousers – the South Yorkshire crowd, who had accessed the venue by the time they took to the stage, gave the band a fair reception that was fortified by Mancunian support near the stage with Paul Doyle having now entered the fray. In return The Drones delivered what was expected, including a jokey aside that the Queen was, "sat over there with Prince Philip" following their trite anti-monarchy number "Corgi Crap". *New Pose* would pen an extremely favourable review of the performance and a sturdy endorsement of the band.

The other support band, London, were managed by Simon Napier-Bell and featured Jon Moss on drums, later of The Damned and Culture Club. I can recollect very little of this band except Drones bassist Steve Cundall later advising me they were decent lads. I also recall the four members of The Stranglers sat at a table within view of the stage during London's act, looking almost like teachers watching a school production.

Everybody knew The Stranglers could play. They may have fallen short of the "prog rock" bands in their musical proficiency but they could hold it together on stage and the pounding bass riffs of Jean Jacques Burnel surely put him in contention in the music polls. Future *Sounds* and *NME* correspondent Ian Wood, then compiling the "Rock What's On" section of the *New Manchester Review* would even describe The Stranglers as "Leaders of the New Wave".

Later in the year, following a live performance on the second series of "So It Goes" Tony Wilson would express regret that The Stranglers' technical expertise would render the rest of the new wave unworthy in the eyes of those "arbiters of culture" that included *Cosmopolitan* magazine whilst reminding viewers, "they're a fine band". Some 28 years on at the Urbis Punk event, and in an effort to perpetuate the legend that it was the Sex Pistols alone who altered the course of musical history, Wilson would somehow remind the more intimate crowd that, "The Stranglers were always shite."

The Stranglers had also been plying their trade for over three years under the supportive gaze of their devotees, The Finchley

Mob and, according to Paul Morley, already had a second album in the bag. Thus their set was already evolving to accommodate newer numbers like "I Feel Like A ★★★" and their homage to tragic Finchley member "Dagenham Dave".

For once Paul Doyle's dress sense was no obstacle to securing a lift home as we were able to offer him a ride. Outside, a Sheffield punkette enquired if Paul's clothing was from the London emporium Acme Attraction. He replied with a simple "no" although he explained on the drive home that he bought most of his clothing(?) from the Antique Market in Manchester.

The thirty-mile journey from Sheffield to Stockport afforded an opportunity to get to know one of the characters of the Manchester punk scene, shortly before the showing of the Brass Tacks documentary in which he would open up for the cameras. Paul was unemployed and living alone in a flat in Chorlton-cum-Hardy, Manchester to where he had moved the previous summer when he turned sixteen. His abiding passion was unsurprisingly the current punk scene, with a favourable nod to the accompanying dub reggae, and the pursuit of live music saw him hitch rides around the country checking out the local punk scenes, particularly when the passage involved any band hailing from Manchester. A recent road trip took him to the city of Leeds, whose punks Paul described as, "really friendly".

On tonight's show, he described Mike Drone as a "good performer" and the headliners as "sophisticated new wave" to which he added, "I really like the music". Steve Shy, who had known Paul for a few years, reminded him of his sharper appearance before he, like Steve, jumped ship from soul music to punk.

Steve also revealed that his previous job had included Slaughter and the Dogs' singer Wayne Barrett as an apprentice. Barrett's favoured subject of discussion was unsurprisingly "Bowie, Bowie, Bowie" and it had been the Dogs' frontman who persuaded Steve to check out his band at the Lesser Free Trade Hall the previous year. A request accepted despite the music on offer seemingly a world away from The Fatback Band, which had been Steve's previous live encounter.

The Dogs' Stones and Bowie influenced pop may not have been too drastic a culture shock for a soul boy but headliners the Sex Pistols and, even more so according to Steve, openers Buzzcocks, definitely were.

After several false starts The Jam finally showed up on Sunday 19th June to play before a teeming Electric Circus. A Top of the Pops appearance followed by the release of their debut album had catapulted The Jam into the league of The Ramones and The Stranglers as a band whose appeal guaranteed a full house, although curiously, not only was the cost of seeing The Jam the same £1.00 charged for Buzzcocks, compared to the £1.50 charged for the other major players including the non-charting Damned, the flyer also described the levy as "Admission" unlike the advance purchase of "Tickets" required for the big boys.

Paul Weller had made the offbeat claim that he would vote Conservative at the next election but greater disquiet existed over their polished routine staged in matching mohair suits with shiny red Rickenbacker guitars. Pete Townshend actually claimed that Rickenbackers were not the greatest instruments but they looked the part, which seemed to be the point where The Jam were concerned. Their slavish adulation of The Who was reinforced with the playing of the Batman theme as an encore. Even playing their only single to date "In the City" twice, had echoes of The Who's occasional double playing of "My Generation" as a crowd pleasing gesture, despite Townshend's avowed indifference to the song.

Although recollections vary as to the reception afforded to The Jam's glossy showmanship, that even involved Weller and Bruce Foxton's synchronised removal of their suit jackets, it was the less than silent minority who took issue with the band. Jon the Postman's heckling and Paul Morley's frustration at being kept waiting to interview Weller were minor irritants to a band whose rehearsed proficiency in performing their r'n'b flavoured pop garnered the approval of most corners of this old building. Local folklore has subsequently maintained that Mark Smith barracked the band for Weller's claimed support of the Conservatives. The fact that Smith was neither a Circus regular nor a follower of The Jam makes the account highly spurious.

Paul Morley, like Kevin Cummins, was ultimately granted access to the dressing room. Morley penned a tentative but largely unflattering critique of Weller's assertive approach for the *New Manchester Review* that quoted Buzzcocks' guitarist Steve Diggle, who was also in attendance "to learn a few things – what not to do" . Diggle compared The Jam front man to Macbeth, stating him "too ambitious" a charge I suspect with which Weller would have been happy. A more exclusive acquisition was Cummins' snap of a casually dressed Weller before the change into his stage suit.

Sunday 26th June 1977

The second Manchester instalment of the Stiff Records tour by The Damned supported by The Adverts whose "One Chord Wonders" would prove to be their only single on that label. Anchor Records were about to put them in the charts and procure them an appearance on Top of the Pops, which would ultimately allow The Adverts to outstrip The Damned. In Stiff's brash style the tour posters had exploited the reported musical ineptitude of anything punk by declaring:

"The Damned Can Now Play Three Chords. The Adverts Can Play One. Hear All Four Of Them At…"

For tonight at least it was still The Damned who the hordes queued to see. For once the waiting line was treated to some ad hoc entertainment. TV Smith and his conspicuous girlfriend Gaye Advert wandered part way down the queue before querying, "How do you get into this place?" I think the advice was to try the front door. There was also a discernible sound check taking place as the strains of "Stab Your Back" could be heard from the side street. By the time I reached the entrance the imposing figure of Rat Scabies appeared with sound check now complete. Maybe he was checking out the dress style of the crowd to make sure it didn't resemble that of the punters who had greeted The Damned back in January at this venue.

Steve Shy enthusiastically asked my view of the ramshackle

outfit whose crude set had opened proceedings, before informing me they were called The Prefects. Furthermore this band, from Birmingham, were proficient musicians whose limited arrangements were a conscious choice. A story later emerged that the band's performance was affected by the consumption of a crate of extra strong lager that had been supplied in the dressing room, a gesture that possibly prompted The Prefects to describe the Electric Circus as "Manchester's finest venue" and "a great club".

Although The Adverts wrote snappy songs that surmounted their limited musicianship, their early gigs always seemed blighted by a poor sound mix and tonight was no exception. Sunday nights at the Electric Circus were becoming an institution and a band that had been sanctioned by Johnny Rotten alongside Manchester's own Buzzcocks were always on safe territory, even when they challenged the audience participation on the third number by stalling the pace for the opening of "On The Roof".

No such issues for The Damned. The set still relied almost exclusively on their debut album that conveniently encompassed both singles. The lack of subtlety in The Damned's approach meant any technical deficiencies that existed were lost in the unwavering barrage characteristic of their live performance. Their repertoire was conveyed with their usual steadfast aplomb and performed more than adequately. Their continued assertion of being a fun band was becoming somewhat specious given their systematic treatment of The Stooges "1970 (I Feel Alright)". Alberto Y Lost Trios Paranoia could have been described as fun, as could The Fabulous Poodles but those bands only fell within the punk parameter because most punks did not differentiate between parody and the real thing.

The one aspect of their previous encounter with a Circus crowd that they may have longed for was a night free from gobbing. Although it never quite reached the incessant level that had plagued them at the Middleton Civic Hall in May, the practice was becoming recognised as an act of appreciation and The Damned's unswerving desire to be recognised as punk originals made them prime targets. I offered a crumb of protection by advising a friend who had tagged along for the evening against demonstrating his approval in such a way. "Doesn't it mean you like 'em?" was his bemused response.

Thursday 30th June 1977

Despite mounting a serious claim to be a crucial port of call on the circuit, there were still gaps in the Mancunian itinerary. A band who commanded total respect from the fanzines, and more than a cursory glance from the nationals, were Generation X. Their last visit to the city was as support to The Drones at Houldsworth Hall the previous December, when Paul Morley had questioned the anomaly of a band whose lyrics cried out for "New Orders" whilst their music suggested "sugar and spice and all things nice". They arrived at Rafters with a double Mancunian support of Warsaw and The Worst.

Watching Warsaw again try to make inroads into their musical ambitions, it was hard to gauge whether their shows would gain sufficient momentum to providing the spark for future generations, just as the Pistols 1976 performance clearly had for them. I could find no apparent flaw within their set but their methodical approach failed to stimulate my interest sufficiently.

One band who attracted my attention, but for all the wrong reasons, was The Worst who were apparently playing their third or fourth gig. Like The Negatives, the three members of The Worst were familiar faces around Manchester. Their major forte would be their capacity to improvise – they were even known to compose the set in the van immediately before delivering it on stage, an act that Mark Smith described as "genius". Tonight there was an awkward distance between performers and audience, who they aimed to meet halfway, with none of the interchange that would render their limited musicianship irrelevant.

In defence of both Manchester bands, Generation X seemed to have brought a sizeable London contingent who imposed their own demands. Kevin Cummins later apologised for the limited choice of live shots as some of the visiting entourage had been obstructive to his task.

I had been introduced by Steve Shy to another visitor from the capital who also went by the name of Steve and was in town selling the fourth issue of *48 Thrills* fanzine. Although I recall chatting to the youth with dyed blonde hair and black leather jacket, I only recently discovered that the person in question was Steve Harrington a.k.a. Steve Strange.

Strange had been through a similar life-altering experience to many a Mancunian when he crossed the picket line of carol singers to witness the Sex Pistols play the Castle Cinema in Caerphilly as part of the 1976 "Anarchy" tour. The encounter would ultimately propel him to London, purportedly in the back of Generation X's van later that week having acted as roadie for the band in Cardiff. Fortuitously, and unknown to the local audience at the time, Strange was also in the throes of launching a punk band known as The Moors Murderers along with Bromley punk face Soo Catwoman.

I assume I partook in the usual fanzine exchange ritual as I recall one of the party, though not Steve Strange who was surprisingly reserved given his loquacious reputation of later years, expressing sympathy with The Clash for my sketched interpretation of the band in issue two of *Ghast Up*, particular my portrayal of Mick Jones which I was assured was "very uncomplimentary".

For their part Generation X were flat and disappointing. Their music lacked energy or commerciality, the two adjectives most commonly used to define their music, if not their politics. Their first session for John Peel would endorse the views of the independent London press, the three numbers being bright and snappy and completely at odds with the general dirge delivered that evening. In a craven act I penned a largely ambiguous review for *Ghast Up* that suppressed my disappointing first impressions of this London band.

Sunday 3rd July 1977

It was the turn of Australia's Saints to play a Sunday night at the Circus and to illustrate the two tier appeal that had developed there. Whereas The Clash, The Ramones, The Stranglers, The

Jam and The Damned had filled the venue to near capacity with the famous queue around the corners of the building, Buzzcocks and now The Saints had to settle for a more humble turnout, with The Vibrators and The Drones subsequent appearances also set to attract a more modest attendance, probably as a result of a lack of chart action and the crossover appeal it generated.

Of the regular attendees present, Drones' guitarist Gus asked if I had seen the support band who went by the name Berlin and who had completed their set before my late arrival. Unimpressed with the band, Gus suggested we interview them as a jape. In Gus's attempts to secure an encounter with Berlin he chanced upon The Saints' Ed Kuepper by the dressing room door, who granted us a more crucial interview after the gig.

The Saints tore through a set that relied on their debut album interspersed with a few of the covers that had helped sharpen their seminal performances including "River Deep Mountain High". The album had received mixed but mostly disparaging reviews, with their single "I'm Stranded" the only product to date to have been fully endorsed by press and punters.

The sound of the Saints had drawn comparisons to The Ramones and, like the New York punks' rapid fire delivery, it was the whole package more than close scrutiny of individual songs that warranted evaluation. And within those parameters The Saints delivered a fair return and earned the right to be interviewed.

The interview panel grew as we ascended the dressing room stairs with Jon the Postman, Paul Doyle and a delegation from the *New Pose* fanzine from Leeds swelling the ranks. Gus became distracted en route by one of the Circus regulars. Adding a touch of formality to the impromptu gathering, the chairs for the guests were arranged in a rough circle around the band members.

Jon the Postman's made a couple of enquiries about the availability of cannabis in Australia and the reported spat with fans that had allegedly resulted in the band pronouncing them "posing pommie bastards." Singer Chris Bailey took umbrage that the press's ludicrous accusation was deemed believable but Jon tried to pacify the singer advising him "No that was good, putting down the poseurs."

The Saints were less than enthusiastic about the musical activity in their native land, although we discovered their reference to "home" alluded not to the city of Brisbane but to London which they hoped would become their permanent base. As was now standard, Kevin Cummins providing a stunning live shot of the band to complement the impromptu interview.

Monday 4th July 1977

"Buzzcocks are playing Crackers in London on Monday. It's a new punk venue. We're hiring a minibus if you fancy it. There's a few of us going. Meet at Virgin to leave about half nine."

And so I found myself in the Virgin store on Lever Street, Manchester. Steve Shy and his girlfriend Ann were in a sound booth listening to the Sex Pistols' interpretation of Iggy Pop's "No Fun" and articulating a preference for the Pistols' B-sides. The said minibus arrived driven by Kevin Cummins and the three of us joined the assembly of Dave Bentley, Francis Taylor and one of tonight's performers, John Cooper Clarke. Clarke requested Kevin stop off at a store before merging onto the motorway, to purchase some fruit and a top shelf magazine.

In a round trip that saw Kevin stay awake for almost 24 hours, the journey down to the smoke was predictably dominated by the subject of the Manchester punk scene alongside observations of band rivalry. The Damned don't like The Clash because Strummer and co think they are superstars but then The Damned think the same of The Clash etc. Local news focussed on the design of the label on The Drones' forthcoming EP that featured an "OHMS" design in ambiguous reference to the royals.

As well as Clarke's poetic musings, tonight's gig would also feature The Fall. "The place is a disco and drinks are probably expensive" I was informed. It seemed all London punks must work or they couldn't afford the lifestyle or clothes prices at the local punk emporiums. I blandly asked John Cooper Clarke what poems he was intending to teach the London audience. Would they know where Salford is? "Yes I think so, they should do" was his response, "perhaps change it to Manchester."

Late afternoon in London had an air of a place of work as Kevin steered the Ford Transit through the West End to Wardour Street and parked up close to Crackers. The order of events became somewhat blurred but I recall visiting a café, glimpsing en route the gangling crew that had loitered so menacingly at Johnny Thunders and the Heartbreakers' gig at the Oaks back in March. When it was mentioned that the Heartbreakers were about to be deported following expiry of their work permit and, it being the fourth of July, they would like to play a farewell for the British fans, I deduced that these people were part of the Heartbreakers' entourage with the band set to gate-crash Buzzcocks' opening night at the Vortex, as Crackers had been rechristened for punk usage.

At my first sound-check proper, having only overheard The Damned through the side wall of the Electric Circus, Buzzcocks acknowledged me among the Manchester support with Pete Shelley observing, "it's Martin Martyn, the civil servant." John Maher suggested I was Mick Middles but a brief debate revealed my identity. Kevin was more interested in a large advertising cardboard cut-out of Elvis Costello and how he could get that into the van.

Buzzcocks played a few of their songs to test the sound, as well as a compressed version of Jonathan Richman's "Roadrunner" that swiftly concluded with Shelley hollering, "roadrunner once, roadrunner twice". Howard Devoto, also along for the ride, offered advice on the sound quality before trading places with Shelley and providing both vocals and rhythm guitar for "Breakdown" and "Boredom". That high point of the day offered some compensation for having missed the reunion at the Band on the Wall. For the second time in a week Steve Shy introduced me to someone from *48 Thrills* fanzine, This time it was the main writer Adrian who was along for the sound check and, unlike his fanzine cohort Steve Strange, was attired in decidedly un-punk gear, unless you count anyone under thirty-five in narrow trousers as a punk.

The Damned were playing two shows at the nearby Marquee so there was time to catch the early evening show along with

Francis Taylor. I still had a few copies of *Ghast Up* 2 to unload which were, as luck would have it, in a Roneo paper box that served to protect the "Stretcher Case" single Stiff Records were giving away free on entry. As it transpired quite a few London punters were eager to purchase my fanzine, particularly with The Clash featured on the cover, although one individual expressed little enthusiasm for the remaining contents.

Dave Vanian was stood by the door in full make up as the crowd filed into the early show that also afforded the chance to catch Johnny Moped in support. Regaled as one of the scene's true eccentrics, Moped looked older than his contemporaries yet despite his bawled delivery and semi-coherent ramblings, his material contained some semblance of a tune.

Johnny Moped, like Alice Cooper, seemed to be the name of the singer and the accepted name of the band and the London crowd reacted the instant they struck up the first number or, as Francis Taylor remarked, "Talk about remote control", even if approval now had to include gobbing and throwing beer. Rat Scabies would join them on drums for part of a number to remind everyone that The Damned and Johnny Moped were friends.

Seemingly oblivious to the swift rise that they and other punk bands had enjoyed, The Damned were visibly piqued by the over-exuberant response coupled with the notorious tetchiness of the locals. Dave Vanian angrily demanded patience as he removed his shirt in the heat and Rat Scabies leapt from behind his kit to throw a drum angrily to the floor. Having confronted the youngsters at Middleton Civic Hall seven weeks prior, Brian James opted to concentrate on his guitar rather than challenge the behaviour of this adult audience, his only vocal contribution being the 1-2s to encourage his band mates to do likewise.

Being on the guest list may have provided a smooth entry at some venues but the security at the Vortex insisted on a full search that required me to explain to an unsmiling bouncer what a phial of insulin was and why I was taking such an item into the venue.

The biggest surprise of the evening was my second encounter with The Fall. Having expected more of the same, the addition of keyboard player Una Baines had suddenly given the band a more colourful edge as Mark Smith led the band through a confident and powerful set that paid little heed to the hordes still filing into the club, unaware of the dramatic transformation that was unfolding, or that The Fall would become more celebrated in these parts than in their native North West. Whatever twists the night would still bring, my abiding memory of the opening night of the Vortex was the discovery of this band from Manchester. How had I failed to spot such an innovative band one month back in the cosier backdrop of The Squat?

If The Fall were the surprise package, the response to John Cooper Clarke was beyond any rational belief. Any attempt to read from his sheets of poetry was overpowered by the ever increasing calls for his removal. His delivery was interrupted the moment the audience deduced that this was not a musical punk act but a man reading poetry as observers noted "What's he doing? He's reading bleeding poetry." That the rhyming couplets were funny and topical and Clarke's broad but clear diction would develop a rhythmic delivery, given the chance, gained no accolades as the first attempt was swiftly aborted with the poet barracked like an interloper.

As a veteran of the northern nightclub circuit, Clarke was accustomed to the odd conflict and re-entered the fray with the more upbeat "Spilt Beans". Alas, this was one battle too many and further voluminous heckling drowned out the Salford bard who quickly conceded defeat and threw his sheets of poetry to the floor.

No such fate awaited Buzzcocks, although they were incensed by the announcement that the Heartbreakers "will be coming on to jam" later on. "Coming on to jam" was of course an ignoble way of notifying Buzzcocks they were relegated to a support slot, a position that the National music press would confirm in the following week's live reviews.

Whatever acclaim punk culture bestowed on Johnny Thunders and the Heartbreakers, particularly with the presence of two former New York Dolls (whose influence on the Sex Pistols was said to have verged into plagiarism in their early days) the night of American Independence Day 1977 has to be close to their nadir. I only say close because of the tragic fates that awaited both Thunders and Nolan.

The dressing room at the Vortex was likened to a broom cupboard by Shelley, the dimensions not proving an obstacle to the Heartbreakers' wish to throw a party to which their large entourage and even larger personalities were not invited. Mark Smith would later recount his one-time hero Jerry Nolan's querying if Una Baines was his "groupie".

The only skirmish Buzzcocks encountered during their set was an impatient remonstration urging Shelley to "get on with it" when he had to replace a guitar string. Such an altercation perhaps illustrated why John Cooper Clarke never stood a chance, but it was a minor blemish on a pretty flawless Buzzcocks performance that even showed Shelley finding a role for his voice in newer compositions like "What Do I Get" and "Whatever Happened To?"

The grand opening of the Vortex did entice a modest smattering of punk celebrity. Brian James made the short walk over following The Damned's second set at the Marquee and a dark-haired Billy Idol approached a disconsolate Pete Shelley slouched at a nearby table. Kevin Cummins grabbed a laconic chat with the Generation X singer before mockingly telling me, "It's Billy Idol".

Forgoing his usual role of image gatherer for the night, Kevin offered to lighten the return journey load by selling the last few copies of *Ghast Up* 2, all of which he despatched making the issue officially a sell-out. It's fair to say he did my job better than I did his when snapping Buzzcocks and AC/DC for the first issue.

Under the Wardour Street lights Buzzcocks were loading their van parked in close proximity to our transport in which I assume Kevin had secreted the Costello artefact. An attempt by Garth to jump repeatedly onto the stage and avert the Heartbreakers performance had been curtailed by the club's security, although the bassist was the only band member with an upbeat persona despite the failed coup, "Think of the publicity!" In fact the publicity in the following week's *NME* was a curt "What gives cocks?" in response to the account of Buzzcocks' intransigence.

Saturday 9th July 1977

As each month seemed to unearth a new venue to showcase punk, it was the turn of the Elizabethan Ballroom in the Belle Vue Amusement Park to provide the backdrop for the tour to support the newly released "The Roxy London WC2" album on EMI's progressive Harvest Label. Unlike the other venues in Manchester where punk rock was sampled, the Elizabethan was a smart venue, in total contrast to the London venue being showcased. A traditional ballroom with a stage for the band and two large wooden dance floors that could apparently hold 4000 dancers it also contained a separate bar and tidy lounge.

The album in question was a series of poor quality live recordings, interspersed with background noise and chatter, captured during the club's brief heyday that had already passed. Being a various artists punk compilation it proved to be a vital acquisition alongside Vertigo's "New Wave" release and to be fair the finished product achieved its purpose, that being to create a recorded memento of the seminal London venue.

The album's inside cover included snaps of Mancunian punks Denise Lloyd and Paul Doyle taken on an excursion to the place, presumably to catch Buzzcocks who contributed two tracks as did tonight's headliners Slaughter and the Dogs.

As one of the four bands who were not making their vinyl debut on the Roxy album (three bands if you discount Buzzcocks who had yet to commit to vinyl post-Devoto) it was the Dogs who were given top billing over Johnny Moped, X Ray Spex and Eater, an accolade they ultimately warranted.

Having been aware of, but not familiar with, the antics of Johnny Moped until this week, I was now witnessing him for the second time in six days. Despite the singer's insistence on portraying himself as less than serious, with his set including a high-pitched, but otherwise true to script interpretation of "Little Queenie", the band were a musically solid outfit whose repertoire hardly required gimmicks. .

"Alright you phlegm gobbing animals" was the Moped method of addressing the now customary spitting and this was one time when humour was the best policy. Johnny Moped were The Damned without the custard pies but with stronger melodies, at least until they chose "New Rose" as an encore.

It did not take a doyen of the music industry to deduce that X Ray Spex were destined to sell records. The piercing vocal of singer Poly Styrene, supplemented by rudimentary bursts of sound from 16 year-old female saxophonist Laura Logic, produced a unique blend that enhanced the quality of their songs. Paul Morley had already supplied an impassioned critique of the band that made some sense when faced with them in the flesh for the first time.

Eater were the band who had chosen to play the youth card, famously describing the Sex Pistols as old enough to be their parents. Dee Generate, the original 14 year-old drummer, had left the band following two single releases, although his mother still chose to employ her famous-by-association status firing letters to the music press as "Dee Generate's mum."

Despite the band being barely out of school, their short career thus far had been quite momentous. In addition to having released two singles, more than most contemporaries, they had headlined over both The Damned and Slaughter and the Dogs at the Roxy and even grabbed the main spot on their debut back in late 1976 that saw them top the bill over Buzzcocks at Manchester's Houldsworth Hall.

In the open spaces of the Elizabethan, Eater cut forlorn figures on the stage. In many ways their ability belied their tender years but a crowd that had been rocking to the first two acts of the package were at once subdued to the point where singer Andy Blade could politely ask people to get off the stage, or at least move away from the band. None of the usual pleading could be heard above the punk euphoria.

If I were more cynical I would suggest this was a wilful act to allow the Dogs a free run. The buoyant charm of X-Ray Spex would always be a tough act to follow, but the hollow ring of Eater gave the Dogs a clean start to build on.

If every dog has its day, this was surely Slaughter and the Dogs'. Their hammy theatrics were a vague distraction as they rode the shower of plastic glasses and their contents to deliver a potent set that suggested that their obvious desire to be contenders for Top of the Pops was getting closer to a reality. Beneath Wayne Barrett's cloak and talcum powder there was a greater level of self-assurance in their own material, even if the selection of compositions didn't seem to grow or vary. Paul Morley's liberal assessment that "They're alright if you don't look at them" tendered on a previous drive home from the Oaks was astutely accurate for this occasion.

A recording of tonight's performance would be released in 1978 as the rudimentarily packaged "Live Slaughter Rabid Dogs" LP. It served to confirm my evaluation of them in what still ranks as one of the better live albums, although the band's petulance at the hurling of glasses was more pronounced than I remembered, making the recorded memento more like a Derek and Clive Live out-take.

Sunday 10th July 1977

After several false starts due to cancelled gigs, partly due to the band securing a support slot on Ian Hunter's nationwide tour, The Vibrators finally played the Circus, which meant our first scheduled interview since the night at the Smithfield Arms back in April when Paul Morley had steered The Drones and us down the interview route.

The inside of the Circus was floodlit due to a BBC crew filming the activities of these punk creatures for an impending Brass Tacks studio debate programme. As the programme's panel featured Manchester punk regulars, the Electric Circus was pretty much the obvious choice and The Vibrators, a slightly older punk band signed to Epic Records with an album released, would seem to represent a more acceptable face of the culture.

The BBC cameras afforded TV exposure to The Drones that

would evolve into YouTube fame many decades later. Despite headlining the following Sunday, it was The Drones who opened proceedings in their own back yard. Penetration were also on the bill and apparently there was some dispute over the running order with the visitors from Ferryhill, County Durham claiming second spot over the local band. The word from The Drones' camp was that they had shown less belligerence than Penetration, merely advising of the extent of their local following. Despite the welcome that was always bestowed on Penetration at this venue, they would never reach the pinnacle of being headliners, unlike The Drones who managed it twice, so perhaps the visitors could be allowed tonight's minor victory.

Since their previous shows in Manchester, The Vibrators had acquired a nineteen-year-old bassist whose input was immediately apparent. The lighter weight pop-orientated sound that had served them well in the cavernous ambience of Manchester's Apollo, gave way to a darker more solid tone here. "They're a lot heavier" was Steve Shy's observation of the new sound. Gary Tibbs' influence on his first band was already apparent.

When visiting Manchester The Vibrators had usually been spared the hard time that certain sectors of the London audiences gave them over their perceived clamber onto the punk bandwagon and tonight they were politely but heartily approved before a TV audience.

The route to the dressing room was populated by Paul Morley and Pete Shelley. Amid the banter Morley made a blurred reference to us being "Observer poseurs" that missed its target, on account of our being oblivious to that day's *Observer* Sunday Supplement featuring an article on the punk movement that listed *Ghast Up* as part of the "avalanche of new wave fanzines" in a list that also cited Stockport's not totally punk fanzine *Penetration*, the publication in which Morley had first cut his journalistic teeth.

An interesting viewpoint would have been Shelley's take on The Vibrators, a band he had previously endorsed, now covering "Jumping Jack Flash", the very act for which Shelley had previously censured Slaughter and the Dogs.

★

In a spirit of camaraderie the band asked what we thought of the new boy. It elicited an easy enough comeback, although the new boy was eager to disparage just about every other punk outfit, most of whom he dismissed as "rubbish" and "can't play".

John Ellis liked the Pistols' singles that he described as, "very clever" although he dismissed the band as "more of a business enterprise than a group". Outside the new wave Ellis was partial to the singing of Barbara Streisand.

Knox suggested The Damned, who he described as a bunch of four misfits who mysteriously worked as a unit, needed to make their mark soon or become the forgotten men of punk. He then steered the conversation back to The Vibrators and their recent album release. They were amenably gracious at our reference to the lightweight production, although Knox likened the mix to Raw Power by The Stooges – a Bowie production and Knox's favourite LP. They briefed us on new material they had been writing and merging into the act, something drummer Eddie had already appraised us of in his regular correspondence.

For whatever reason, the dialogue drifted to spitting and the then current groundswell of violence against punks, which the elders in the band understandably denounced. The topics we failed to explore and, which they certainly did not volunteer, were any bawdy tales of life on the road with Iggy Pop or Ian Hunter.

★

Departing the Electric Circus with some scribbled notes as a record of the interview, tonight would not be our last encounter with this group of visiting musicians.

Driving back from London several weeks later on the evening of Monday 25th July, having visited Rough Trade records among other London haunts, we stopped for a drink somewhere in the proximity of Stafford around 9:00 pm. An average looking man with short dark hair, perhaps in his mid–twenties wearing a black jacket and black jeans, strolled by. Mick jokingly suggested it was John Ellis, noting the stranger's passing resemblance to the guitarist but assuming it was no more than a likeness.

A second stranger disappeared down the same trajectory causing greater bewilderment. Far more outlandish in appearance in punk leather jacket and shiny drainpipe jeans with a shock of dark hair, the question "Is that Knox?" was probably more rhetorical. In 1977 thirty-something punks were far from common, particularly in a residential Staffordshire pub.

The enigma was solved when the less outlandishly garbed John Edwards appeared and Mick felt confident enough to address the drummer. The conversation went something along these lines.

Mick: Are you John Edwards?

Eddie: Yeh. Why?

Mick: Mick and Martin from *Ghast Up*. We interviewed you the other week in Manchester.

Eddie: Oh of course you did. I recognise you now. So are you here for the gig? We're playing in Stafford tonight.

Mick: Er! We were just passing through on our way home from London.

Eddie: Well seeing as you're here, there's no excuse for not coming down to the gig.

Despite travel weariness, the generous offer could not be forsaken and the next phase of the adventure occurred in the back of a Transit van driven at an unnerving speed by John Edwards towards the Top of the World venue in Stafford. The brisk journey afforded a chance to catch up with the other three Vibrators. They recalled our friends from Manchester, The Drones, supporting them at the Electric Circus, although John Ellis was unmoved by their recent EP release suggesting they were perhaps just not good enough. I recall offering a word in their defence reminding him that John Peel had confessed to liking one of the tracks.

Whatever Ellis's views on The Drones' capabilities at that time their future careers would become entwined. Drones drummer Peter Howells would, like Ellis, be chosen to accompany Stranglers' bassist Jean Jacques Burnel on his solo tour to showcase the "Euroman Cometh" album in 1979, Howells even being selected to contribute drums on three of the album's tracks. Their paths would again cross the following year when Ellis played guitar on The Drones' single "Can't See" which many would argue was their finest recorded moment.

An interesting anecdote shared by the band was of a gig arranged for the following evening at Crackers discotheque in London as a showcase for their record label's parent company CBS. The reward for a stirring performance would be a series of dates in America.

Arriving at the Top of the World we were escorted into the venue by the band, whilst others dealt with such matters as the equipment. The venue was the usual large auditorium with plenty of standing room. As I recall it was smarter than the Electric Circus and, for some inexplicable reason, punk gigs in such towns seemed to attract a small element who dressed like regular club goers but behaved in the surly manner that the tabloid press suggested was "punk".

The Vibrators could have no complaints with the reception, being given two encores as they delivered a set similar to the one staged at the Electric Circus, although their all-round good guy image was tested when thirty-one-year-old Knox deemed it appropriate to spit into the front row before departing the stage at the end.

The night would deliver a further twist. We were invited backstage without the need to explain that we now required a lift back to the pub where the band were staying, as a road crew member genially enquired, "Do you want to come and meet the band?"

The dressing room already accommodated a generous smattering of locals, mostly of the female variety, to whom the assorted Vibrators gave similar beliefs and anecdotes to those offered to ourselves back at the Circus, Knox describing The Damned as a bunch of misfits. The followers from Stafford were particularly struck with the articulacy of Knox who one young lady pronounced, "A real intellect, I'm amazed".

Gary Tibbs' continued tirade against fellow new wavers also struck a chord. Seemingly these locals were granted access to their idols at the Top of the World and were somewhat disparaging about many including The Boomtown Rats who were described as, "really chronic for the first twenty-five minutes" by the lady who swooned over Knox's eloquence. Paul Weller was labelled "boring" for devoting his attention to his girlfriend whilst ignoring the backstage multitude.

The indifferent review of The Vibrators debut LP by the *NME*'s Julie Burchill was challenged mainly by the band member who played no part in recording the album, Gary Tibbs noting that Burchill was roughly the same age as him and adding that the band had been informed the writer actually liked the LP.

As time was called on the gathering it appeared there were insufficient hands to remove the gear with the guy I presumed was the road manager asking, "What about you lads?" Thus I was appointed an auxiliary roadie charged with the fastidious task of lifting and shifting valuable and weighty equipment down a flight of stairs and into the van to such directives as "Careful that's an SXT11".

Sunday 17th July 1977

Having meticulously ploughed their furrow around Manchester and beyond, willingly lending support whenever given space on the bill, The Drones returned to headline at the Circus.

Well almost. The Worst had become regular interlopers on the scene, often borrowing other band's equipment to make their noise. Allan and Ian made the regular excursion from Preston in a van, which may or may not have held their rudimentary gear in its storage space. Either way the equipment belonging to the advertised bands, even those at the foot of the bill, probably represented a step up in calibre, not that the sound produced was in anyway a departure from The Worst's norm.

Tonight The Worst were presumably there by invitation as Ian Hodge sat behind a distinguished Chad Valley drum kit. Allan Deaves used the exclusivity of the audience to remonstrate on whatever issues he considered worthy of reflection, be it the police or the fast breeder reactors, musical arguments delivered via the usual battery of expletives.

There is a certain irony that a crowd who would later dance wildly to The Drones, a former cabaret band who still took the act of performing relatively seriously, would lift The Worst, an apprentice punk band learning on the job, to their highest plane so far.

Being an abstract concept, it was a tricky proposition to constructively measure The Worst alongside their peers. Less polished than The Drones. Less enchanting than Buzzcocks. More political than The Fall (Mark Smith would later class their extemporisation as genius). More improvised than The Negatives or Jon the Postman? Ultimately the hands of The Worst were tied by their indebtedness to the surrounding multitudes who had countenanced their inclusion on the next level above the Circus regulars of Paul, Denise, Dawn, Joan etc.

Tonight everything seemed to fit perfectly. There was even a measure of deliberation to Allan's bluster between numbers as the free form music soared and tumbled in equal measure, with their rapid set coasting rather than drifting to its conclusion. Although I remain of the view that any successful attempt to record The Worst would almost certainly have detracted from their fabled status, a recording of tonight's gig may have supplied the definitive Worst record.

And so to The Drones. Unlike the last occasion, the band had little to prove this time around and the crowd obligingly participated from the opening riff and throughout a set that was augmented with a preview of both sides of their forthcoming single, the band having signed a deal with Valer Records.

The band still sat haughtily behind Buzzcocks as the closest challengers, alongside Slaughter and the Dogs who certain Drones were beginning to acknowledge as equally worthy contenders. Maybe the looming emergence of The Fall and John Cooper Clarke, who was about to release a record of poetry recited over an electronic soundtrack, should have served as a warning that the bar was being raised and competition within Greater Manchester was about to get a whole lot tougher.

For tonight however The Drones could savour their position and delivered the kind of sharp, capable, risk-free set that had become their forte. Mike Drone's traditional homily of "I've got a message for all you people, you just wanna be yourself" would have been dispensed at some point. The Circus crowd in turn were happy to indulge via the usual ritual of compressed dancing with encore. The Drones had come through their very own Sunday night at the Electric Circus, thus cementing their position in 1977 Manchester folklore - as had The Worst in their own parallel universe.

Thursday 21st July 1977

Stiff Records were given the plaudits for releasing the first bona fide UK punk single. "New Rose" by The Damned appeared on the label in October 1976, produced by another Stiff Artist Nick Lowe. Thus any release on the Stiff label qualified for rational evaluation from members of punk culture. Even Max Wall's recording of Ian Dury's "England's Glory" earned a favourable review in *Sniffin' Glue*.

In his defence, Elvis Costello did not just share a label and a producer with The Damned, he seemed to have an attitude and his debut single "Less Than Zero" referred to Oswald Mosley, which in turn echoed The Clash's anti-fascist stance.

However I did not know what to expect of the man about to preview his debut album to a packed Rafters. One person who seemed to know what to expect was TV's Tony Wilson who had donned a white suit and fedora for the occasion and, in what looked like a vainglorious attempt to share the spotlight, danced throughout Costello's stream of crafted songs performed on this occasion with US West Coast band Clover who got the gig prior to the Attractions becoming a permanent fixture.

My knowledge of a man to whom Stiff Records had given considerable backing was limited to both sides of his first single and a solitary radio play of the follow up "Alison". And the fact he was 22 and married with a young son. The debut single had garnered favour from the media with its clever arrangement and lyrical composition, drawing comparisons with Graham Parker and even Springsteen. Costello would curtly deny such charges before the gig when Paul Morley secured a fleeting interview in which he insisted "I don't sound like those people."

Having the entire "My Aim Is True" album together with selections of the following year's "This Year's Model" at his disposal, Costello could confidently pace his set from the opener of "Welcome to the Working Week" through to the finale of "No Action" although the song that imprinted its beguiling chorus on everyone's memory was "I Don't Want to Go to Chelsea".

Unlike the punk norm of unleashing the single at the outset, Costello made the audience bide their time before rewarding their patience with "Alison" and "Less Than Zero". "Red Shoes" was introduced as his "single out tomorrow" with the added enquiry, "are you gonna buy it?" The resounding affirmation was at variance with the single's lack of chart action, although it was probably the album containing the single, also released the following day, that persuaded the devotees within to make a purchase.

In the live environment Costello was clearly a more gifted vocalist than his records suggested. The comparisons to Graham Parker, who had also been tested on the pub rock circuit, had some rationale, even if Parker's songwriting followed a more traditional route.

It was the suited and booted Wilson who led the calls for "more" whilst swapping notes with Morley whose pre-gig interview technique suggested he was slightly less enamoured with the bespectacled singer/songwriter than the TV presenter.

Earlier, in the dressing room, Costello had advised Morley of his fulsome praise for Stiff Records, who he had alighted upon following years of fruitlessly hawking his tapes around various record companies. Stiff were in the throes of a bountiful publicity drive entitled "Help Us Hype Elvis" and had provided the musicians who backed him in recording and were now lending musical support on the road. Moreover Stiff granted what was generally referred to as "artistic freedom" although in Costello's case that was presumably the wrong terminology as he refuted that his creation of music constituted neither art nor entertainment nor showbusiness. Costello reasoned that rock was art but pop was not and he was content to be grouped with the latter.

Thursday 28 July 1977

In spite of, or maybe because of, the "Snuff Rock" EP that contained punk parodies "Gobbing On Life" "Kill" and "Snuffin' Like That" along with the reggae spoof "Snuffin' In A Babylon", Alberto Y Lost Trios Paranoias found themselves weirdly acknowledged within the punk audience. The Albertos' credibility within the punk clique was certainly not hindered by their EP being released on Stiff Records.

Reviewing the EP in *New Manchester Review*, Ian Wood even suggested that the humour within the Albertos had been dragged forward a decade by their contact with the new wave producing a more accessible comedic thread than their preceding album releases.

What the punk audience failed to anticipate was the level of esteem and support that the Mancunian comedy troupe had acquired on the club and college circuit prior to the punk explosion. Thus for the first time accessing Rafters was not the simple task of arriving at the door and paying the admission fee as it had been thus far. With an expanding queue stretching along Oxford Road and around the block, any hopes of catching tonight's show would require a dogged level of perseverance. The new wave may have been growing in popularity but these old school entertainers showed the way to draw a real crowd.

Sunday 7th August 1977

Possibly the most bizarre double header to present itself at the Electric Circus was the visit of two acts signed to the Step Forward label run by Miles Copeland and Mark Perry.

The Cortinas arrived with their debut single "Fascist Dictator" and the flipside "Television Families" gaining airplay on the John Peel Show. The band from Bristol were described as being among the youngest on the scene with an average age of 16.

They had a calculated stage routine that involved each member being introduced as "Johnny" as they ran through the band line up which was actually the peak of a monotonous set that was becoming the lot of too many punk bands. Presumably some of the audience appreciated The Cortinas as vocalist Jeremy Valentine, in thanking the crowd for their approval, gave the now hackneyed request to stop spitting.

Although I penned a curiously favourable review of the night for a two page supplement given away with later copies of *Ghast Up* issue 3, the only aspects of Chelsea's set that stuck in my memory were of vocalist and poster boy Gene October bounding on stage, towel in hand and at the end of their set leading the band straight back to play an encore that was not requested. I also recall Chelsea having a song called "Pretty Vacant" but I don't recall the song being any less of a dirge than the rest of their music.

CHELSEA

Gene October, clad in white boiler suit, (make that WHITE boiler suit) and towel in hand, threw his verbal punches at the crowd in between almost every number. Why Gene? Why storm off in temper towards the dressing room, don't you like Manchester?

The show began OK as Gene jumped up and down, laughing at the crowd gobbing at him, the gobbers were, after all, the kids who were flipping head over heels to the music down by the stage. In between songs Gene mopped his sweating face with his towel and hurled the odd comment like "I thought Manchester's crowds were supposed to be really great" or how about "You're not from Manchester." Half the crowd bared their teeth whilst the other half shook their heads in total confusion.

Believe it or not, I think he's great, one of the best, the only trouble being his ego which can't quite accept all this heckling that exists to add spice and above all else, a real challenge to someone like Gene October, who does have some strong ideas and feelings in his lyrics. Which brings me round to his songs.

RIGHT TO WORK is far too easy to dismiss, mainly because it's rather too subtle, I mean how am I supposed to know it's an anti-Trades Union chant? Given this meaning the song sounds so much stronger and Gene's voice much more convincing.

"Having NO FUTURE it's a terrible thing", being the operative words. I think it must be remembered that such sentiments apply equally to many small bands who're trying to start playing gigs around the country.

RIGHT TO WORK was played twice tonight, once during the set, before that highpoint when Gene stopped the music and delivered his main speech of the night, "I know the ones, you just come in here to cause trouble, you want to throw a can at my head. We'll play that number again." Considerable applause, and again RIGHT TO WORK was the encore after demands for something "faster".

There are other good songs, I know, but there is a sameness about them which gives RIGHT TO WORK that "Comet among the stars" feeling, THE LONER perhaps slightly escaping the gravitational pull being a very personal song.

Tonight was good because both bands (no, I haven't forgotten The Cortinas who supported) brought back some of the early flavour of the new wave which has been eroded by time. Gene October's a sensible bod, perhaps Chelsea'll always provide an alternative.

And now for something more adventurous with a typewriter.

Thursday 11th August 1977

A further chance to assess the worth of XTC, whose disjointed keyboard driven rhythm had last been heard at the Roxy headlining over The Drones. Although a respectable crowd greeted the Swindon outfit, entry to Rafters had reverted to normal service after the previous week's overwhelming demand for Alberto Y Los Trios Paranoias. DJ Rob Gretton took the decision to include The Monkees' "Last Train to Clarksville" among the night's offerings of customary punk and reggae that had occasionally widened to include pub rockers Count Bishops' "Train Train" or Dr Feelgood's "Sneakin' Suspicion".

XTC had joined the growing list of the new bands to be snapped up by Virgin Records and were supported by another Virgin act who went by the name of The Table and had released a punk novelty single entitled "Do the Standing Still". Suggestions from the music press, that had themselves been involved in an act of deceit over a band called The Snivelling Shits, were that The Table were not a real band and the single was just another punk spoof with Brian Eno being named in one publication as the man behind the myth.

Tonight a real band performed as The Table and ploughed through a non-confrontational series of out-takes variously based around their single, culminating in the track itself before exiting to a ripple of polite applause. There was a degree of perplexity as to whether the outfit on stage were a group who had formed and adopted the name The Table before growing into the unit that released a single or whether they were a random bunch of musicians put together after the single to maintain the pretence. Either way, The Table's general banality rendered the dilemma irrelevant.

By contrast XTC seemed to have gathered pace, with their songs now bouncing with poppy choruses and snappy futuristic titles like "Radios in Motion" and "Into the Atom Age". They still insisted that their reading of "All Along the Watchtower" was a worthy inclusion but they balanced the sombre mood of the Dylan track with an up-tempo version of "Fireball XL5" that garnered the approval of Jon the Postman who led the calls for an encore through the stage microphone.

Tuesday 16th August 1977

Granada TV presenter Tony Wilson seldom, if ever, ventured into Collyhurst to visit the Electric Circus, however it was performances recorded at that venue that Wilson introduced as "Some live musical excitement at Electric Circus in Manchester" on the second series of his teatime TV music show "So It Goes".

This was also the date that Elvis Presley died at his Graceland mansion in Memphis, Tenneesee – meanwhile over in Collyhurst, free admission got you an audience with The Jam, Buzzcocks and Penetration. This may also have been the first time that Jon the Postman was referred to on a handbill, although the flyer in question omitted to disclose The Jam's appearance and called the local legend "Ted the Postman".

Of the three bands captured for the series it was probably Penetration who left the most alluring imprint. Their debut single "Don't Dictate" may have been another cliché-ridden punk anthem but their effervescent performance mirrored the vibrancy that personified their live shows in Manchester. Embarrassingly the cameras caught a steady volley of beer and spit that culminated in a fight with one of the assailants.

Wilson suggested that, "Good rock music should have an aggressive violent edge" that went over that edge when fuelled by the "drug of the seventies – alcohol" further observing, "Electric Circus in its day is no more prone to the punch up than half a dozen pubs in a two mile radius of the Circus". In fact the "violent edge" that Wilson referred to was conspicuously absent at the Electric Circus, at least away from the television cameras. I cannot speak for the pubs around Collyhurst as I only ever frequented the one regular call en route to the venue, emerging unscathed on each occasion.

Buzzcocks performed a loose version of what Pete Shelley termed, "a nice pop song called 'What Do I Get?'" complete with a "tricky guitar solo" that quickly disintegrated and the unique clamour of Garth's backing vocals echoing "What Do I Get". Maybe Shelley's initial request "don't gob at me" should have been better heeded. The main story that emerged tonight, aside from the passing of the king of rock'n'roll, was Buzzcocks signing a contract with United Artists at the Circus bar.

The Jam's glib professionalism fell somewhat flat in their attempt to be both flash and impulsive, resulting in a lacklustre showing that shrouded any melody within their music or indeed any depth to Paul Weller's snarled vocals. The guitar chords were sharp but the final product was distinctly mediocre making Weller and Bruce Foxton's gymnastic leaps somewhat futile. Weller left the Circus crowd with a pledge to "see us in November" by which time the Electric Circus would be no more and the ambitious Weller would have upped his game to play the Apollo.

In a slightly rash defence of The Jam, Wilson suggested it was a symptom of an elitist snobbery creeping into punk culture that The Jam were being knocked for being, "too popular or not sufficiently avant-garde" adding that, "The Jam on their day are great." A further addition that, "They are making big waves in The States, spiking up the myopic scene over there, leading the way for other bands, we hope they all follow" indicated that Wilson's keen patronage of The Jam was somewhat previous.

Friday 19th August 1977

For Friday 19th August, the Electric Circus flyer proclaimed –
"??Surprise Top Recording Star ?? – plus Zhain"

According to Ian Wood, who was now compiling the Rock What's On listing for the *New Manchester Review*, the Circus had described the surprise act as "an artist with several chart albums to his/her/their credit but who has not appeared here (presumably Manchester) for several years." Names speculated on by Wood were Bob Dylan, John Mayall or Spiggy Topes – a satirical figure invented by *Private Eye* magazine.

Zhain were a standard combo with long hair and denims who had plied their trade since the early seventies and were continuing to do so despite line-up changes that saw guitarist John Milner obtain a PhD from Leeds University before re-joining the band.

Why the Circus management chose the cloak-and-dagger approach was a minor mystery, although the clandestine nature of the gig possibly attracted a wider audience of curiosity seekers. There was another element in that the Sex Pistols were in the midst of a closet operation performing under various aliases, although any plans to hoodwink the punk crowd were well and truly thwarted by the Sex Pistols themselves. Not only were they to play the same night at the Lafayette in Wolverhampton as The S.P.O.T.S. (Sex Pistols On Tour Secretly) but word had reached the Manchester punk crowd and a coach arranged. As a final irony the pick-up point for the coach was the Electric Circus.

For those left back in Manchester a blackboard by the cash desk contained a hand chalked announcement, "Tonight Alvin Lee". There had earlier been a sizeable collection of equipment being delivered as a reflection of the magnitude of tonight's performer.

The story ran that Alvin Lee was one of many performers who had become aware of the growing reputation of the Electric Circus and had consequently made contact to offer his services for a modest fee, later recalled by Drones' bassist Steve Cundall who was assisting the Circus management with bookings at the time, to be a few hundred pounds.

Saturday 20th August 1977

Were Bethnal a rock band or a punk band or part of the "new wave"? Their music employed a violinist but their short hair and narrow jeans suggested a loose alliance to the punk movement. An alliance reinforced with the approval bestowed upon the Londoners by Steve Cundall and M J Drone, both present tonight at the Circus and both of whom denounced the hostile reception from the long-haired crowd due to the band's punk veneer.

I had to concur with the two Drones members, Bethnal being the best band I had seen on a Saturday night for several months. Their music consisted mostly of short, sharp, though never angry, bursts and the violin was gainfully employed during their cover of The Who's "Baba O'Riley". However even that failed to reassure the crowd of the band's honourable intentions. That said The Who had never enjoyed the status of Rainbow or Ted Nugent or even Led Zeppelin as mainstays of the Circus soundtrack, so maybe "Stargazer" or "Stranglehold" would have been better choices. And drop the violin...

Steve Cundall was eager to recount the previous night's passage to Wolverhampton, "The Pistols were great!" Despite his smiling enthusiasm for what other reports described as a truculent encounter, with fighting and setting fire to the stage being part of the show, the journey home was recounted less pleasurably. The coach driver had taken a dislike to many of Manchester's punk clientele including Steve's band mate Gus Gangrene, whose passage home had to be secured following the plea bargaining of others. The driver had called the police, who took a resolute interest in the coach and its occupants with Gus – real name Gary Callender – reportedly providing the name Gus Gangrene to officers. The final leg of the journey saw an altercation with some characters at Piccadilly bus station who were offended by Steve and Gus's choice of clothing.

★

Drawing together the loose ends for the third issue of *Ghast Up* proved a laborious pastime. The big news across Manchester was the impending closure of the Electric Circus. As the story went, the club was visited by some official inspectors whose job, it was suggested, was to order large amounts of food late in the evening to test the venue's ability to cater for the numbers of attendees that often reached the thousand mark. Of course there were more serious matters such as the number of fire escapes, but safety issues were not paramount for music lovers.

There were the usual conspiracy theories that it was the Circus' reputation as a punk venue that singled it out for such attention and, naturally, we at *Ghast Up* had to fight their corner. Steve Cundall, erstwhile bassist with The Drones and by now a valued friend, alerted me to the "Save the Circus" campaign recently instigated. M J Drone would wear a customised black T shirt with the slogan, "Why Close the Electric Circus?"

For us there was a more pressing issue in that the Roneo Printing Machine was not functioning as it had when we assuredly cranked out Issue two. Despite the mechanical setbacks, there were acts of benevolence that have remained with me through the years. In an attempt to streamline costs we sought the purchase of blank electronic stencils. A stationery shop in Manchester sold these but only in boxes of one hundred.

Having wrestled with whether the future of *Ghast Up* could justify such outlay and foolhardily decided it could, the shop manager offered us the loose stencils he had in stock with his compliments. Although I am sure I courteously offered our gratitude, my single biggest regret is that we didn't acknowledge the shop in print. Here was a city centre manager of a stationary suppliers who, I would surmise, had no specific interest in punk rock, although I doubt we burdened him with the details of our publication, making it a totally altruistic gesture.

The other act of generosity that we did at least offer printed recognition of was Kevin Cummins' lavish supply of photos for which he declined payment, suggesting, "Just buy me a coke next time we're in the Circus" being Kevin's usual response. In a further act of co-operation Kevin secured a Vibrators band photo from fellow photographer Richard Chang that he suggested would be more exclusive than the record company promo pictures that the band had kindly obtained on our behalf.

If the episode taught me the generosity of humans, I also learned the unreliability of machinery. The ink that had flowed freely through the cut stencils of Issue 2 was now clogged within the roller, denting the quality of photos and artwork and making an enforced return to "artlessness", as Paul Morley had kindly pronounced our blurry images in Issue 1. Morley had referred in print to our having, "stuttered out our first issue". The term definitely applied to the onerous task of yielding what circumstances would dictate was our final issue, although I managed to create a two page supplement that was inserted into later copies of Issue three that included a review of Chelsea at the Electric Circus. Ironically, Richard Boon had generously termed *Ghast Up* "regular" in his *New Manchester Review* rundown, compared to *Shy Talk*'s, "unfailingly late appearance".

From Morley's point of view, an article on Patti Smith that had been his wish to write since first contact, again failed to materialise. I seem to remember him blaming the post. Mick did pen a clipped article on the New Jersey singer, although we chose to leave Patti Smith to Sandy Robertson and his Patti-enamoured fanzine *White Stuff*. We had the succinct articles on

The Slits and X-Ray Spex from Morley that swelled the contents to a record fifteen pages of photos and prose as well as the "fax on the negatives". Although submitted under the Modest Young moniker, Morley had asked to be credited as Seven Up after his favourite drink, which I modified to Severn Upp.

Shamefully, we played along with the private in-joke that was The Negatives, publishing unduly favourable reports of their appearances at the Oaks and the Squat Club and most dishonourably we ran the bogus story of their having recorded and released an EP entitled "Bringing Fiction Back Into Music". Rather than sticking to the original story that the record was deleted before it was released, it seemed judicious, as well as plausible, to explain away the record's scarcity (or non-existence) by poor sales.

And we had an advert for the debut single by Generation X on Chrysalis Records. As well as Valer Records having secured The Drones' services, Buzzcocks had landed a deal with United Artists and, in an echo of their capture of The Rolling Stones, having previously spurned The Beatles, Decca Records took a chance on Slaughter and the Dogs, placing them as ne'er-do-well rebels next to Buzzcocks' fab four. Yet it was the company who had opted for the London quartet of Generation X that granted us advertising space and a freebie single which, at 1977 prices, equated to a seven per cent bonus on the £15 cost of a full page ad.

Sunday 21st August 1977

The Boomtown Rats and their fanatical frontman Bob Geldof had spontaneously appeared from the darkness to occupy major standing alongside the new wave clique. They were given a track on the "New Wave" compilation album that subsequently became a hit single. They were somehow granted a main story in the music weeklies when Geldof was assaulted on stage at Camden's Music Machine. Why such a little-known band were playing the Music Machine and why the regrettable incident was major news was unclear. True, it occurred alongside a reported spate of punk bashing with Paul Cook and Duncan (Kid) Reid among the victims but who exactly were The Boomtown Rats?

It isn't quite true to describe the Boomtown Rats as an unknown quantity prior to "Looking After Number One" the opening track of one side of "New Wave". They had been billed to support Tom Petty and the Heartbreakers at the Free Trade Hall back in April but the concert was cancelled when Petty's allure failed to generate the minimum requirement of 300 ticket sales or, to put it into context, considerably less than the numbers who turned out to harangue The Damned or Wayne County at the Circus. There were no such problems at the Electric Circus on an August Sunday night with the usual steady stream making their way into the venue, except there were to be no Boomtown Rats. For whatever reason the headliners had pulled out, elevating Eater to top slot leaving a space for The Fall.

Seeing them for only the third time and following their landmark appearance at the Vortex, the prospect of a Fall gig was infinitely more exciting than either of the advertised bands. Having extolled The Fall to anyone who would listen, including the delivery of a glowing reference in the forthcoming *Ghast Up*, my only fear was that they might fail to justify my commendation.

I was not alone in my admiration for the band formed by Mark Smith and named after Albert Camus' last complete work of fiction. "Great band, The Fall," was Paul Morley's response when I mentioned the band's Vortex appearance. He had marked them highly in his Manchester article in the *NME*, ranking them, along with The Worst, as the serious pretenders of the second wave of Manchester bands.

Buzzcocks manager Richard Boon, possibly as a diversion from my trying to prise an advert for Buzzcocks' debut single out of him, asked my opinion of both the Vortex and The Fall. I was probably indifferent to the merits of the venue, although I stopped short of calling it a "shit hole" as Mark Smith later would but I was fulsome in my praise of the band to which Boon enthused, "Yes they're very different."

As the gig went, The Fall were even better than last time. The confidence in delivery right through the band belied the statistics that gave this as their seventh outing. The original "You got The Fall" opening routine had evolved into the more assertive "We are The Fall" ritual that would evolve with each gig as Smith laid claims to be one of the voices of the new wave. Like Hell or Verlaine or Rotten, here was an anguished vocal delivery that epitomised the new movement.

The musicians behind the singer had yet to demonstrate the singularity that would give each a role within the whole but their collective togetherness was exquisitely disjointed by the intrusion of Una Baines discordant electric piano laid sparsely around Martin Bramah's guitar.

From the opening bars of "Last Orders" the set ploughed through their early standards around topics ranging from psychiatric hospitals to industrial estates. And then the crashing intro that pronounced the haunting riff that had lurked in my memory since the Vortex. The song was called "Repetition" and indeed it was but was that not the point? Although the song touched on the use of Electroconvulsive Therapy it also gave an early indication of Mark Smith's disenchantment with the slavish conformity of so many new wave bands hence, "Repetition in the music and you're never gonna lose it."

Eater's best effort of the night was advising that, "A lot of bands don't like Manchester crowds, but we think you're fucking alright". After The Fall, Eater were never going to hold my interest and, true to form, they were hackneyed and somewhat pointless.

Thursday 25th August 1977

Maybe there was something in the beer supplied by The Nosebleeds' management. Not only had I composed a fair but favourable review of their debut single curiously entitled "Aint Bin To No Music School", I had made the journey into Manchester to witness the unveiling of The Nosebleeds as a headlining act. Not that I judged it a chore to gauge the band's new look, but Ed Banger and the Nosebleeds had always come as a free add-on to both the Dogs and The Drones, so it was a new concept to be paying to see them.

The Nosebleeds' single release proved that Rabid Records was not, as I had assumed, a convenient and apt name to place on the label of the Dogs' single. Rabid Records was an actual label run by Tosh Ryan with Martin Zero as in-house producer. Before the year was out Rabid would also release the first recording by John Cooper Clarke with the "Innocents" EP that saw the poet placed over a musical landscape held together by Zero's electronic percussion.

Although Rafters was not brim-full, Vini Faal and the band looked suitably gratified with the assembly that greeted their arrival. A collection that included label-mates Slaughter and the Dogs with Howard Bates and Mike Rossi each procuring a copy of *Ghast Up* three. I recall they both proffered the twenty pence cover price but Mick waived the fee for these featured artists.

Bates reappeared to feedback his views on the chronicling of the Dogs' Roxy Tour appearance at the Elizabethan Ballroom given an extensive write-up in our pages. His amiable response confirmed the article met with approval, although he was keen to clarify a point I made about their musically youthful approach, reminding me he had only just turned seventeen. The update on their recording activities was that Slaughter and the Dogs had been encamped in the studio with someone Howard described as "Lizzy's producer". The producer in question was Nick Tauber whose credits included Thin Lizzy's original hit "Whiskey in the Jar" and two subsequent albums the Irish rock band cut when they too were Decca recording artists and had yet to break into the major league. Tauber would do a similar service on the Dogs' early Decca releases. As Howard put it, "We've got the money now."

The Nosebleeds produced their usual set, now extended to include their single. Vini Reilly offered an alternative focal point to the ever-animated singer formerly known as Ed Banger, Reilly's immersion in his instrument altered the dynamic from their previous somewhat guileless approach. From aiming to make the simplistic sound worthy, the objective had now shifted to conspicuously understating the artfulness in Reilly's playing to make guitarist and band appear compatible.

Ultimately The Nosebleeds came through the test with Garrity having the self-assurance to swing from the celebrated rafters that informed the club name, although he was somewhat previous in leading the band straight back on stage before the pleas for an encore had reached any sort of crescendo.

Friday 26th August 1977

The unlikely pairing foretold by Paul Morley in his *NME* Manchester article occurred with The Drones and Slaughter and the Dogs putting their differences aside to embark on a joint tour. The billing presented both bands as co-headliners reading thus –

"SLAUGHTER and the DOGS plus THE DRONES
THE DRONES plus SLAUGHTER and the DOGS"

Given that Slaughter and the Dogs' previous form included devising a poster that suggested equal billing with the Sex Pistols at the Lesser Free Trade Hall, and the fact the Dogs had seen some chart action, albeit as just one part of the "Roxy London WC2" live album, the indications were that the Dogs would court main status, even if The Drones still had the slicker stage show.

True to expectations it was The Drones who opened proceedings at Middleton Civic Hall with a set that now contained their reading of The Ronettes' "Be My Baby". Whilst the inclusion of a pop standard executed in a punk style was becoming a routine practice, and M J Drone was one of the more competent vocalists, the band's previous incarnation as pop cabaret act Rockslide made it look like a reversion to previous form.

The appearance of two of these punk bands had attracted a selection of curiosity seekers who had not purchased the threads but felt duty bound to behave in an antisocial manner. Thus a few random obscenities were yelled that were largely ignored by the band but not by Denise and Joan who rebuked one offender. M J Drone's token response was to blame the sound man.

On a night when The Drones' rehearsed musicianship was beginning to sound limited, their act drifted through the usual motions without the conviction and swagger usually paraded in their home town.

After the pinnacle of the Roxy tour, coupled with the landing of a record deal, Slaughter and the Dogs were equally predictable and unconvincing, despite carrying an impressive array of shiny new equipment courtesy of Decca Records. Their one point of note was provided unsurprisingly by Mike Rossi who, maybe sensing the safe musical parameters that had contained The Drones, gave a short virtuoso display on his newly acquired Gibson to remind us the Dogs were no three chord wonders, despite a review in one national paper inferring their musicianship was non-existent. Although as Johnny Ramone once observed, many "prog rock" guitarists could play endless solos but none were Hendrix.

Sunday 28th August 1977

It was a surprisingly packed house that greeted The Adverts return to the Electric Circus as headliners. They had enjoyed chart success and a Top of the Pops appearance that featured a live vocal from TV Smith, even if the band enacted the usual mime. On top of that their tunes were becoming familiar with a session on the John Peel Show that was becoming the main radio outlet for punk music.

Unusually on a Sunday night it was conventional rock act The Slugs, featuring Circus manager Allan Robinson on drums, who supported. Equally unusual was the vibrant anticipation that greeted the announcement of their arrival on stage. The Slugs were well known within rock circles, but clearly not with the hordes of Sunday night punks who thought S.L.U.G.S might be an abbreviated euphemism for a secret appearance by the Sex Pistols as S.P.O.T.S had been. A point duly made by the visible disappointment that saw numbers leave the venue following the Pistols' non-appearance.

Whether it was a deliberate act of deception on the part of The Slugs' drummer or not, the full house attracted a visit from local police curious to discern the attendance.

More apposite support was provided by 999, whose frenetic

pop driven via ex-Kilburn and the High Road Nick Cash and his powerful Noddy Holder-like vocal, struck the right chord with the bouncing hordes in front of the stage.

Whether The Adverts were aware of the extraordinary events that had preceded them was unclear but they were always going to struggle to prevent the night being an anti-climax. To their credit their increasing familiarity with their material and the incessant catchiness of songs like "We Who Wait" or "The Great British Mistake" prevailed despite bassist Gaye Advert struggling to keep pace with drummer Laurie Driver, reminding the audience that perhaps the Pistols were not the only band worth seeing. Such was their newly discovered esteem they could even defer "One Chord Wonders" until the encore.

Thursday 1st September 1977

The ink having dried on a contract with United Artists, it was a thriving Buzzcocks who took their turn to play Rafters. Like the Dogs, a deal afforded them new and better equipment, most notably Garth's exalted Gibson Thunderbird bass that was replaced early in the set to make way for its less cumbersome predecessor. The precise worth of the deal with UA was the subject of much speculation in the music press but Shelley would quantify the value at three quarters of a million. To this revelation Mick suggested that they had better be good to which Shelley countered, "I am good."

More promising than the money or Shelley's bluster, was a tape that DJ Rob Gretton played between sides described by Shelley as "just mucking about". The four tracks premiered were "Orgasm Addict", "What Do I Get?", "Whatever Happened To?" and "No Reply" that not only confirmed a forceful pop sensibility but assuredly demonstrated that Shelley's voice was not the obstacle to delivering Buzzcocks' music that I had feared.

As well as The Prefects, who had brought their raucous bluster along in support and were to have their Mancunian cult status rewarded with an *NME* interview that Paul Morley was ready to conduct, Rafters was to witness an early showing of Stockport's own Distractions. Pete Shelley had described himself as more a "punk Mod" than a "punk rocker" and like Buzzcocks, The Distractions' music was unashamedly pop oriented with bespectacled singer Mike Finney offering a strong singing voice that steadied the nerves of the apprentice musicians behind him. They in turn seemed slightly unsure of the worth of their short sharp bursts of soulful pop music that had a familiar ring even on first hearing.

Buzzcocks had to contend with a lone dissenting voice protesting, "Our money for your rubbish" between the first few numbers but the silent majority decreed that the shadow of Howard Devoto had been truly eclipsed as Buzzcocks delivered a fresh assertion within their music, as if the recording studio examination had removed any seeds of doubt. Even harmonies were beginning to adorn their music which was formulating into potential singles, with the remainder suggesting a strong debut album. Such was the rapport between artist and audience, it was a bemused Steve Diggle who queried after the show if such a level of acclaim was really all for these four ordinary lads.

Not unusually Jon the Postman was on hand to wrap up proceedings with another local legend Martin Heywood, later known as Martin X, adding musical accompaniment. Unusually for the postman, both he and his musical accomplice were forced to endure some close range gobbing as he pleaded, "Louie Louie, don't spit" although it was the harmonica-playing Heywood who seemed to collect the lion's share of the phlegm.

★

Although we still had Howard Bates' number for an intended Slaughter and the Dogs interview, any such plans were put on hold while we pursued contact with The Fall. Warnings that Dogs' singer Wayne Barratt liked to answer, "Baked beans" to most questions had been a concern, although the Dogs would surely have featured if our Roneo machine had obliged with more issues. But it was the articulate and musical approach of The Fall that demanded cross-examination.

The first approach was to guitarist Martin Bramah who was in the audience at Rafters and seemed a little detached in asking,

"What exactly is it you want?" We did swap phone numbers and he gave a wry smile that we shared the same forename. After a few phone calls an interview was arranged to take place at the Kingswood Road flat that Mark Smith and Una Baines shared in Prestwich. The first time we had invaded the private space of artists.

Sight of their record collection was a first insight into The Fall's inspirations. Nestled amongst the collection of budget priced reissued albums such as Captain Beefheart's "Safe As Milk" or The Velvet Underground's "The Velvet Underground Featuring Nico" was the re-released "The Birthday Party" by The Idle Race, the band formed and led by Jeff Lynne, before joining The Move and ultimately The Electric Light Orchestra. I tentatively asked if ELO held any interest, given that they were the current outlet for Jeff Lynne's song writing, Smith responding that their day ended with the departure of Roy Wood.

I don't recall being offered any reggae to devour, although Smith spoke highly of Rupie Edwards' first dub reggae release "Ire Feelings" and cited Big Youth as a major influence. He also had praise for multi instrumentalists Henry Cow, to whom The Fall had been likened. Smith described Henry Cow's John Greaves as a "good singer" although he was modest enough to admit that it was probably the politics in Henry Cow's music that drew the comparison.

In Paul Morley's *NME* round-up of all things Mancunian, it was suggested that The Fall's political stance put The Clash's prominent anti-fascist position in the shade. Smith thought his band's politics had been overstated suggesting they only played three or four political songs in the whole set. Or to clarify, "we're not a dogma band like The Clash". Smith admired and respected Joe Strummer while describing "that guitarist" Mick Jones as, "just a poseur" like "that bassist" Paul Simonon.

Of the current breed Smith described The Adverts as "psychedelic", the Pistols' "Holidays In The Sun" as having great lyrics but no tune, noting "I wish I could write lyrics like that" and The Damned's version of "I Feel Alright" as being vastly inferior to the Stooges original. A point raised when he conceded the likeness of the recurrent riff of "I Feel Alright" to that used in The Fall's "Stepping Out". Borrowing a riff was okay but covering The Stooges was better left well alone as Smith illustrated with The Vibrators reading of "No Fun".

One band who he thought trod a similar musical path to The Fall were Subway Sect, who employed similar chord changes, and whose recent debut session for The John Peel Show did not accurately represent the complexity in their music. For The Fall, Smith preferred simplicity "but not badly played simplicity".

After the supply of several cups of tea Smith noted, "I think I'm addicted to caffeine." As for what The Fall wanted from the music business, Baines confessed to "I don't know what bands who play the system have but I definitely do not want it!"

I recall Smith stating, "It's getting a bit stale fanzines – some of them are really bad." He did recall having been in Vibes music shop in Bury, who had recently approached us to stock *Ghast Up*, and being surprised, not just by my complimentary remarks on The Fall's appearance at the Vortex in Issue three but by actually finding a local publication that mentioned the band.

In more general discussion Smith asked if the fanzine was what we did for a living, showing a reassuring naivety similar to when I first approached Buzzcocks. He also declared an interest in Astrology, asking what our star signs were. For the record I am Libra, Mick Middles is Aquarius and Mark Smith is Pisces, although he claimed a phobic aversion to water of any volume. And Mark Smith harboured a universal dislike of students.

Friday 2nd September 1977

The overwhelming response to the Sunday nights at the Circus, at least in terms of attendance, persuaded the management of Graham Brooks and Allan Robinson to more or less extend the genre to the entire weekend. A far cry from The Damned and Wayne County's ill-fated appearances, although the widening appeal of the likes of The Stranglers, together with the wider classification of "new wave" made it a less risky move.

August had witnessed bands like The Count Bishops, whose blend of R'n'B had undergone a transition from pub rock via their releases on the Chiswick label and Gary Holton's Heavy Metal Kids who pre-dated punk but seemed content to accept the renewed interest the trend had afforded them.

Maybe the booking of Chiswick artists Radio Stars was the first real test. They were built around the athletic stage presence of ex-Johns Children singer Andy Ellison and bassist Martin Gordon, who had a brief musical association with the Mael brothers in the British version of Sparks that ended after the breakthrough "Kimono My House" album and the hit singles it spawned.

There were few if any punks there to greet them, so their crossover appeal had to be resolute. In fact there were few of any faction in as sparse an attendance as I would witness at this venue. The stories may have insinuated that the Circus was being compelled to close by the powers that be for its willingness to showcase punk bands but tonight the venue had fashioned its own air of impending doom.

At 32 Ellison, a talented artist but always on the fringe of success and never quite making it, perhaps accepted such nights as an inescapable consequence of his position, but surely Gordon thought he had risen above this level when he joined the Maels on Top of the Pops as they sat one place off the summit of the pop charts in 1974.

Radio Stars' resolute professionalism in delivering their neatly fashioned pop music at least brought an acceptable response from the few who had made the journey along Oldham Road to check them out, even if that involved Ellison stepping down to join the audience at one point to augment the applause.

Saturday 17th September 1977

Another Saturday night and just as Ultravox! had replaced The Enid in March, it was Mark Perry's Alternative TV who would stand in for Ultravox! whose advertised attendance to promote their second album "Ha!-Ha!-Ha!" failed to happen. Word had spread before the night that Alternative TV's Manchester debut would supplant the return of John Foxx and Ultravox! so the crowd were primed to evaluate the band.

Alternative TV had made their recording debut with their reggae tinged "Love Lies Limp" being given as a free flexi single with the final issue of Perry's *Sniffin' Glue* fanzine. *Sniffin' Glue* had, of course, spawned the rich fanzine culture throughout the UK from *Ripped and Torn* in Cumbernauld to the tiny hand-written *Stranded* in Devon, not forgetting other notable publications such as Sheffield's *Gun Rubber* or London's *Situation 3*. Whether *Sniffin' Glue* was the best or just the first was a debate that would rage on but the one incontestable point was that it had shaped an environment where major record stores would gladly stock duplicated and photocopied fanzines such as ours without quibble.

Alternative TV's live shows had received favourable press although this came most profusely from *Sounds* writer and Patti Smith obsessive Sandy Robertson, who was an associate of Perry and a close friend of Alternative TV guitarist Alex Fergusson. While not wishing to question Robertson's objectivity, my mind was still open as to the worth of Perry's transition from fanzine writer to musician.

Perry chose to drink amongst the Circus crowd rather than remain in the sanctuary of the dressing room for much of the evening, taking in the predictable soundtrack that would invariably see Patti Smith's "Gloria" played alongside Junior Murvin's "Police and Thieves" with Wire's live rendition of "Lowdown" carrying more power when fed through the house PA.

From a musical perspective the nascent ATV struggled with the dilemma as to when the soapbox approach of written journalism should give way to the more abstract art of music. The between song rants blended into bellowed lyrics as Perry seemed intent on retelling how he went from a nine to five existence but was ultimately disillusioned with the sheltered lifestyle that was now the lot of the punk clientele and which drew accusations of hypocrisy from several of the local punks.

Intriguingly their one release "Love Lies Limp" which had shifted at least 15,000 copies (that being the final circulation figure of *Sniffin' Glue*) had been favourably received for its subtle blending of punk and reggae guitars but was not played that evening. Or perhaps it was on the set list but the band curtailed proceedings before its arrival, given the uneasy truce that existed between band and audience.

As the set petered out to indifferent applause, the regulars of the Manchester scene delivered the final affront. The Worst's attempt to educate the London visitors in the northern way was thwarted as singer Allan Deaves delivered the message, "We're just the same as them but they won't let us use their equipment."

Another punter grabbed the microphone to strike a rendition of "We have a right to Worst, yes we do!" Whether that was a deliberate act of parodying one of Mark Perry's Step Forward signings is unknown but that was the last transmission from the stage microphones as the plugs were pulled before Jon the Postman could lead the house through a further deviation of "Louie Louie". The Circus DJ's attempted resolution of inviting GPO Jon to use the DJ booth came to little but the point had been made to the unfortunate Perry and his fledgling band.

Wednesday 21st September 1977

A rare midweek visit to the Electric Circus with the promise of an appearance by Glen Matlock's newly formed Rich Kids. There had been favourable reviews in the music press with Matlock being described as the "ex-Pistol" or more vehemently as the "fired Pistol". In addition to being a vastly superior bassist to Sid Vicious, Matlock had co-written all of the Pistols' songs up to his departure and word was that "Pretty Vacant" was his composition with the exception of two lines added by Johnny Rotten. Furthermore "Pretty Vacant" had been included in the sets reviewed in the papers that had seen The Clash's Mick Jones help out on guitar which, given the Sex Pistols reluctance to perform live anywhere near this city, was the closest thing to seeing the Pistols.

There was support from Birmingham's The Killjoys, whose animated bassist Ghislaine "Gil" Weston provided the visual lynch-pin to the fast paced punk served up by Kevin Rowland's band. Rowland and backing singer Heather Tonge were later seen drinking at the bar while The Worst delivered a restrained and surprisingly less challenging set. Allan Deaves closed proceedings by thanking The Killjoys "for letting us use their equipment." Many years later Steve Shy advised that Kevin Rowland, whose later successful career as the soul singing frontman of Dexy's Midnight Runners often saw him portrayed as arrogant and aloof, was a keen champion of The Worst during his punk days.

What followed seemed a lengthy delay with the rumour mill buzzing that there would be no Glen Matlock or his new band. Sure enough it was the reliable but already acquainted Subway Sect who steered us into the early hours. Vic Godard maintained his nonchalant approach holding a dignified silence when required to allow the level of applause to flourish. Although the evening represented a anticlimax for most of the audience, the Subway Sect set list revealed a sharpness in parts within the guitar chord changes.

Friday 23rd September 1977

A return to blond locks for Billy Idol and a more spirited showing this time around. It was a more congested Rafters that saw the commercial appeal of Generation X shine through the feeble doctrine within their lyrics. The overuse of punk clichés remained but that was outshone by the auditory allure of the music, despite Idol's unnecessary reference to "brown acid" in an anti-drug tirade.

Before their sparkling performance Billy Idol even directed me to a man called Jeff who would settle the £15 bill for the advert in *Ghast Up* now that the fanzine was available to view in Rough Trade, as was the stipulated condition for payment.

Sunday 25th September 1977

There were two choices for this particular night. Iggy Pop, the "Godfather of punk" to many, returned to the Apollo without the keyboard skills of David Bowie this time but with The Adverts in support. Meanwhile on the penultimate Sunday night at the Electric Circus it was The Slits' turn to headline with Birmingham's The Prefects and inevitably Manchester's very own The Worst in support. Or as Steve Shy put it, "there was only one choice" describing the Iggy Pop tour as, "Nothing to do with what's currently happening". Paul Doyle possibly had split loyalties as he could be seen making a hasty entrance before the Slits' set to face accusations of "I thought you had gone to Iggy Pop".

Tony Wilson and his "So It Goes" team opted for the old school punk, driving their cameras along Ardwick Green to capture Iggy's performance of "The Passenger" and "Lust For Life" for the upcoming second series. Despite having just released his second album of the year, "Lust for Life" was a further collaboration with David Bowie recorded in Berlin and probably his most commercial record to date, the word from the Apollo was of intense disappointment. The same gig received a disparaging review by Tony Parsons in the *NME* who deemed Iggy Pop "boring" having kissed the singer's well-licked Cuban heeled boots in the previous week's issue.

A legend that did emerge from the Apollo was of Howard Devoto presenting a copy of Spiral Scratch to Iggy Pop with the explanation, "I've got all your records. Now you've got all mine". The tale appeared in the music press and was also relayed by Tony Wilson on "So It Goes" who oddly referred to Buzzcocks as "The Buzzcocks".

The only positive comment I heard uttered by anyone who was at The Apollo was the crystal clarity of The Adverts. Far from exposing the musical limitations of Tim Smith's band, the theatre's PA provided the perfect amplification for their intelligent compositions to sparkle.

Back at the Circus, The Worst's set comprised the usual mix of the planned and the impromptu. Maybe they were buoyed by manager Steve Shy's assertion that the bands on show had more relevance than the legendary Iggy, as there was an element of conviction in their delivery, with Allan Deaves following the song "Fast Breeder" with the accusation, "You're the fast breeders, you're just sitting there."

The claimed rehearsed ineptitude of The Prefects was beginning to formulate into recognisable slices of songwriting as titles like, "Going Through the Motions" and "The Bristol Road Leads to Dacca" took on the semblance of actual songs carrying power and conviction.

Maybe Iggy Pop had stolen the thunder, along with a quantity of the audience from The Slits but their first full-length show at the Circus lacked everything that their clipped set on the White Riot Tour or their frenetic appearance at the Oaks had delivered.

In a conventional attempt to engage the audience Ari Up attempted to direct the crowd to mimic her swaying dance routine to little response other than odd catcalls of "boring". The four Slits performed in an uncomplicated manner and their musicianship never lacked cohesion, but there was a sense of aimlessness to much of their material.

The muted response to the band's exodus from the stage was countered after a few minutes by Ari Up's return to the microphone to declare, "Ladies and gentlemen, The Slits" before the band reconvened to deliver an encore that had not been requested.

The abiding memory of the night was of guitarist Viv Albertine dancing on stage to T. Rex's "Ride a White Swan" five days before the elfin singer's final journey.

the final act

Saturday and Sunday 1st and 2nd October 1977

The final weekend arrived and true to form the queue snaked its way around the sides of the building providing Kevin Cummins with a final opportunity to capture the spirit that was to be no more. The queue offered ample opportunity to snap away as movement into the club seemed unusually tentative.

Until tonight the purchasing of advanced tickets had ceased to be a requirement to gain entry. If being a fanzine writer failed to convince the door management to let us in, paying the requisite one pound or one pound fifty would always sway the issue. Tonight the rules were different. Dave Bentley arrived by taxi, ambled straight into the venue and explained there was "a blanket no guest list" for the evening, the show being for the Pat Seed Scanner Appeal. Bentley gained entry not as a guest of The Drones, which he had sometimes managed, but by the more traditional proffering of a ticket.

For once the queue presented an unassailable obstacle for some whose resolve to see The Drones and Birmingham's Steel Pulse headline over many lesser Mancunian acts was broken by the house full claims of those inside.

The second night began in similar vein, although the slowly-moving queue managed to make its way around the side street and inside the venue.

My abiding memory was that Warsaw had in fact been cast among the Saturday night crowd. However a revisit to Paul Morley's review for the *NME* suggests they appeared early on the Sunday evening and their performance was marked by some progress on their part. That I have no recollection of what would have been a much abridged selection, listed as three numbers only in some parts, would suggest they made less impact than The Fall's clipped and crafted set or The Prefects, whose Midlands roots had proved no obstacle in entering into the folklore of the place. Mark Smith had claimed that Sunday night was earmarked for the elite of Manchester's musical offerings, so presumably Warsaw's Sunday night presence suggested that someone assumed they belonged in another category.

Whether Steve Shy and Dave Bentley had tired of the joke or they had uncovered musical differences, they no longer played a role in the running gag that was The Negatives, whose numbers had expanded to include, among others, an assemblage of female backing singers with Buzzcocks' manager Richard Boon on saxophone and even a guest appearance by Pete Shelley himself.

As each number dissolved into a largely free form improvisation, Paul Morley used the opportunity to direct a slight at his former employers The Drones announcing one title as "Sick of Rockslide", The Drones having chosen to stay away having been placed on Saturday's bill. The disparate instrumentation gained some unity towards the end as the collective members worked the marching rhythm of Buzzcocks' "Sixteen" culminating in Morley offering the only vocal with the song's abrupt climax of "I wish they would stop" signalling the band's cue to withdraw.

Given their numerous planned and impromptu appearances, along with their member's ubiquitous presence within these walls, it was inevitable The Worst would play their part. There was a degree of predictability around The Worst's final Circus appearance. As expected there was no sloppy sentimentality but the overriding sense was that the liberal mind-set of the Circus crowd, possibly The Worst's greatest ally, was about to be removed.

Unlike most of their contemporaries, The Worst's lasting legacy is that they left no recorded output as testimony to the band's existence. Kevin Cummins apparently owns many taped recordings of their live shows but the legend in these parts is that John Peel, having shared a panel on the Brass Tacks programme with Allan Deaves and Ian Hodge, offered a loan of £100 via Dave Bentley for the band to enter the studio. Richard Boon also expressed an interest in financing a Worst record with the differing offers cancelling each other out.

If the final night delivered one surprise it was the return of Howard Devoto. The stage announcer, whose introductions had been uncomplicated and straight to the point, chose the more inventive declaration, "Don't believe everything you read in the papers, or magazines" as the cue for the maiden performance of Devoto's Magazine.

In two brand new numbers "Shot By Both Sides" and "The Light Pours Out Of Me" followed by Devoto's renowned interpretation of Captain Beefheart's "I Love You Big Dummy", the latter announced by the draping of a life sized dummy over Devoto's shoulder, Magazine provided the high point of a satisfying but largely predictable evening.

If the use of Beefheart's "Dummy" was an indication that Devoto was merely picking up where he left off, the unfamiliar handling of rhythm guitar duties on "Shot By Both Sides" and the immediate impact of the two new songs, suggested Magazine were to be, at the very least, an equal force alongside the now established Buzzcocks.

A final night would be incomplete without the rhythmical wit of John Cooper Clarke whose readings were densely applauded, as the Salford rhymester was encouraged to overstay despite his reminder that "the Buzzers are on next". If Buzzcocks had earned their position as the cream of the current crop, the placement of John Cooper Clarke as an inclusive alternative had, in the cities of Salford and Manchester at least, widened the net. In a complete antithesis of Clarke's reception at the Vortex, the crowd were urging the poet to continue reciting at the expense of some bona fide music.

The Circus DJ had included T. Rex's "20th Century Boy" closely followed by Elvis Presley's "Way Down" to mark the recent passing of Marc Bolan and The King, and in a final stroke of irony the arrival on stage of Buzzcocks was preceded by the DJ reminding those present of the Circus's impending ending with the playing of Wayne County's reading of the Stones' "The Last Time".

The Electric Circus began life to cater for a serious rock audience for whom punk was seen as an unwelcome irritant. The treatment of The Damned and the Electric Chairs, as well as the scant numbers that attended to gauge the worth of Buzzcocks or Chelsea at the beginning, was surely testament to that fact. And now, twelve months on, it was the crooning of Wayne County and the loosely crafted pop music of Buzzcocks that symbolized the end of the venue.

Diehard rock fans had seen their beloved Electric Circus host its final night of revelry on the Friday when Jenny Haan's Lion played the last "serious" rock gig. The impressively voiced Ms Haan and band were described as "absolutely brilliant" by a musician friend and former associate of Bill Nelson. The same individual had offered the advice that The Drones "can't play" and that "they were a drone". Maybe they asked for that.

However tonight was the real finale and, despite the crowd's reluctance to see John Cooper Clarke make way for Buzzcocks, the band drifted through their now standard set with an assuredness that peaked with Garth replicating the car ignition sound on the bass intro of "Fast Cars" achieved in the recent John Peel Session. The one tentative act still maintained was the continued retention of the tracks from the Spiral Scratch EP, particularly given that those songs belonged to, as Paul Morley had described them, "the Howard Devoto quartet" as opposed to the "pop group" that Buzzcocks now were.

Pete Shelley could be forgiven for playing the sentimentality card between numbers, culminating in a reminder before "Time's Up" that time was up for the Electric Circus. The final act of nostalgia came with Shelley inviting Jon the Postman to the stage with Steve Diggle striking up the familiar "Louie Louie" riff. The prospect of one of the few original fans, who supplemented the sparse crowds at early Buzzcocks' gigs, performing to a full house backed by some of his heroes never really materialised in the ensuing commotion, although the Postman's legendary status was confirmed by the unreserved encouragement levelled at Shelley's invitation.

★

There had been other less inspiring Sunday nights spent in the confines of the Electric Circus where attendance had probably been more as a sense of duty to the venue and to the bands who had taken up the challenge.

The visit of Cyanide at least revealed what type of punk band attracted the attention of a record label like Pye, the York band having signed to the label whose chart interests at the time were "Magic Fly" by Space and Meri Wilson's novelty hit "Telephone Man". Following tiresome performances by two nondescript support bands, Cyanide were issued the directive by one drained individual to "play something decent". Presumably their repertoire did not extend to that.

The Only Ones arrived with credible endorsements, particular from the other bands. Unfortunately the deadpan vocals of Peter Perrett failed to ignite a spark within their infectious tunes compelling many of the Circus crowd to denounce them as "boring".

The closure of the Electric Circus had been a contentious issue that divided opinion among the locals. Obviously the final weekend had demonstrated an intense level of partisanship from bands and punters as it seemed that every Mancunian band was either there, or wished they had been there. The Drones had already nailed their colours to the mast even writing a new song, "Lift Off the Bans" that was interpreted as being a reaction to the Circus closure. At the other end, the fast-emerging Fall were less perturbed at the club's passing with Mark Smith, who at twenty already had a well-developing level of cynicism, even expressing approval that the Circus was to close describing the place as a "shit hole" although ironically he would talk up the prestige of playing the second night of the final weekend.

Our contribution to the "Save the Circus" campaign involved the publishing of my phone number in issue 3 of *Ghast Up. It* elicited a solitary response from a young lady who introduced herself as a friend of Graham Brooks and offered the Electric Circus as a contact address. The published number was also utilised by future writer Jeff Noon who rang for any help or advice I could give in his desire to produce a fanzine based around various lyrics from Mancunian artists.

The most fundamental void that would be left was the absence in the city of a certain kind of venue. One that could squeeze in the thousand or so people wishing to witness The Clash or Ramones, but could also provide enough atmosphere for the more modest numbers attracted by The Drones or The Vibrators. There was an easy solution for those in the latter category as both Pips and Rafters existed alongside the Students Unions at the institutes of further education within the city. The capacity at the main Students Union at Manchester's Victoria University (now The Academy 2) was even said to be close to that of the Electric Circus, although I can't recall so many being shoehorned into that venue around the time.

For bands for whom the Circus had been chock full to capacity with t-shirt sales being forced behind the bar, the only solution was to try their luck at a major concert hall that sat more with the lofty ambitions of some as well as providing a foyer to peddle their merchandise. Therein lay the problem. The continued expansion of rock concerts that culminated in the "Led Zep at Earls Court" scenario was completely at odds with the allure of the "sweaty club" that the Circus had been at its most congested. Could any seated theatre match the exclusivity that The Ramones and Talking Heads granted the Circus audience? Furthermore, would the chasm be too wide? A thousand people turned the Circus into a heaving cauldron of bodily fluids. The Free Trade Hall required more than that number just to eliminate any hollow ring.

Friday 7th October 1977

The Dogs and Drones tour rolled into Salford College with three more Manchester bands in tow. V2 and Fast Breeder were the advertised support with Warsaw deigning to join the entourage. All three held with the steadfast, if unadventurous, vocal-bass-guitar-drum formula, although Fast Breeder could boast two guitarists. Fast Breeder, as the name suggested, wore their political hearts on their sleeves whereas V2 were allied more closely to Slaughter and the Dogs with their visible glam roots.

Warsaw were beginning to acquire an unyielding reputation

that said more about their long standing resolve at the foot of the bill but fleetingly suggested that within their rigid format was a stubborn belief in the sounds they produced, despite Peter Hook's bass playing and Ian Curtis' baritone both conspicuous by their anonymity. There was a curious observer in the house whose name had appeared on both "Spiral Scratch" and "Cranked Up Really High" although both releases drew acclaim in spite of, rather than because of, Martin (Zero) Hannett's production.

With Slaughter and the Dogs again headlining, the auspicious victory over their local rivals added a new layer to their show with Wayne Barrett sporting deadpan face make up and attempting a mime routine during "Cranked Up Really High". If that represented a new level of amateurishness in their stage craft, it also displayed an element of self-deprecation that their clumsy theatrics had longed for. It also hit me that Barrett's broad interpretation of the Velvet's "White Light White Heat" was turning the Dogs' rendition into a definitive Mancunian take on the pop art aspirations of the original.

The infamous feuding between the teds and the punks had always seemed to occur just out of my earshot despite being repeatedly reminded that I should ignore them at my peril. Whether the events after the gig represented a clash of cultures or an episode of gratuitous violence, I never did find out, but the mindless shattering of plate glass windows, that sixties further education structures were famed for, was in stark contrast to the Dogs' affected innocence.

Friday 14th October 1977

A planned visit to assess the Tom Robinson Band at Rafters was thwarted by the extortionate admission price for, what I perceived to be a relatively unknown and untested band. "2-4-6-8 Motorway", their debut EMI single, was only a week old and £1.50 seemed a hefty price to establish whether the adulation from the music press was justified. Had I realised the sudden impact of this band when the sold out board displayed at Salford University later on the same tour I may have coughed up the admission price.

And so it was off to the now familiar Squat Club where Jon the Postman was performing with a newly-assembled band. Arriving late following the aborted visit to Rafters, the band christened Puerile were up and running and unsurprisingly playing, "Louie Louie".

Despite a basic but steady riff holding the song together, the Postman still appeared to be ad-libbing lyrics throughout what seemed an endless rendition. Whether the band were waiting for a cue from the singer or whether they themselves took the decision to wind up the performance was never clear, although the song did eventually splutter to a staggered halt.

A brief attempt at free-form instrumentation should have signalled a different number but instead evolved back into "Louie Louie" that moved at a marginally slower pace than the machine gun delivery of the first a cappella rendition back in May.

Saturday 15th October 1977

Whatever the true story behind the threatened deportation of Johnny Thunders and the Heartbreakers back on American Independence Day, tonight at Manchester University Students Union they were definitely back. There were one or two familiar faces in the queue on Oxford Road from that Oaks gig. Faces I had not seen since that unforgettable Tuesday night, suggesting the Heartbreakers possessed an exclusive following in addition to the generic punk audience. And yes, the tall Americans were conspicuously present.

Although seeing this band again could never replicate the mood that existed the first time around, the quality shone through with Walter Lure and Billy Rath justifying their status alongside the two former New York Dolls Thunders and Jerry Nolan. Writing about the New York scene in issue three of *Shy Talk*, Paul Morley referred to the legend that the Heartbreakers were so named because the breakup of the New York Dolls had caused many broken hearts. Morley described the Heartbreakers as "just as good as the New York Dolls" which was a judgement that could have been substantiated had the duration of the Heartbreakers existence ever equalled that of their predecessors.

With the "L.A.M.F" album released, the practised quartet demonstrated how accurately they could replicate the songs from that album with "Born To Lose" being almost as close to the record as the New York Dolls' performance of "Jet Boy" on the Old Grey Whistle Test back in 1974 although, unlike the Dolls' television appearance, the Heartbreakers were actually playing.

Friday 21st October 1977

With the big guns from the Circus days yet to test their allure at the larger halls, it fell to Elvis Costello and his new backing band the Attractions to return to the city and present his music to a seated audience when the "Live Stiffs Tour" arrived at the Apollo Theatre.

A week before The Clash would make their debut at the same cavernous hall, it was first blood to the Stiff setup, whose £1.25 ticket prices undercut The Clash by 50 per cent. And if The Clash remained the current punk frontrunners, the Stiff package at least offered strength in depth, despite Wreckless Eric's illness making him the sole absentee from the label's roster.

Fittingly it fell to performer and label producer Nick Lowe, whose "So It Goes" single had set the Stiff label's ball rolling, to open proceedings backed by a revolving door of musicians christened Last Chicken in the Shop. Lowe's set verged on the bland and predictable at times, although his longevity in the business seemed to give him the self-confidence to carry on regardless, with Dave Edmunds emerging from behind the drum kit to perform his most recent hit and Lowe composition "I Knew the Bride".

A brief rendition of Ex-Pink Fairy Larry Wallis's Stiff single "Police Car", drew generous approval from the modest audience despite Wallis' long hair and discernible "hippy" connections, the surprise package of the night was the Manchester debut of Ian Dury and the Blockheads.

"Have you got your new boots and panties?" was the whiny introduction by the compère, before the charismatic Dury took an instant grip on the audience. Backed by an experienced six-piece band and with a wealth of material from their recent debut album, Dury charmed all before him from the lilting opener of "Wake Up and Make Love to Me" through to the inevitable finale of "Sex and Drugs and Rock and Roll."

Unlike the demonstrative approach of much of the new wave, the Blockheads' music hall approach was completely at home in the expansive theatre, allowing the thirty-five-year-old Dury to foster an affable rapport, his easy-on-the-ear voice reassuring the audience that faster numbers will follow.

Dury and the Blockheads' exultant performance paved the way for Elvis Costello and his now permanent backing band to settle into the large auditorium, although the initial sight of the singer, who had turned Rafters into a hallowed hall for the evening back in July, now gracing the big stage caused some consternation. "He's had a bonehead" was one remote observation of the distant figure that delivered a mixture of the familiar and the not so familiar, "Radio Radio" being one of the new numbers introduced.

Elvis and the Attractions delivered a capable set, it even became apparent that Costello was a proficient guitarist in addition to possessing a resilient voice but perhaps tonight was the first realisation that the new wave was moving out of the clubs and into the halls with something lost in the transition. It was not yet the "Led Zep at Earls Court" scenario that Mick Middles had suggested could occur but maybe the first step.

The night at least finished on a high with the collective musicians delivering an encore of "Sex and Drugs and Rock and Roll" and the main man Costello calling for the crowd's appreciation of Ian Dury.

Friday 28th October 1977

For the first full length show by Magazine, following their concise triumph on the last night of the Electric Circus, Howard Devoto was unleashed at Rafters with The Fall, rapidly becoming the go-to band if you wanted a credible support act, in tow.

It was a sneering Mark Smith who opened his spiel with "The Clash registers will be ringing at the Apollo tomorrow night at two pound fifty a throw" before launching into the "We are The Fall" prologue that tonight offered "as in from heaven, as in internally untogether". The latter descriptor referred, not to bassist Tony Friel, who would soon be packing up his instrument to form The Passage, but to unsettled guitarist Martin Bramah, who in the words of Smith had "wanted to do his own stuff for a long time".

The Fall had achieved a notable level of assuredness in such a short passage of time with Mark Smith and Martin Bramah striking up an assertive bearing on an audience now familiar with the content and delivery of a Fall show. Whether those present would heed Smith's condemnation of The Clash and withdraw their patronage was doubtful, although a definite collective was emerging who would cite The Fall as the genuine article. I recall Jeff Noon, who was present towards the back of the club, delivering the rhetorical question, "Who needs The Clash when you've got The Fall?"

If The Fall's rising stock was evident, Magazine's prolonged set was a disappointment as the full repertoire, on initial hearing at least, failed to equal the sample delivered on the closing night of the Electric Circus. Maybe I was expecting too much too soon. Devoto's peers, most notably Buzzcocks, had been developing their craft during Devoto's sabbatical from the business, although even comparing this showing to Buzzcocks at the Oaks back in April, Magazine felt long and drawn out. They were a work in progress, although the word was that Virgin Records were about to tie them down.

Saturday 29th October 1977

The Clash's "Get Out Of Control" tour arrived in Manchester at the Apollo Theatre. Like the Circus and the Universities, the Apollo was situated a drive or a bus ride away from the city centre and, in spite of its location in the satellite district of Ardwick, the 2634 seater Apollo was set to depose the Free Trade Hall as Manchester's calling point on UK tours.

The Clash had much to prove this Saturday night. "Get Out Of Control" was a reference to their recent "Complete Control" single, a riposte to their record label for lifting "Remote Control" as a single from the debut album. As Mark Smith wryly observed, the punch line to the whole episode was that the single was released on CBS. A more crucial issue was the £2.50 ticket price that represented a 60% increase on the £1.50 charged at the Electric Circus back in May.

Before a note was played it was clear the cavernous Apollo was never going to match the condensed atmosphere created within the Electric Circus. There was none of the usual interaction and swapping of notes with the regulars. We were in a large auditorium watching a show on a distant stage.

The surge from the seats that greeted the opening band quickly receded when it was noticed that the act on stage was not Richard Hell and the Voidoids but a group of females. The Lous were a French all-girl group who Mick Jones apparently rated highly and who made all the right noises. They were politely applauded but this was a night when the audience had bigger fish to fry.

What exactly the issue with the sound was during Richard Hell's first attempt to play was unclear but his tetchy response in throwing his guitar aside and storming off prompted a chorus of "I'm So Bored With the USA". In an act of diplomacy to the American guests, or maybe a jokey slight on the audience's xenophobia, Joe Strummer would later introduce the same song as, "I'm So Bored With the UK".

The Voidoids ultimately returned to complete their set with Hell offering an overly courteous, "Thank yooo" after each number, but the damage had been done long before they closed with a rendition of The Stooges "Now I Wanna Be Your Dog" complete with dog howling backing vocals.

The way was clear for The Clash to make a further conquest – whether the excitement generated by the music justified the level of exuberance that saw rows of seats smashed was doubtful but, in an act that mimicked the scenario when The Clash played the Rainbow on the White Riot Tour, the front rows of seats were forcibly ripped from their anchors. Still playing the insurgent, Strummer advised to pass the seats forward and out of the way.

There was little to actually fault the Clash for within their set, although Mick Jones and Paul Simonon employing the big stage to strike guitar hero poses only compounded the shattered myth that the band were now force feeding music that had been so unaffectedly vibrant the last time around.

There was no air of bewilderment outside after the gig. The Apollo is situated on a main bus route by the Ardwick roundabout and, in the first real act of camaraderie, the crowd made their way to whatever mode of transport would ferry them home. It was reported through the departing throngs that Paul Morley hated it.

★

The month of November 1977 saw two crucial releases for differing reasons. The Shelley-fronted Buzzcocks unleashed their first single for United Artists. The choice was the Shelley/Devoto composition "Orgasm Addict" coupled with "Whatever Happened To…?" a song credited to Pete Shelley/Alan Dial. As Mark Smith informed us while enthusing over the adroit lyrics of the B-side, the Alan Dial in question who composed the lyrics was Buzzcocks' manager Richard Boon.

"Orgasm Addict" sounded slightly pacier than expected but the final mix was justification that Buzzcocks would be a worthwhile investment. The buzzsaw guitar sound was already evident and Pete Shelley's lead vocal even threatened to overreach in parts. But for the fact that the subject matter would keep it off radio playlists, Buzzcocks probably would have seen early chart action with a catchy and well-produced debut.

The flip was even more promising. From the driving bass intro (what would be Garth's last on record) to the harmonious backing vocals that typified so many Buzzcocks' singles, "Whatever Happened To…?" was a joyously euphoric pop ditty, crafted without the continued involvement of Devoto.

Slaughter and the Dogs may have enjoyed the reputation of being quick workers in the studio but it was The Drones who won the race to release the first album, "Further Temptations" being released on the Valer Label. Being first and being the best are not automatically analogous and if Paul Morley's spiteful review in *NME* was indicative, The Drones had failed on every level, although the bold sleeve design earned more than a few plaudits.

The album contained all the familiar stage favourites, including re-recordings of "Lookalikes" and "Corgi Crap" from their debut EP but without the feedback that had remained on the initial recording through financial constraints. Production duties were handled by Simon Humphrey whose studio credits apparently included work with John Williams, George Melly, Bruce Forsyth and The Glitter Band to name but a few.

As a softener for the melodic limitation of much of their material, the album included a recording of Greenwich and Barry's "Be My Baby" and a venerable reading of "City Drones" complete with piano - a track dismissed by the band as, "not commercial enough" when pondering singles material. In a bold move a recent song "Underdog", written in response to the media's classification of the band as the poor relation to Buzzcocks and Slaughter and the Dogs, was given a dark production complete with electronically distorted vocals. Not that scrutiny of individual tracks was the purpose of a Morley review that brutally dismissed his former charges as "a product for consumers".

The Drones had, in the main, endured a torrid time within the pages of the *NME*. Their debut EP had received an unconstructive dismissal at the hands of Tony Parsons who deemed the "Temptations of a White Collar Worker" title a paradox given the band's conformity to the punk blue print, suggesting that the image of the white collar worker as adversary to the renegade had been lifted from Jimi Hendrix's "If Six Was Nine". The follow up "Bone Idol" was met with indifference on first review but the classification of the single as a Double A-side seemed to prompt the powers at IPC to revisit the single, granting Parsons a second opportunity to twist the knife in a review of the single's flip side "Just Want To Be Myself" where Parsons informed us that he had his crosses to bear but he didn't "drone on and on about it". The same writer had been equally compelling in his dismissal of the "Streets" compilation on Beggars Banquet that included the original recording of "Lookalikes" on its track listing, suggesting the label should not stick their shoddy creations under his nose.

That the *NME* gave the LP to Paul Morley to review was strange given that his previous involvement with The Drones, including production credits on the debut EP, was one of music's worst kept secrets. That he and the band had drifted somewhat acrimoniously apart, and it was the likes of Shelley or Devoto or Mark Smith whose causes he now defended, was an equally well known fact, although this was hardly a "build 'em up and knock 'em down" situation given The Drones only positive press in the *NME* had been alongside the collective acclaim Morley bestowed upon most of the current Manchester music community in his "They Mean It Maaaan-Chester" piece.

While Morley had every right to revise his view, no doubt recognising that the band had never justified his initial overzealous support of it, it did beg the question what would have happened if he had been pleasantly surprised by the album. Would the *NME* editorial have sat easily with a glowing review of an album being penned by the band's former manager?

The Drones sat more easily on the more sensitive pages of *NME*'s closest rival *Sounds*. In a more generous assessment Editor Alan Lewis assumed the job of reviewing "Further Temptations" himself and compassionately suggested that any detractors should think long and hard about what their expectations of the average punk bands was if they wished to avoid a reversion to the boring old wave. Lewis summed up the derivative nature of The Drones and their ilk as imitation being an honourable tradition in rock, even comparing the doomy treatment of "Underdog" to the Velvet Underground.

Closer to home, *New Manchester Review* writer Ian Wood shared Alan Lewis' view that "Further Temptations" should not be too rapidly dismissed for its simplistic approach, even commending the studio sound achieved as infinitely better than the other Manchester bands. Presumably both Lewis and Wood had approached the review with full expectation that the album would fall short in the minds of many new wave commentators, although I suspect Wood felt a certain loyalty to a Mancunian act while southern contemporaries seemed to avoid the worst of the abuse.

Paul Morley would later explain away The Drones as music that appealed "because for a while we just wanted to dance" in the sleeve notes of the ten inch "Short Circuit" EP recorded over the last two nights at the Electric Circus, echoing his earlier description of The Drones and various others as "'77 pop". Presumably "'77 pop", or as he expounded the definition, "music that you can dance to", had ceased to be a term of endearment in the seven months that had elapsed since Morley used the term to convince us of The Drones' worth.

Maybe the new breed should have reverted to the old tradition that you needed a live band to dance to before a certain DJ apparently decreed that records would suffice. Certainly The Drones were not the first and would definitely not be the last band to come up short when attempting to transfer their live act into a recording studio.

Slaughter and the Dogs had also unfurled their debut single for Decca by this time. The potential hit "You're a Bore" coupled with their anthemic "Where Have All the Boot Boys Gone?" was released in September 1977 in both seven inch and twelve inch formats supported by an onslaught of weekly ads in both *Sounds* and *NME*. The shortcomings of the Dogs single was not Decca's marketing but the insipid mix of their most commercial song.

What should have been the Dogs' passport to Top of the Pops, "You're a Bore" was a flat and lacklustre affair only marginally better than the boorish chant on the other side. Like their debut "Cranked Up Really High" the song was evidently an anti-drugs tirade, although their cause may have been lent more credibility had someone apprised them that in recreational drugs terms "acid" and "LSD" were the same thing. Phil Wainman, or some like-minded pop producer, should have been tasked with turning the song into a hit single. Unfortunately the job was handed to "Lizzy's producer" Nick Tauber who turned it into a bland rock number that even John Peel pronounced inferior to their debut single.

The flip side "Where Have All The Boot Boys Gone?" would at least prove a useful anthem to some when, a few years later, a certain sector of the music press decided that real punk stemmed, not from the Stooges or Velvet Underground but from the football terraces and as such should be distinguished from the developing sound structures of The Fall, Joy Division or even The Clash. Curiously the same redrafting of history would also rank "Further Temptations" as a punk classic. As for the question posed by the Dogs… maybe some grew their hair and started wearing make-up and listening to David Bowie and Roxy Music. I am sure some also drank tea from a cup!

Monday 7th November 1977

The Free Trade Hall's position as the main venue in the city may have been seized by the Apollo but the old theatre still managed to deliver a few gigs of significance. Tom Verlaine brought his band Television over from New York with Blondie in support and New England legend Jonathan Richman was witnessed by Mark Smith who said to be in awe of the Modern Lovers' ability to change the atmosphere within the hall with their musical approach and Richman's mystification when faced with chants of "Wally".

Tonight it was The Tubes, whose lampooning of the punk culture had, like Alberto Y Los Trios Paranoias, somehow endeared them to some of its membership. Thus the upstairs bar witnessed members of The Worst and The Drones in town to check out the American entertainers whose choreographed stage routine involved several costume changes.

Conversation in The Worst camp was less about tonight's gig and more about manager Steve Shy's failure to keep in regular contact. Before the days of mobile phones or Facebook this involved regular phone calls that for some necessitated a walk to the nearest phone box. I swapped notes with Drones guitarist Gus over my recent catching of the re-recorded "Lookalikes" on the John Peel Show as a sample off the forthcoming album. Gus suggested the cleaner version without feedback was an improvement although he still harboured concerns with the production.

Presumably the brains behind this UK tour had decided The Tubes could rationally be defined as a punk group, giving a support slot to Wire, a band whose work experience on the "Roxy London WC2" had earned them a full-time position on the album's Harvest label. Although some Mancunian punks were willing to admit The Tubes to their exclusive club, an insufficient number were sold on them, on the basis of the West Coast band's debut album (which had featured a song called "White Punks On Dope" apparently written as a satirical swipe at their middle class audience) to grant Wire a fair hearing.

So it was left to the predominantly mainstream audience to ensure that Wire died the proverbial death. Running through a set containing songs of ever decreasing length, with several numbers clocking in at well under a minute, Wire could never be accused of testing the audience's perseverance. Their minimalist approach to the craft of song writing received the loudest cheer when singer Colin Newman announced their last number. Newman's most notable interaction prior to this had been a robotic "Get stuffed cunt" aimed at the many detractors within the hall.

No such fate awaited The Tubes whose big band sound attracted an early roar of approval as it blended into "Young and Rich" before the inevitable series of musical sketches that provided a perceptibly literal interpretation of the songs such as singers Fee Waybill and Re Styles performing pseudo sex during "Don't Touch Me There".

If there was a punk moment in the big show, it was a scene involving a shade wearing punk dressed in black who had been planted in the audience to spit his beer at Waybill who in turn spat back before the character mounted the stage to be ferociously beaten up by Waybill in time to the music, complete with blood capsules.

Saturday 12th November 1977

I was aware that Buzzcocks gigs were not confined to Manchester but appearances in the city always had the feeling of parochial one-offs. Tonight at Manchester Polytechnic's Cavendish House was the first time one of their gigs felt like part of a wider tour. They had a United Artists single to promote and, although it should have made little difference, they had acquired a new bassist with nineteen year-old Steve Garvey replacing Garth whose services had been publicly terminated by band and management.

The Cavendish House venue was an old ornate brown and white brick two storey building at the end of Cavendish Street with a series of oval windows and leaded lights on the first floor windows. You could gauge the crowd size by the point on Cavendish Street at which you reached the queue. Entrance was through a set of double doors and the most memorable feature of the inside were the cartoon pictures on the wall depicting characters from The Beano. Maybe I didn't venture far enough into the venue but my recollection is of always watching the band side on with the stage to the left.

As if to emphasise the point that this was one stop on a tour, support was from London's Lurkers, who had spawned a couple of singles released on Beggars Banquet but were not the usual Mancunian support act for Buzzcocks. The Lurkers were one of many bands of the time whose structural influence was unashamedly based on The Ramones. With that limitation their repertoire struggled to suggest anything inventive despite smiling singer Howard Wall encouraging each and every one to have a great night.

Pete Shelley's one act to incite audience participation was to waft a copy of Jeff Noon's *Noisy People* fanzine that had been published after several setbacks with printing costs and was being sold on the night. The fanzine was Noon's first creation and contained montages of cuttings from the music press with handwritten observations mostly on the worth of the music being reported. The main articles were typewritten lyrics of current songs layered over a montage background that included Buzzcocks' "Sixteen", Warsaw's "Novelty" and most tellingly

The Fall's "Repetition". Shelley suggested the crowd use the fanzine to sing along with "Sixteen".

★

Although I can recall much of the earlier interview with Mark Smith and Una Baines, said interview was not captured on our Dansette tape recorder due (probably) to human error. That said, although the likelihood of a fourth issue of *Ghast Up* was becoming increasingly unlikely, it seemed prudent to try and arrange a further interview. A second visit to Prestwich would lead to many more, beginning a friendship that lasted a few years and considerably longer in Mick's case.

Although our visit kicked off at the Kingswood Road flat, the timing of our stay resulted in our first visit to the Forresters Arms on nearby Bury New Road. The flat had acquired several posters through their association with Buzzcocks and Magazine. The large yellow Orgasm Addict poster designed by Linder Sterling that Smith described as "horrible" nevertheless adorned the wall alongside a poster of Christ Carrying the Cross by Dutch painter Hieronymus Bosch. Smith asked, in what seemed like an expectant manner, what we had thought of Magazine. My unenthusiastic response was echoed by Smith who concurred, "Yes, they are a bit disappointing".

While Paul Morley had been generous in any of his assessments of The Fall within *NME*, *Sounds* had featured a review of the final night of the Electric Circus in which Jon Savage had been summarily dismissive of the band.

"I think they cop out, if it isn't obvious to them" was Smith's response to Savage's lack of enthusiasm, already developing a healthy disdain for negative reviews which he would later claim were among his favourites.

The visit to the pub established that the 20-year-old Smith had been visiting such hostelries for years, "Cos I've always been, like, tall for my age." He also remarked that Prestwich was a good place to drink as there were many nice people who lived there.

The drink lubricated a business proposal to finance a Fall record. I had no plans to become a music mogul, indeed I had no idea of the costs of studio time but the thought of a Fall record alongside the Buzzcocks, Slaughter and the Dogs, Drones and even Nosebleeds releases, of which Mark Smith observed of Vini Reilly "he has been to music school" seemed all too alluring. Perhaps wisely Smith gratefully declined our offer, explaining that plans were afoot to record an EP for Buzzcocks' label New Hormones with Richard Boon agreeing to finance the recording. I don't recall Smith going into detail of the tracks to be recorded but I managed to establish that "Repetition" would be tackled in the studio.

Sunday 13th November 1977

A Sunday night in the genial confines of the Band on the Wall, the ideal location for The Fall to step out on their own, free from the shackles of a main headlining band and with some offbeat support in the form of Trevor Wishart and the Tent Poles. Despite Mark Smith's insistence that The Fall were not overtly political in content, the running feud with the big boys continued with the flyer, created by the Manchester Musicians Collective, for whom this was one of a series of Sunday nights proclaiming "Your Alternative To The Clash Registers!"

With a respite from the volley of spit and beer that this traditional jazz venue offered, The Fall delivered a near flawless set that was growing to include instrumental breaks as in "Futures and Pasts" and alternative vocal passages as in "Rebellious Jukebox" both supplied by want-away guitarist Martin Bramah. Smith and Baines lodger and sometime manager Kay Carroll offered an accompanying dance routine to the rhythmic tempo that encompassed many Fall songs.

With a further issue of *Ghast Up* seeming less likely, despite my parents' house still containing the bulky Roneo Machine, Mick Middles penned a commending review for the newly launched *Trick* paper that published articles submitted by the general public proclaiming, "We are our readers". I assume they never paid for their contributors' freelance work, although it only existed for two issues. The article was credited to Mick Middles, *Ghast Up* so it was arguably the last ever article attributed to our fanzine –

NO HIP-OCRISY, NO CLASH REGISTERS

THE FALL – Band On The Wall, Manchester

The Band on the Wall is a Manchester jazz club, filled from wall to bar with the beard'n'glasses/real ale/student/Ivor Cutler intellectual sect. They swarm to cast their highbrow views over ridiculous individuals who perform on tent poles/biscuit tin lids/horrible pianos etc. avant garde? art? music? who really knows? (or cares).

The Fall are cold/hard/cynical leftists who thrust their views/songs upon usually all too-willing crowds. The Fall are tight, and superbly different. They are in my esteem Manchester's No.1 new wave outfit. (Buzzcocks not excepted).

Place them in an unpublicised gig at the Band on the Wall, supported by (tent poles?) and you have an amazing night on your hands. I'll never forget it anyway.

The Wall was moderately filled with the usual crowd, only twenty or so new wavites to be seen. The feeling was fresh and interesting like a trip back in time, a couple of years. Beautiful.

I laughed my way thru the unbelievably horrible support acts. From the stage came "This one is a piece in three movements" followed by clank, plonk, varoooom! I fell about laughing, unable to control myself, nobody else laughed (aside from me mate). What's a pile of bricks in the Tate to me? Whereas next to me the conversation continued in the "Now, Jeremy, this it's really relevant" view. I spotted the Fall's vocalist, Mark, sneering at the bar.

"Hey, Mark, you're not actually gonna play are you" I asked, amazed.

"Oh yeah, should be interesting, Mick," he replied.

An understatement if ever I heard one. But sure enough, given ten minutes and the Fall onstage, uncompromising, brutal and as always (to me anyway) compelling.

"Hey Fascist" kicked the band into gear. A bottle to the Nat. Front with nursery rhyme chorus "Psycho Mafia", "Bingo Masters", "Industrial Estate" (Yeah, yeah, Industrial Estate) followed in true casual form.

This band are so intense, your alternative to the Clash registers. No hypocrisy here, just pure, fresh Iggyism, at its finest. The highbrow shuffle uneasily. Mark's casual sneer. Una's (fragile keyboard) fresh suffragette looks, Martin's (slash guitar) mimicking all add together, providing stunning visuals (Don't leave, Martin, you fool).

The Fall's classic "Repetition" finally arrives. It's a slow, drawn out, massive song. "This song's gonna last for three hours" based around Siren, combine guitar Mark spits out his slurring vocals. "All you shithead creeps who are into Mozart music better clear cos we'll show you how to do it, we dig repetition, repetition, repetition".

Appropriate to the end, that's the Fall then as the bar switches off, the Fall lock into "Last Orders". And it's over. The bewildered highbrow wander off to their waiting Jags, thinking about the Fall. I wander away, smiling, glad to have recaptured that wonderful early new wave feeling, amazement and ecstasy. Sadly the harsh realities of the clash registers soon filter through and I return to 1977.

See this band with new light.
The Fall. As in eternally untogether
As in national murder
As in Heaven
(Lyrics courtesy of the Fall)
And this is not a biased report.

MICK MIDDLES (*Ghost Up*)

Tuesday 15th November 1977

Back to the Elizabethan Ballroom in the Belle Vue Amusement Park for an occasion that would be preserved in part by the Granada TV cameras, here to capture footage of Siouxsie and the Banshees and The Clash for Tony Wilson's second series of "So It Goes". Subway Sect had returned to The Clash fold but were not on the agenda for the TV show, or if they were their support slot ended on the cutting room floor.

Attempts to collect the admission charge were abandoned almost immediately. I don't recall the level of destruction being on the scale reported, such as all the glass doors being shattered. I am sure a few managed to tender the admission charge before the door security became resigned to letting the majority in free. Whether the cost of seeing The Clash was less than the exorbitant £2.50 at the Apollo I don't recall, not being one of the handful who actually paid.

The whole débâcle could have been a preconceived stunt. Presumably Granada TV's funding of the event ensured there would be no financial loss and anyway, were the audience not effectively extras? Mick Hucknall's visible presence has been pinpointed on re-runs of the footage.

Joe Strummer was quick to garner integrity from the proceedings, announcing the opener "London's Burning" as "Getting in for Nothing". Despite the guileless politics to which Strummer sometimes religiously adhered, this was an incontestable return to form for The Clash who regaled the swaying masses throughout with most of the debut album and the customary stage reworking of "Capital Radio" with Strummer announcing that, "twenty five English pounds" was being offered for the *NME* giveaway single of that title.

To mask any wrongdoing for their co-operation with the big business that this TV company constituted, the by now guitarless Strummer pointed to a cameraman with the rationalisation, "see that, that's money talking. Your money". Or maybe the singer was attempting to divert the beer and glasses and the obligatory phlegm away from the band as the cameramen were suddenly fair game. A further petty act saw Strummer revise the lyrics of "What's My Name" to "Here we are on TV, what does it mean to me? What does it mean to you? …. fuck off", again pointing his wrath at a (no doubt) union card holding cameraman.

But this was a night of payback as the underwhelming appearance at the Apollo was displaced by what was, for all the questionable political sloganeering, a spirited performance played to a once more upright audience allowed to dance without the bouncers throwing them back into their seats. There was talk of some rough handling of fans at stage side, which Tony Wilson insisted was the work of The Clash entourage but as a live rock band The Clash were once again back among the elite.

Probably the most tellingly political statement of the night was Joe Strummer questioning if the audience thought punk was dead. The inquiry brought a vociferous response, although the follow up question delivered a more rousing thumbs up to confirm punk was alive and well as Strummer added, "Thank god for that."

Thursday 24th November 1977

A second chance to assess the worth of Mark Perry's Alternative TV in town supporting Wayne County and the Electric Chairs at Manchester Polytechnic. Despite *Ghast Up*'s continued absence, ATV's label Deptford Fun City had written to suggest the gig may be of interest to our magazine and offered to put our names on the guest list, as well as furnishing a copy of the Electric Chairs notorious new single "F★★k Off". The act of generosity had been prompted by Buzzcocks manager Richard Boon who had given our details to the record label.

Since the September visit to the Electric Circus, Perry had acquired a guitar that he appeared to still be in the process of learning, although he was unafraid to deliver a few lead licks early in the set, consistent with his recent stated preference for jazz. As the new slightly more musical approach engendered an acceptable if indifferent audience response, Perry took the cue to revert to the soapbox rhetoric with an ode to the "punk from Manchestaar" who "wore a swastikaar".

As the set dwindled to an inconclusive end, the one aspect of live performing that Perry clearly understood was when to withdraw gracefully rather than force an encore. Sensing the lack of enthusiasm that still existed around an ex fanzine writer turned performer, Kevin Cummins asked if we were going to, "slag them off." I must have indicated something in the affirmative as Cummins turned to Paul Morley, who was in the midst of discussing the rebirth of Howard Devoto's career, to pose the same question. Morley appeared about to concur when he delivered an unequivocal "No".

Wayne County and the Electric Chairs were every bit as good as they had been at the Circus back in May, although lyrics like, "F★★k off" or "wash me in the blood of rock and roll" carried less shock value when not used as a bargaining tool with a hostile crowd. County had faced some scepticism among the punk contingent over his earlier shock act that utilised big hair and make-up, *48 Thrills* fanzine dismissing him as "bleedin' entertainment" but such misgivings were never shared by the Manchester punk crowd.

Even without the dressing up, Wayne County still possessed a self-assurance in front of the solid unit that the Electric Chairs clearly were and his intrinsic showmanship saw the band glide through a repertoire that featured titles such as "Stuck On You", a song that rhymed the title with "Elmer's glue", the more suggestive "Cream In My Jeans" and County's homage to their native New York "Max's Kansas City".

If tonight demonstrated anything it was that Wayne County and the Electric Chairs were morphing into a latter day Screaming Lord Sutch and the Savages, destined to remain a celebrated live act on the club and college circuit rather than a band who would shift records. The extrovert County possessed the verve to steer most audiences and tonight, playing to the converted, the band delivered a vibrant live show but maybe this was to be their peak.

Friday 16th December 1977

Whilst most Fall gigs had more than equalled expectations, their appearance at St John's College, a small student venue close to Granada TV Studios that garnered some approval for its low admission price and non-requirement of a students union card, was the first non-event they would produce and perhaps an early indicator of the unreliability for which Mark Smith would later become infamous.

Both Manicured Noise and The Elite delivered uninspired

but, at least, complete sets in support. Whilst it was the custom of Manicured Noise to drift through their performance with minimal rapport, the youthful singer of The Elite left the stage with a curt, "Good night boring old farts, seeing as you probably don't know what BOFs are." Mark Smith, not renowned for his verbal generosity to any of the current breed, would later praise The Elite as worthier contenders than most.

The first sign that the best laid plans were about to flounder was the sight of Mark Smith wandering amongst the audience acknowledging those he knew whilst loudly and drunkenly condemning the student population of this and every other educational establishment. The drunken tirade continued as The Fall stuck up the first chords with the usual assertive, "We are The Fall" intro replaced by a slurred, "Good evening and I hope your grants have come through."

Martin Bramah tackled the crowd's antipathy towards the band's failure to establish anything musically by advising he could play fancy riffs before demonstrating with an impromptu guitar burst that never threatened to evolve into a Fall number. If tonight was memorable for anything it was the debut of the drunk and incapable caricature that would envelop Smith in later years.

Sunday 18th December 1977

Somehow the Elizabethan Ballroom, Belle Vue seemed to have become a much larger venue accommodating ever larger numbers, and the throngs that filled the venue for the appearance of Buzzcocks almost gave the hall a cavernous feel.

That Siouxsie and the Banshees were the support act was a clear indication of the rapid acceleration that had propelled Buzzcocks' status in recent months. Like Buzzcocks, the Banshees were now delivering a more tailored act although the commanding vocals of Siouxsie remained the fulcrum around which the Banshees' loose musical arrangements drifted.

The growing acceptable face of punk meant more innovative bands like Buzzcocks and the Banshees were now subject to the same constant stream of beer and spit that had blighted The

▲ Shy Talk fanzine. Probably the first punk fanzine in Manchester, published from Wansford Street off Maine Road in Moss Side.

▲ Ghast Up fanzine that augmented the Mancunian punk press in 1977. Curiously the labour of producing a D.I.Y. publication meant both Shy Talk and Ghast Up stalled after their third issue.

▶ The last item to be produced by the Ghast Up stencil machine - Punctate was a two page supplement given away with later copies of the fanzine.

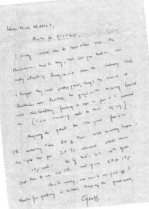

◀ A reply from Geoff Travis of Rough Trade requesting 25 copies of Issue 1 of Ghast Up, for which Travis paid in full without prompting.

▼ Monthly flyers from the hectic summer of 1977 at the Electric Circus. The "Surprise top recording star" proved to be blues rock guitar legend Alvin Lee.

▲ A communication from Modest Young a.k.a. Paul Morley complete with more of Morley's musings on the envelope.

▲ The self-released debut EP by The Drones on their OHM...S. label.
A move no doubt inspired by Buzzcocks' Spiral Scratch debut.

▲ Some artwork of The Clash created with a typewriter based on a photo that appeared in the NME. This was included in Ghast Up 3 as a loose flyer in some copies. Nearly forty years later one such flyer found it's way to Philadelphia to appear in a Clash exhibition.

THE ELECTRIC CIRCUS and **So It Goes**

invite you for an evening of boredom and frantic non-commodity music with **Buzzcocks**, **Penetration** and **Ted the Postman**

Tuesday Aug. 16th 6·30 to 10·30

starts early - don't you?

Please note, as from the 2nd October the Electric Circus will be closing due to pressure from the Local Council and Fire Service.

We would like to thank all our members for their support over the last 12 months we have been operating.

We would also like to take this opportunity to thank Piccadilly Radio, Granada T.V., the B.B.C. and all the Music Press for all the help and support they have given us.

Thanks once again.

> GRAHAM BROOKS
> ALAN ROBINSON
> (Managers)

◀ Tuesday 16 August 1977 was the day Elvis Presley died at his Memphis Graceland home. Over in Collyhurst, the Electric Circus hosted Tony Wilson's "So It Goes" programme.

▲ The final Electric Circus flyer for September 1977. The management team of Graham Brooks and Alan Robinson expressed their thanks to their members and the media.

Damned's custard pie approach. Steve Severin informed one offender, "You're spitting right" before inviting the character, whose leather bomber jacket and wide trousers suggested he was no punk, onto the stage. The individual was more than happy to milk the attention, grinning throughout the hail of beer and gob that the Banshees' guitarist had persuaded him to sample.

With a contract to fulfil, Buzzcocks' set began to grow in the countdown to releasing their debut album. The commercial and harmonious arrangement of "I Don't Mind" was premièred in Manchester as was "Fiction Romance" with Shelley warning the song was so fresh it might crash and burn before reaching the end.

The widening of songwriting duties was also disclosed with Shelley generously advising, "This one's catchy" before playing Steve Diggle's "Autonomy", the memorable hook of the song aided by its partial debt to The Ramones' "53rd and 3rd".

Obviously getting the hang of this showbiz thing, Shelley announced the next number "What Do I Get" was to be their upcoming single due out in January and managed to dedicate "Sixteen" to bassist Steve "Paddy" Garvey whose birthday was imminent and who was nineteen. His handling of revellers was less proficient. An attempt to quell the now customary flow of beer and spit, with Shelley suggesting "it distracts us" was repaid by the contents of a beer glass being thrown at the singer's face.

★

1977 ended almost as tranquilly as it had begun. A year that saw the Electric Circus briefly become the Ad Lib of the North, although this being Manchester, regulars never clustered around Buzzcocks like courtiers around royalty. More likely Pete Shelley would cadge a cig. As well as the implosion of the Electric Circus, the Oaks as a punk venue also came and went in 1977. The only regular haunt to survive into 1978 would be Rafters, with the Students Union Bars at UMIST, Manchester Polytechnic and the main University reaping a larger slice of the action.

As usual around the Festive Season gigs were thin on the ground, although the listings always had a select number of

Christmas shows including a 24-hour punk festival at a club in Keighley, West Yorkshire that featured a Mancunian line-up of The Drones, V2, John Cooper Clarke and, representing Yorkshire, Rudy and the Zipps.

1978

After the relentless activity of the previous year, 1978 was always destined to be the quiet after the storm, or the start of the post-punk years as commentators have subsequently come to define it.

An early outing was to catch up with Mark Smith who recounted a tale of a disastrous Rock Against Racism benefit gig at the Stretford Civic Theatre on 23 December that had seen his then famous silk shirt liberally drenched in gob by a surly audience. The Stretford show also marked the end of bassist Tony Friel's Fall career as he left to form The Passage alongside Dick Witts of the Manchester Musicians Collective.

We were also given a preview of the prospective debut EP that Richard Boon had financed Smith proffered a cassette tape to sample on the car stereo en route to the pub. The opening track "Psycho Mafia" prompted Smith to concede his embarrassment at listening to himself singing but the four tracks that also included "Bingo Masters Breakout", "Frightened" and a lengthy reading of "Repetition" provided a rounded assessment of The Fall to date, including Una Baines' still disjointed keyboards and Smith's propensity to rant as demonstrated on the protracted spoken intro to "Repetition".

Despite Smith's self-conscious retort to the sound of his voice, three of the four tracks would emerge unaltered as The Fall's debut EP, the casualty being "Frightened", that the band would re-record for their debut album. The original recording of "Frightened" remains one of the more enigmatic Fall songs. Mick Middles would describe it in a later *Sounds* review as "slow and climatic and reminiscent of Black Sabbath's 'Iron Man'".

★

The Fall's growing clamour had struck a chord with the national press beyond the Mancunian brotherhood. *NME* writers Tony Parsons and partner Julie Burchill had attempted to conduct an interview based around The Fall's anti-fascist political stance that had, according to Mark Smith, culminated in Burchill storming out with Parsons following, "like a lapdog".

A more fruitful encounter occurred with former *Sniffin'*

Glue scribe Danny Baker, whose activity with the punk fanzine resulted in his later contribution to the monthly glossy fanzine *Zigzag*. Baker caught up with the band at Huddersfield Polytechnic on Friday 13th January 1978, or rather they fell into his lap being an unlikely support for his cherished Sham 69.

According to the *Zigzag* article that transpired this was Baker's first encounter with The Fall, a band he only knew from Tony Parsons' published appraisal that there were few bands, "fit to lick The Fall's plectrum". A chance meeting saw Baker swiftly converted to the band's cause in whom he seemed to perceive an atypical originality, despite The Fall's appearance being the subject of a wrangle with the other support act, The Doll, who, according to Mark Smith and Fall manager Kay Carroll, seemed to believe their inclusion on the Beggars Banquet compilation album "Streets" should qualify them as second on the bill. An argument settled in The Fall's favour by the flip of a coin.

Baker's endorsement, together with that of *Sniffin' Glue* creator Mark Perry would ultimately sway Step Forward Records benefactor Miles Copeland to release The Fall's debut EP.

Saturday 11th February 1978

The swift call to arms following the release of an album had seen The Drones expand to acquire a diminutive keyboard player. Although Mike Koman's limited stature was less apparent when sat behind the keyboard, clad in a suit and bowler hat to reflect the "White Collar Worker" that had graced the title and the cover of their debut EP, it was laid bare by the glossy "Further Temptations" package issued by Electric Circus Management – an organisation that included former Electric Circus manager Graham Brooks in its employ – and under whose wing they now fell. The group photo, supplied naturally by Kevin Cummins, depicted Koman alongside the much taller figures of Gus Gangrene and both Howells brothers and to reinforce the point the accompanying blurb supplied details of each member's (inaccurate) dates of birth and heights.

In a straight steal from their associates The Stranglers, The Drones' live show also now included a couple of erotic female dancers clad in lingerie as a continuance of their "Further Temptations" theme, the album cover having featured a prostitute on the front with the same individual on the reverse being propositioned by the four band members outside a seedy sex shop. Quite why they had chosen to run with the cover art subject matter was something of a mystery. The album title was presumably a follow on from the "Temptations of a White Collar Worker" EP but the songs on the album gave no clues as to any preoccupation with the seedier side of city life, unlike later releases by Marc Almond or Morrissey.

And so it was that The Drones arrived at the Barnes Wallis Building home of UMIST as part of their tour to promote the album with an even less spontaneous approach to performing than their previous studied method. Despite the misplaced ideals of the accompanying sideshow, the home support still guaranteed a warm reception although there was a certain air of perplexity that The Drones' development had turned into this.

The mood was best summed up during a delay before returning for an encore. Roadie Sarge had addressed the crowd calling for fewer missiles if they wanted the band back on stage. Jon the Postman, never one to stroll by an unguarded microphone, took the opportunity to perform a few lines of The Fall's "Industrial Estate" before suggesting we give The Drones another chance, opining that, "they're alright, a bit of a cabaret band, not as good as The Fall."

Mick Middles response was to pen a quizzical review of The Drones move into all round entertainment which *Sounds* published. I was to encounter Mike Drone and Steve Cundall the following week during a coffee break from their rehearsal room. Far from being angered by Mick's review, they appreciated the constructive assessment and vowed to keep a copy of the *Sounds* review in their "scrapbook" echoing their previous response to Paul Morley's initial blunt evaluation. I was later informed that Steve Cundall had been less appreciative of Morley's review of "Further Temptations" and had made the journalist fully aware.

Friday 3rd March 1978

The first event proper of 1978 saw Wayne County and the Electric Chairs at Rafters as part of their "Eddie and Sheena" tour and in keeping with the forbidden love theme of the song in question (a Ted and a Punkette making out within a late-fifties pastiche that only Wayne County could pull off without sounding hackneyed) youthful rockabilly band Levi and the Rockats were the support. There was an additional bonus in Manchester with The Fall making up the bill.

Mark Smith, never one to indulge punk sartorial style with the exception of a pair of Shoeworld brothel creepers that he mockingly suggested made him, "the Eddie Cochran of the blank generation", appeared wearing sunglasses to deliver the "we are The Fall" intro.

After the shambolic appearance at St John's College and an even edgier Rock Against Racism gig in Stretford just before Christmas, it was a return to form from a band who were arguably Manchester's most inventive at this point. Buzzcocks had established their recording career, following their first two excellent singles, with a debut album that contained flashes of brilliance but was mostly the tying up of loose ends that had constituted their set from the beginning. "Another Music in a Different Kitchen" had received plaudits from the music press but many of their standard numbers lost their edge when restrained within the studio.

Although The Fall were yet to commit to vinyl their set was growing and evolving constantly. They could, like all their fellow Manchester bands, still deliver much of what was expected live but there were always surprise elements that set a Fall gig apart. As John Peel would later describe his favourite band, "always the same, always different" and never was this more true than in their formative years.

Whereas The Fall were yet to appear on record, Mark Smith had provided the spoken intro to the debut release by Jon the Postman's Puerile with Smith declaring amongst other things, "The Postman is the music scene" before the postman finally delivered his recorded version of "Louie Louie" that

Smith would pronounce "definitive". Mark Harris, the guitarist with Puerile, was keen to exploit their early venture into vinyl advising Wayne County, who was eating a sandwich at the time, that Smith appeared on "my band's record".

Wayne County and the Electric Chairs were again in their element performing live. Mark Smith would later praise the showmanship of the American as "great" although the acclaim came with the rider that it had all been done before. Smith was particularly impressed that County had made a record entitled "Fuck Off".

Saturday 18th March 1978

Despite Rafters' survival as the one regular punk haunt from 1977, the scene it could reasonably create was limited by the bands available. The requirement to showcase Beatles copyists The Pleasers somehow forced the management, or maybe the band's management, to offer a prize for the shortest mini skirt, a gimmick that the audience declined to participate in.

Support was provided by five piece band The Heat, whose considered approach necessitated their explaining the songwriting source within the band of each number performed. Despite their unadventurous approach and the overall lack of any sparkle within their music, The Heat's performance would be remembered as honest and inventive compared to the supper club style cabaret that the headliners delivered.

In an attempt to gentrify the beast that punk and the new wave had become, the media had borrowed a term first coined by Pete Townshend who described The Who as "power pop". In an attempt to cement the terminology, radio DJs steered Buzzcocks' "What Do I Get" and Glen Matlock's new band Rich Kids into the description. Record companies' eagerness for any cash-in saw a wave of bands like Tonight and Yellow Dog appear to complete the genre as well as deciding the time was ripe to inflict The Pleasers on us.

Whether The Pleasers failed to grasp the irony of their position as musical archivists who sought to recreate a sound of yesteryear, their part in the new movement was unclear, but they showed genuine appreciation when sections of the crowd delivered mock screams and cries of "The Rutles". As for their set, it contained original compositions that sounded derivative almost to the point of plagiarism interspersed with covers such as Pete Townshend's "The Kids Are Alright" all delivered with smart suits and shiny guitars and a grateful "cheers" following any applause.

Friday 12th May 1978

Back again at Rafters and in an attempt at keeping the spirit of 1977 alive the Vibrators returned to Manchester to promote their second album V2. Unusually Rafters had begun to operate an overzealous door policy more in keeping with the type of nightclub it had been before the invasion of rock bands. On entry there was an unhappy, though not hostile, individual pleading to no avail that he was nineteen, a claim that seemed about right.

If I was to utilise my place on the guest list I also had to furnish proof of my 22 years. It was approaching a year since we last wrote about The Vibrators in a fanzine, but the band and their record label had generously remembered us.

Since the standard pop punk fayre that had served The Vibrators well over the previous two years, the sound had developed a darker edge that Mick Middles described in a *Sounds* review as, "A fun time Doctors of Madness". Gary Tibbs led the audience through a hand clap as the band delivered their finale "Troops of Tomorrow" suggesting he was destined for bigger and greater things, though sadly for the likeable blokes that were Eddie and Knox, it was not to be with The Vibrators.

★

It was inevitable that the closure of the Electric Circus would leave a cultural void in Manchester's musical landscape. Rafters, like the Students Union venues in Manchester and Salford, continued to stage new wave bands but they had co-existed alongside the Circus and never seemed to share the spontaneous bonhomie that fell into place at the Collyhurst venue.

The Squat Club was probably the nearest contender, offering

the occasional intimate gathering of punk's inner circle, never more so than the night Steve Shy carried a large brown envelope with a message written across it to donate generously to help buy equipment for The Worst. But the size of the venue ensured you would never wake up sweat-drenched and ears ringing having witnessed The Clash or Ramones the night before. As for the bands who packed the Circus on a Sunday night, they had outgrown the club and college circuit with the exception of The Damned whose showbiz aspirations had predictably stalled after their debut LP. I don't know why, I guess these things have got to be.

Ironically there was a ready-made replacement already in Manchester. The Mayflower on Birch Street, Gorton, had, like the Electric Circus, been a former Cinema (the Corona) the building's white-tiled frontage still exhibiting the outward appearance of a palace of a bygone age, even retaining the "Corona" lettering above the entrance. The club was also situated away from the city centre close to Belle Vue Amusement Park and had existed for many years as Stoneground.

Stoneground was a rock venue in the fundamental mode of the Electric Circus that had showcased acts like Sassafras, Babe Ruth and the Heavy Metal Kids several years before the Circus would do likewise and even managed several gigs by the Sensational Alex Harvey Band with Alex. In the early seventies, Stoneground was the place to check out bands such as Can, Gentle Giant, Amon Duul II and the Edgar Broughton Band. Even relics from the sixties such as Love Affair's Steve Ellis, reinvented in a serious rock band called Ellis, and the operatic voiced Arthur Brown, now of Kingdom Come, performed to a standing-only denim clad audience at the early seventies venue.

In fact the Mayflower did present a handful of gigs involving Manchester punk bands in 1978, without becoming a natural habitat for the scene. As part of a short tour following the release of "Another Music in a Different Kitchen" Buzzcocks played two nights supported by The Slits with John Cooper Clarke being added to the Manchester line-up. Also the band christened Stiff Kittens by Pete Shelley (or Richard Boon) and briefly named Warsaw, had finally chosen the name Joy Division to escape confusion with another band named Warsaw Pakt and would appear as part of a frenzied gigging schedule throughout the year.

Furnished with the basic décor characteristic of seventies venues catering to a rock audience, the Mayflower was many things the Circus had been and did in fact emerge as a regular venue, if not really a home from home, the following year. It adopted the name "Funhouse" for certain evenings that peaked with the all-day "Stuff the Superstars" gig on Saturday 29th July 1979, that featured both The Fall and Joy Division along with a host of Greater Mancunian acts including Karl Burns' post-Fall Elti-Fits and Mick Hucknall's pre-Simply Red band Frantic Elevators. The headliners were Stockport's own Distractions who, at that moment in time, had signed a deal with Island Records making them the one featured band who were on a major label.

Sadly my one attempt to visit the Mayflower in 1978 consisted of standing outside the venue with about twenty-five other people, including Stuart Grimshaw, at the time a bandmate of A Certain Ratio's Martin Moscrop in glam punk outfit Alien Tint. Somehow word had reached the waiting crowd that Edinburgh's Rezillos would not be turning up, prompting an exodus to another watering hole where live music was not on the menu.

The Rezillos would swiftly return to the city to play the Apollo following success in both the singles and album charts. Their attendance was confirmed on that occasion by Mark Smith who advised the Scottish band were amongst a growing list who described themselves as "Fall fans". I don't think Smith reciprocated the admiration but his attendance was required as one of the support bands.

the russell club

If the Electric Circus was to have a successor, the Russell Club in Hulme would at least prove a worthy candidate. Or more accurately it would do so on the nights run by Tony Wilson and Alan Erasmus when the club was christened the Factory. These nights would also see the prominence of the artwork of Pete Saville, who would come to define Factory as much as any of the bands or its TV personality co-owner.

Situated in the shadow of the infamous Hulme Crescents, the club's unusual layout saw the bar directly opposite and facing the stage, a point demonstrated at the Christmas gig when surprise guest Pete Shelley pleaded with Buzzcocks' manager Richard Boon to "Please get me a drink." Although still not the most salubrious of venues, there was an upstairs where food was served and you could even spot men in suits and ties dining, albeit those probably involved in the management of the club. Despite the stated capacity of some eight hundred, the downstairs always seemed small and intimate, the stage never far away.

To cement its position as a regular haunt, the Russell Club would also see the re-emergence of fanzine culture as the fabled publication *City Fun* sold its first issues for a bargain, and non-negotiable, ten pence a copy in this club. The earliest issues of *City Fun*, appearing towards the tail end of 1978, fit the customary punk fanzine format as defined in *The Observer* Colour Supplement of the previous year. That being "printed by the very cheapest methods", "stapled together at the corners" and "contents typed or hand written". Early editions had substandard and occasionally illegible printing that, for whatever reason, used a variety of colours of ink on different coloured paper.

From such rudimentary beginnings *City Fun* would become a part of the fabric of Mancunian popular culture, in spite of some purposeful opposition from within the city, not least from

Factory themselves who, among other gripes, took umbrage at a live review that suggested Joy Division, A Certain Ratio and Section 25 "sounded the same". The comparison forced Factory Records to remove *City Fun* from their mailing list as they were "not happy in the role of encouraging third-rate music journalism". In launching such a scathing critique, which by that stage famously included many unsolicited contributions, Factory managed a side-swipe at *Sounds*, the paper that Tony Wilson always considered a poor relation to *NME*.

The first Factory night took place on Friday 19th May 1978 and featured ex-Nosebleed Vini Reilly's new band The Durutti Column and Jilted John, an eighteen-year-old student from Sheffield named Graham Fellows, who was studying drama at Manchester Polytechnic.

Jilted John's project at the time was the recording of two novelty songs, both narratives by the singer in character as the awkward teenager. "Going Steady" was a satisfied recount of his contented life in a steady two month old relationship with a girl called Sharon, whilst the other song entitled "Jilted John" was the tale of the unlucky-in-love teenager of the title who is jilted by his girlfriend Julie. The songs were to be the latest release by Rabid Records with Martin Hannett producing. The record would be issued in a picture sleeve with the front cover depicting the happy couple of "Going Steady" and the back cover showing Jilted John being sneered at by his nemesis Gordon (the Moron) and his ex-girlfriend Julie while eating chips. The record curiously took a while to reach the local shops following Fellows performing it on Granada Reports.

Durutti Column had been put together by Alan Erasmus and Tony Wilson, built from the ashes of Fast Breeder whom Erasmus had recently managed. Moreover Durutti Column were one of several bands who would exist around the Factory bubble like courtiers to label royalty Joy Division.

The Factory nights would also aid the flourishing Liverpool scene with Julian Cope's A Teardrop Explodes featuring on a bill behind Joy Division, as would Orchestral Manoeuvres in the Dark who went as far as releasing their debut single "Electricity" on Factory.

Friday, 26th May 1978

"A Boeing 707 is about to l-a-a-a-a-nd" was the unusual intro from Mark Smith as The Fall returned to the Squat Club for one of many gigs at the venue in support of Rock Against Racism. The remark was in reference to a recent *Sounds* review in which the journalist's appraisal seemed more concerned with the excessive decibels used by The Fall, even suggesting that the difference between punk and Heavy Metal was that HM was the quieter genre. The writer had summarised The Fall's arrival as akin to a jet plane crash landing on the venue.

Before the gig Smith had smiled at the review asking "Don't you think that's great?" thus spawning a convention of accepting good and bad reviews with equal grace, even citing some bad reviews as his favourites. There was a question mark as to whether the writer had mistakenly reviewed another band on the bill as The Fall. Despite Smith's grinning acceptance of the review, he was at pains to point out that there had been a lengthy delay before The Fall's entrance at said gig and one of the earlier acts had made a thunderous noise.

As well as showcasing parochial punk gigs, the Squat also hosted the decidedly un-punk Manchester Mekon, who were present to lend support to The Fall and the Rock Against Racism movement. Originally just The Mekon, this long haired collection of folky rockers had grown out of the Manchester Musicians Collective of which Smith was a keen advocate. A favourite description of them was of failed prog rockers who fell short of delivering anything truly progressive. Thus their even-tempered music allowed them to slip under the radar despite their looking more like a collection who would scoff at the entire punk movement.

The growing confidence within The Fall saw the band developing into a unit that were ready to commit their songs to record with the interplay between Smith and Martin Bramah, who remained despite his desire to make it on his own, growing. Bramah's opening vocal on "Rebellious Jukebox" even served to highlight the strength of Mark Smith's vocal phrasing that was about to be captured in the first of many sessions for the John Peel Show recorded at the Maida Vale Studio in London the following Tuesday.

Thursday 15th June 1978

My only visit to London's legendary venue the Hope and Anchor on Upper Street, Islington. The venue that had staged all the legends of London pub rock including Dr Feelgood was hosting Clayson and the Argonauts. Neither a punk band nor a Manchester band, we were there at the invitation of the band and singer Alan Clayson had opted to fulfil the gig rather than attend one of Bob Dylan's shows at Earls Court, or as he put it, "rather than see Bob Dylan, I'd rather be Alan Clayson."

More crucially the drive back to Reading, where we were staying, somehow steered us from North London into the city and over Tower Bridge, which is where I first heard Jon the Postman's Puerile's "Kowalski of the Seaview" being played on the John Peel Show.

There was a particular reason for the car radio being tuned to the show that night as it saw the broadcast of The Fall's inaugural session with "Rebellious Jukebox" and "Industrial Estate" premièred alongside the more basic rock fayre of "Mother-Sister" and "Futures and Pasts" that resonated over the airwaves as we finally headed northwards out of London and back to Berkshire for an aborted attempt by Mick to interview Clayson and the Argonauts for a *Sounds* feature.

Thursday 13th July 1978

This was the first night of the three-day Manchester Rock Against Racism Carnival in the city's Alexandra Park. A similar event had occurred in London's Victoria Park a few months prior with the Tom Robinson Band headlining over The Clash, X-Ray Spex, Steel Pulse and Patrik Fitzgerald. Steel Pulse would again proffer their support, as the Midland reggae outfit joined the cast that also included Manchester reggae band Exodus alongside The Fall and Buzzcocks. There was also a space for Lancaster's China

Street whose backing for the cause would be reinforced by their debut single being entitled "Rock Against Racism".

The other big name to lend support were tonight's headliners Graham Parker and the Rumour, whose strong showing compensated for the non-appearance of The Fall. The story would later emerge that the show went ahead without the issue of a music license, so effectively those present witnessed Parker and his band run through a practice set in preparation for playing the Picnic at Blackbushe Aerodrome Festival the following Saturday along with Bob Dylan and Eric Clapton.

There had been a degree of scepticism from The Fall camp about the execution of Rock Against Racism's principles, some of which Mark Smith suggested "suck" so their absence was not a complete shock. It was clear The Fall were not about to appear when the compère repeatedly announced "I heard a rumour".

From the opening "Thunder and Rain" through to the encore of "Hold Back the Night" Graham Parker and the Rumour supplied a rich cocktail of blues and soul, the highlight being Parker's donning of an acoustic guitar for "That's What They All Say". The strong Parker voice, backed by the multi-instrumentation within the Rumour, augmented by a guest appearance on saxophone by the formidable figure of Albie Donnelly, provided the perfect blend for a warm summer evening in South Manchester.

And still no sign of The Fall.

Friday, 14th July 1978

Apparently the conspicuous absence of The Fall the previous evening had been unavoidable and, according to Mark Smith, regrettable as he was at pains to apologise to any Fall fans who had ventured into Moss Side expecting the band to play. Tonight the Rock Against Racism Carnival adjourned to UMIST with The Fall supporting Glen Matlock's Rich Kids.

Following Mark Smith's unusually grovelling intro due to Thursday's non-appearance and after a delayed start that was rumoured to be attributed to Smith's refusal to play before the arrival of their "number one" fan Jon the Postman, The Fall swept through a routine, slightly underwhelming set that included an early reading of "It's The New Thing" that would become the band's second single, although their debut, recorded the previous year provisionally for New Hormones, had yet to surface.

Smith also gave an early indication of his blasé attitude to drink and drugs dedicating "I Like To Blow" to Scottish footballer Willie Johnston who had just tested positive for a banned stimulant contained in a medication prescribed for his hay fever at the World Cup Finals in Argentina. The incident cost Johnston his international career but Smith preferred to make light of the footballer's predicament welcoming Johnston to the rock and roll junkie fold.

Unlike Mark Smith, Midge Ure was quick to point out that Rich Kids' purpose in being here was to support Rock Against Racism. Not to plug their forthcoming single and album both of which shared the cumbersome title, "Ghosts of Princes in Towers".

What followed was a lightweight stab at middle of the road blandness. Glen Matlock had always offered a more melodic route to the Pistols otherwise snarling delivery, but with ex-Slik singer Ure now acting as his foil, Rich Kids lacked the cutting edge balance that Rotten or Jones had provided. Where their own material fell into a rut of sameness they borrowed "Here Come the Nice" from the Small Faces, somewhat ironically given Midge Ure's subsequently fervent anti-drugs stance.

Saturday 15th July 1978

Large sections of Manchester congregated back at Alexandra Park on a warm Saturday afternoon. Steve Shy was back in his neighbourhood to advise he had been working on a building site for the past few months and stockpiling some of his earnings with a view to persuading his former charges The Worst to reform.

Exodus played and went. Their mainstream reggae was more palatable than Mark Smith's description of "rubbish" perhaps warranted, as they entertained the arriving hordes who had partaken in the Anti-Nazi League march from the city centre to the park in Moss Side.

As the last marchers filtered into the park, John Maher's drumming intro to "I Don't Mind" was the first indication that Buzzcocks had arrived, with no prior announcement and with many in the crowd assuming that they would be headliners in their own back yard. What reverberated around the park was a throwback to their early days with the reedy sound flowing from the faraway stage around the vast park making Buzzcocks sound like a transistor radio in the distance.

With the band now selecting from a chart career, the action was less forced and predictably less intimate with Pete Shelley attempting to bridge the chasm by glibly referring to their music as "jungle rhythms". Naturally both sides of the current single were performed with Shelley informing that "Love You More", a single that had gained negative reports for its short duration and was still well under two minutes despite it having been extended to please the critics, had penetrated the top forty at number thirty-eight, Shelley wistfully hoped for better in future saying, "maybe next week". The record would peak at number thirty-four in a chart that had been expanded from a top fifty to a top seventy-five in May 1978.

It was the turn of China Street to unfurl their reggae tinged set. From a distance the Lancaster band struggled to make a sufficient impact other than with the zoned out few whose stimulus was not the music or political message within.

It fell to the temperate rhythm of Birmingham's Steel Pulse to soothe the audience on this summer afternoon. With an Island deal having already supplied two hit singles and their debut album about to go top ten, Steel Pulse's growing reputation, together with their harmoniously restrained blend of reggae, made for a smooth passage as the afternoon sunshine began to fade.

The Midlands outfit were familiar guests in Manchester having played the penultimate night at the Electric Circus, even being captured on the ten inch compilation recording "Short Circuit: Live at the Electric Circus" released a few weeks earlier with the herb anthem "Makka Splaff".

To cement a carnival atmosphere that managed to persist

despite sections of the crowd drifting away after Buzzcocks' set, Steel Pulse were joined for the encore of their Island debut single "Ku Klux Klan" by members of the other 3 bands including Steve Diggle on guitar.

Friday 21st July 1978

To mark the second anniversary of the Sex Pistols' gig at the Lesser Free Trade Hall on 20th July 1976, the same venue was commandeered by Granada to record a TV special, only this time there was to be no Sex Pistols or Slaughter and the Dogs.

Despite recording and releasing an album via their Decca contract, Slaughter and the Dogs had announced the first of several break ups, the split actually occurring prior to the release of their debut album "Do It Dog Style".

Likewise the Sex Pistols were no more, having announced their break up in January whilst performing at Winterland Ballroom in San Francisco. The only Pistols album proper, released towards the end of 1977, comprised much of the set delivered at their two Manchester shows in the summer of 1976, suggesting they may have been approaching a spent force when others picked up their mantle.

The business that was the Sex Pistols persisted in the form of their current single "No One Is Innocent" that featured exiled old lag Ronald Biggs yelling vocals recorded in his Brazil hideaway, suggesting "God save Ian Brady", "Myra Hindley" and "Martin Boorman" among others. In two years the band that were said to have altered the course of musical history in Manchester had themselves become a novelty act, which only reinforced the arguments of many serious rock fans where punk was concerned.

In a final show of irony the Sex Pistols were belatedly nominated "Band of the Year" in the 1978 *Sounds* Poll, narrowly pipping Ritchie Blackmore's Rainbow to top spot. The Stranglers and The Clash also entered the fray that was otherwise business as usual with the old guard of Genesis, Led Zeppelin, Yes, Queen, Thin Lizzy and Status Quo making up the numbers. Whether it betrayed a sense of humour or merely confirmed that the best musician category was a pointless assessment given that many readers could not play a note, the best bass included Sid Vicious and Gaye Advert either side of the Wings' Paul McCartney.

Tonight's event was a word of mouth affair with a man on the downstairs door suggesting there was nothing going on here before motioning to go upstairs and handing some large paper tickets when asked "aren't Buzzcocks on?" In fact the night featured two bands whose existence can be traced to the Sex Pistols appearances of 1976 with Pete Shelley now fronting Buzzcocks and their original singer Howard Devoto opening proceedings with Magazine.

Both bands had, like the Sex Pistols, released their debut album. Unlike the surviving Pistols they continued to plough a musical furrow with a focus on creating music of substance. Magazine had released a stunningly powerful debut single in January "Shot By Both Sides" quickly followed by the admirable "Touch and Go" before the release of their long player "Real Life". Mark Smith had advised Devoto of his preference for the less accessible "Touch and Go" to which an indignant Devoto apparently described "Shot By Both Sides", originally a Shelley and Devoto composition to which Devoto had added the lyrics, as "the greatest record ever made".

Not to be outdone, Buzzcocks issued one of their optimum moments, also in January, having finally crafted the definitive version of "What Do I Get". Their equally fine follow up was the result of United Artists lifting the track "I Don't Mind" from the album "Another Music in a Different Kitchen". In a nod back to the days of "prog' rock" the band had been at pains to stress that the LP contained no singles, a move that may have been to safeguard Buzzcocks from Pete Shelley's own accusation at The Damned's album debut being reliant on two previously issued singles. To lighten the issue the advertising for the single would self-mockingly refer to the action as a "marketing ploy". Either way it would join their strong procession of singles and earn Buzzcocks the Top of the Pops appearance that had paradoxically evaded Slaughter and the Dogs, though not Magazine who had also mimed on the show with "Shot By Both Sides".

Although both Devoto and Shelley would cite Velvet Underground, The Stooges and Captain Beefheart among their influences, Magazine betrayed a Roxy Music/David Bowie flavour whereas Buzzcocks had evolved into an all-round pop group whose development had been likened by Paul Morley to sixties beat groups such as The Searchers or Herman's Hermits.

Footage of both bands would form the link on the Pistols anniversary Granada TV programme that featured Tony Wilson interviewing both Devoto and Shelley on the story so far of both bands following Buzzcocks formation that night in 1976.

Buzzcocks' set would culminate with Tony Wilson mounting the stage to question whether the audience had noticed the diminutive stature of Pete Shelley before announcing a reunion. What followed was the inevitable coming together of the Shelley/Devoto axis with Steve Garvey sitting out the final number allowing Steve Diggle to resume bass duties and Shelley to provide sole guitar and backing vocals as Buzzcocks reverted to their original line up to again perform The Troggs number, "I Can't Control Myself" as they had done for the first time on this stage two years before.

Friday 18th August 1978

My first visit to the Russell Club was for a bill that listed a protracted line-up of Giro (or Gyro as they would be billed at Eric's in Liverpool the following evening), Ed Banger, Gordon the Moron, Jilted John and John Cooper Clarke. The evening was billed as a Rabid Records night, although Clarke had risen above the local label to be signed to CBS and Gordon the Moron had not featured on the label as an artist in his own right.

A packed downstairs saw a few old faces including Paul Doyle, whose first response at being reacquainted after more than a year was the offer to share a joint if he could find somewhere discreet to roll his stash and Jon the Postman who had, for now at least, reverted to his original role as spectator.

For whatever reason John Cooper Clarke failed to appear as did Jilted John. Since his previous appearance, the Rabid Records single had been flipped to make "Jilted John" the A-side and licensed through EMI, a union that would provide the drama student with a top ten hit single and Top of the Pops appearance, so maybe he had bigger fish to fry at that moment. Those who didn't were Gordon the Moron and his illusory girlfriend Julie.

Gordon the Moron was portrayed by Bernard Kelly, a six-foot five-inch individual from Didsbury in Manchester, described by Graham Fellows as "a proper punk" and "like an Andy Warhol figure". Kelly had appeared on the single sleeve and performed a hand jive alongside Jilted John on the Top of the Pops appearance. Tonight he had utilised the character for a comedic musical routine accompanied by a Rabid in-house band and the young lady who portrayed Julie on the single sleeve.

Gordon would become a regular figure at the Factory nights but for now his act consisted of adopting an American accent complete with a regular, "Thank you, you're beautiful" in between pastiche numbers.

His take on Magazine's "The Light Pours Out Of Me" somewhat banally became "The Light Pours Out Of My Arse" with a further dig in Howard Devoto's direction, this time his receding hairline, with "Boredom" becoming "Baldy". In between Gordon taunted current flavour of the month Devo with "I can't get me back to Akron" and, despite the triteness of the humour employed, managed to entertain and amuse during a brief set.

Ed Banger had reinvented himself as a solo performer. He retained a backing band who would remain uncredited although they appeared to be more or less the same assorted musicians who had just played behind Gordon the Moron. Having previously gone to the lengths of removing the "Ed Banger and" from the original band name in a bid for serious deliberation, Eddie Garrity had now decided that as a madcap solo artist, Ed Banger was the way forward.

What the solo Ed Banger delivered was a series of quirky and loose observational snippets that nestled somewhere between songs and mischievous horseplay. As a taster he had a lengthy semi-spoken declamation recounting the tale of a loaf of bread from the oven to its journey and evacuation through the human digestive system told from the bread's viewpoint.

There was also a single in the offing via Rabid Records entitled "Kinnel Tommy" an armchair fan's commentary on an average footballer – passable when performed live but maybe lacking sufficient intelligent wit to sustain appeal for the duration of a single.

For tonight Ed Banger was, like Gordon the Moron, entertaining and likeable enough. Unlike headliners Giro who ploughed a furrow through rock music that Mick Middles would define in a *Sounds* review as "rock theatre". Steve Forster in *New Manchester Review* described Giro as one of Manchester's most capable bands suggesting that a muffled PA system had contributed to their off-colour performance.

Thursday 7th September 1978

The Drones had parted company with guitarist Gus Gangrene, who was said to have found a position in the early incarnation of Blackpool punk band Skrewdriver. Gangrene had briefly fronted the band Bitch, whose short tenure had seen them support The Clash at a low key appearance at Rafters in July, the night after The Clash again brought the sound of the Westway to the Apollo. Bitch's set on the night had been described by Steve Forster in *New Manchester Review* as a mixture of punk and pop with snatches of heavy metal, with particular praise for a cover of The Shangri-Las' "Leader of the Pack" that Forster labelled "remarkably good."

It was reported that The Clash road manager had refused to allow The Freshies on the bill at Rafters, despite the band being asked along by Dougie James who was promoting the gig. It was left to Freshies singer Chris Sievey to comment, "The Clash will never play one of our gigs again."

Another ex-Drone was keyboard player Mike Koman, whose tenure had lasted less than eight months. Tonight they would play the Russell Club as a three piece with Mike Drone handling guitar and vocals, and bassist Steve Cundall still weighing in with the occasional lead voice such as on the cover of "Then I Kissed Her" that had supplanted "Be My Baby" as the band's Spector tribute. A smiling Pete Howells greeted Mick and I shortly before The Drones continued where they had left off at the start of the year.

1978 had seen Buzzcocks shave the charts and now saw them playing the Apollo. The Fall continued to foster a reputable status, even if their recorded output had stalled at the solitary "Bingo Masters" EP that had only recently gained release via Step Forward records. John Cooper Clarke had signed a major record deal and issued a single "Post War Glamour Girl" that saw his poetry coupled with an electronic disco beat and his wrapping of poetry within a synthesized landscape arranged by Martin Hannett would continue on his "Snap, Crackle and Bop" LP later in the year but as Mark Smith observed, "they don't know what to do with him". The harshest move was to include the Salford rhymester as support to Be-Bop Deluxe on their Drastik Plastik Musik tour, a booking that would put him back in a firing line similar to his attempts to perform at the Vortex, when music fans in such places as Glasgow and Bradford were unprepared and unwilling to endure some Dylan lookalike regaling them with poetry.

By contrast The Drones had bided their time following their ill-judged "Further Temptations" cabaret roadshow and were back in the familiar territory of playing it straight to a club audience. Opening without any preamble and launching straight into a new song with a chorus that asked a question along the lines of "What will it be like in twenty years from now?" first impressions were of a band that still strove to make their music presentable, despite Mike Drone later confessing that he was more a rhythm guitarist than a lead.

As more new songs emerged that contained memorable hooks, there was a growing feeling that The Drones were perhaps equipped to ride the second wave in a traditional manner, despite repeated calls for the old stuff which drew a reassuring "your family favourites will follow" from the singer.

Before the "family favourites" there was time for Mike Drone to explain the origins of a recent composition inspired by a TV documentary of the same name before unleashing "Johnny

Go Home" a song that both Howells brothers would later show boundless enthusiasm for, even describing it as, "one of the best songs they ever wrote" when re-recording it in 1997 following a reformation the previous year.

The evening concluded as a modest triumph for the returning Drones, although the band's deserved encore of "My Generation" was preceded by Mike Drone's sad announcement that Who drummer and self-confessed Worst fan Keith Moon had died that evening at the age of just thirty-two.

Thursday 12th October 1978

It was the turn of Wayne County and the Electric Chairs to play the Russell Club with the artist in transition. In fact the show was delivered fully in the character of Jayne County despite the billing suggesting the artist remained Wayne.

Naturally the set retained a huge element of brashness but played in the female persona, as opposed to the burlesque drag of previous years, there was a curious slickness to the performance that allowed the band to introduce several new numbers early into the set. Even the finale of "(If You Don't Wanna Fuck Me Baby) Fuck Off!!" seemed to stop short of complete outrage as County and the Chairs entered the next phase of a career that would further their reciprocal love affair with this city.

Monday 16th October 1978

Monday was now a regular night at the Band On The Wall and it was the chance for Ed Banger to prove his worth as a solo artist when playing as the main act. Although he would drop the band in favour of an electronic beat the following year, for now his act relied on the traditional line up of guitar, bass and drums, with his old Nosebleeds cohort Toby Toman behind the drum kit.

At least the genial confines of the Band On The Wall, coupled with the oddball humour that was now a core ingredient of the act, ensured that Ed Banger's days of attacking members of the audience were behind him. Not that Paul Morley was available for a re-match, Morley having curiously declined to evaluate Ed Banger in an *NME* review of a Rabid Records night in

Liverpool, citing his close friendship with the singer as the reason.

Ed Banger's delivery was oddly restrained tonight with a possible explanation being his revelation that EMI were in the throes of attempting to do for Ed Banger what had been done for Rabid stablemate Jilted John in licensing the "Kinnel Tommy" single through its major label. Perhaps the artist now considered his material could stand alone without improvisation.

Present tonight were Tony Wilson and his Factory partner Alan Erasmus. Wilson was amiable enough, requesting Mick to inform "Eddie" that he "thought he was entertaining", although he chose to tackle Mick Middles regarding his loyalty to *Sounds* suggesting it was the *NME* that held the credibility in the music press.

Ed Banger gave a knowing laugh at Mick's relayed message from Wilson, although he had an air of jovial contentment with his current position. Perhaps this was his niche within the music industry, even if the EMI deal would fail to deliver.

Friday 20th October 1978

One of many Factory nights at the Russell Club that would showcase a variety of what was becoming termed "post-punk" fronted by the main men of Factory, Joy Division.

The support were both of the electronic variety opening with The Tiller Boys, who were another vague concept, or as Richard Boon would define them "this conceit". Boon would liken them to The Negatives, who he had joined as a latter-day member, as "a group that didn't really exist". Boon's demarcation of The Tiller Boys and The Negatives as "fiction" referred to their playing of the media rather than a complete lack of existence. Whereas The Negatives had maintained among other claims to have recorded an EP, The Tiller Boys would invent numerous gigs, commonly at different locations on the same night.

The given line-up of Peter Shelley, Francis Cookson and Eric Random admit to having played around four gigs, of which Shelley featured in two of them according to Random. There was no evidence of Pete Shelley's presence tonight as the live show consisted of taped sounds played without the obvious presence on stage of any actual performers.

A more apparent presence were Cabaret Voltaire whose jerking electronic sound would draw early use of the term "industrial". The insistent beat within Cabaret Voltaire's music/muzak was accentuated by a flickering lightshow and the electronically enhanced vocals echoing the dark skies and factory sounds of the steel industry of their native Sheffield.

Having persisted, despite the reluctant acceptance of the band previously known as Warsaw, Joy Division were beginning to forge an individualism that had looked unlikely back at the Electric Circus or the Squat Club the previous year. A further endorsement came from Mark Smith, who singled out Joy Division's "At a Later Date" from the "Short Circuit Live at the Electric Circus" LP as a highpoint of an otherwise disappointing memento of the final nights of the Circus.

Joy Division's persistence had caused Mick Middles to refer to them as "the long standing Joy Division" in a light-hearted round-up of all things Mancunian in *Zigzag*, a descriptor with which Rob Gretton, now managing said band, took umbrage, issuing in turn a challenge to come and sample his charges in whom he had paramount confidence.

Gretton had always been a helpful ally back in the fanzine days and Mick was now a regular northern contributor to *Sounds*' live pages, so the mission was accepted and a review of Joy Division at the Band on the Wall written of the same gig on 4th September 1978 was coincidentally reviewed by Paul Morley in the *NME*. The favourable review conceded that the band's artistic turnaround had resulted from tenacity including a description of Peter Hook, who had famously and instinctively made the purchase of a bass guitar his first priority after seeing the Sex Pistols, as a bassist "who could eat Jean-Jacques for breakfast".

There was a further development, with Gretton now eager for Mick to write the first feature on Joy Division in the national press. Before the main act appeared, a now bearded Gretton was on hand to rearrange a date for Mick to interview the band at

Tony (T J) Davidson's Practice and Recording Studio on Little Peter Street where JD rehearsed. A previously aborted rendezvous had resulted in Gretton missing a home match at Maine Road, a forfeit that the devout Manchester City supporter accepted with grace and humour.

And so Joy Division appeared amid flawless lighting and sound. The band who had laboured under the guise of Warsaw were now a tightly synchronised unit who left nothing to the fates, with the composed drums, the sharp pounding bass, the intricately honed guitar and the deep baritone all blending into a singular hum.

The first hand experience of the crafted sound that flowed steadily from the stage, was that the doomy though not depressing timbre of the music provided a clear channel through which these four men would deliver their music. There were no tapes or synthesizers in use but the close co-operation between voice and instruments gave the music a recurring pulse that befitted Ian Curtis's rigid yet flowing dance moves.

The main reservation about the worth of this band was how such an unswerving approach would create any individual gems. The impression left was of an overall musical concept rather than a collection of individual tracks that could stand alone. Such misgivings aside, it was fair to say that on tonight's showing Joy Division had joined The Fall, Magazine and Buzzcocks as graduates of the Manchester punk scene who had eclipsed the "punk band" pigeon-hole.

The sudden development of this four-piece, who had shown little or no promise to the vast majority of observers during their Warsaw apprenticeship, was something of an enigma. The parochial support offered during 1977, most notably from Paul Morley who had initially suggested Warsaw had the aura of Rod Stewart's Faces and would doubtless develop that force into something more singular, had never been repaid in their formative year and was swiftly amended with Morley tentatively suggesting that their destiny may remain as a support band.

Although the observation made by Rob Gretton that people had taken their eye off the band in the first half of 1978 was reasonably accurate, there was a rationale in that, despite having witnessed Warsaw almost as many times the previous year as the swiftly burgeoning Fall, they failed to leave any indelible imprint on the memory.

Whether my failure to grasp last year's Warsaw reflected a shortfall in my perception was open to debate given a couple of factors. Warsaw had performed "At a Later Date" on the closing night of the Electric Circus within an extremely condensed set. The song "Novelty", that would appear on the B-side of "Transmission", Joy Division's debut single for Factory the following year, had existed in some form during the days of Warsaw, the lyrics having appeared in Jeff Noon's *Noisy People* fanzine.

For tonight what I had witnessed was a band who would attribute their formation to having witnessed the Sex Pistols some two years earlier, before the less influential members of the Mancunian community who would wait for Bill Grundy and the Anarchy Tour to alert them to the punk phenomena. For their part Joy Division's only palpable debt seemed to be to The Doors, their music bearing no resemblance to the Sex Pistols or for that matter, the band who assiduously plied their trade lower down the bill as Warsaw in 1977.

Almost a decade later guitarist Arthur Kadmon, of Manicured Noise, Ludus and The Distractions, would accuse The Doors of being "responsible for so much crap in music". Whilst Jim Morrison and company almost certainly inspired one too many "goth" bands, perhaps Joy Division were the exception that justified the charge. Some 38 years later sound engineer and Deeply Vale Organiser Chris Hewitt would also question the level of importance that history has granted Joy Division.

"There's all these outsider bands and they all get written out. There was a time when The Drones played to more people than Joy Division. The Fall are another one. A lot of people tell me The Fall were a better band than Joy Division and they've got the longevity."

Saturday 21st October

Another date with The Fall, who tonight headed a bill playing a benefit for *The Leveller* magazine at Manchester Polytechnic. It was also an opportunity to reacquaint with Jeff Noon who had recently returned from time in London displaying a more luxuriant hairstyle than his former punk look. Jeff had always been a devotee of The Fall and, for his part, Mark Smith had praised Jeff's fanzine *Noisy People* suggesting "he should have done another".

Despite their one single release to date, The Fall had developed a level of assuredness where they were not above indulging an audience, they played a set that had evolved between their inception and late '78 and would furnish their debut album that appeared early the following year.

But tonight belonged to Stockport's Distractions. Described by Steve Forster of the *New Manchester Review* as "one of Manchester's best kept secrets" and praised by Mark Smith following a support slot to The Fall at Droylsden's Concorde Suite back in June where Smith suggested the band's set was "primarily covers but delivered with considerable power and prowess".

Here The Distractions played an original set with a strong commercial flavour that may have suggested a recognisable familiarity to Mark Smith's ears. But the factor that set The Distractions' well-crafted pop sound apart was the formidable vocal of singer Mike Finney. Described at the time by Mick Middles in a *Sounds* review as "a superb rock'n'roll singer" the sound of Finney's finely-tuned voice resonated around the venue.

Kevin Rowland and Mick Hucknall had both played in punk groups prior to forming bands whose calling card would be soul music. The Distractions should have been ahead of the game having no need to reinvent themselves but sadly the rise to pop stardom never materialised despite the best efforts of the music press.

Saturday 28th October

A return to a familiar haunt to witness two local bands. The Trend hailed from the Tameside area of Greater Manchester whilst support band The Freshies were from the then lesser-known area of Timperley, a suburb that would gain future fame as the locale of Freshies' frontman Chris Sievey's alter ego Frank Sidebottom.

But tonight was more about the venue as it marked a return to the re-opened former cinema on Collyhurst Street that had existed as the Electric Circus up to a year ago. Whatever factors had forced the local council and fire service to deem it necessary to close the Circus, forcing the building's short-lived usage as a cabaret club, presumably they were no longer an issue as the place was back on the circuit trading as the Venue.

There was no queue to gain access, although a respectable if modest number had made the journey into Collyhurst to assess the bands and venue or perhaps both. The Electric Circus backdrop was no longer in place behind the stage, although the layout was surprisingly untouched since the heady nights of 1976 and 1977. The one familiar feature was the sight of Kevin Cummins stood by the stage holding a camera.

The Freshies had been dismissed in the press as just another third-rate punk band, a strange descriptor for a group who displayed more than a nod towards The Beatles. Their song-writing craft contained intelligent arrangements around some strong melodies that could well have helped them onto the punk bandwagon but their choice of song titles such as "Ballrooms and Moon" or "Two of the Same Girl" suggested their interests lay elsewhere.

An oddity of The Freshies' shows was the playing of several numbers consecutively announcing all the songs at the outset. That may have implied a reluctance to engage with the audience but Chris Sievey was more than happy to communicate with the front rows, dedicating a number to an audience member who identified himself as "Head banger number one".

Meeting the band would not involve ascending the stairs behind the bar, as Mick had arranged to meet with Chris Sievey who was stood by the bar. Sievey asked what we were drinking informing us "that would be ten pence" before purchasing the drinks supplementing the shortfall!

Sievey was eager to inform us of his main mission for the evening, which was the avoidance of a record company A and R man who was desperate to sign The Freshies. The singer and main songwriter did not consider his band were ready to start the process of making records, although The Freshies had already recorded an EP that had been released on their own Razz Label. The record was packaged in a plain white sleeve, information handwritten thereon and the label featured a design of hand painted circles drawn on a spinning record deck. By contrast The Trend delivered a more confident and professional set even if the music nestled within safer parameters. Their poppy edged and memorable tunes were best summed up by Chris Sievey's description of them as "Sex Pistols crossed with the Boomtown Rats."

★

The second coming of the Electric Circus as the Venue was a short lived and inconsequential episode that never saw the glory days return. The highpoint was probably the Sunday night appearance of Joy Division who, like the previous year as Warsaw, remained one of the hardest working bands on the circuit.

The end of an era happened early the following year when the club disappeared from the *New Manchester Review* weekly listings and ultimately from existence. Symbolically it was on a visit to the North Manchester home Mike Drone shared with his wife Maggie and their baby son Michael John Junior that I first caught sight of the flattened landscape where Manchester's inner circle had queued to sample so many life-changing moments, including the first of The Drones' seven appearances.

The journey to discuss the current activity of the post-Valer Drones and listen to a recording of their prospective single "Can't See" as well as delivering a painted portrait of Mike, took us via Rochdale Road out of Manchester involving a stopover in Collyhurst for Mike to drop off a hired van, which is where the reality dawned that Collyhurst Street had lost its only venue to the demolition crew.

index

acknowledgements

Thanks are due to the following for their help and involvement in producing this book: Martin Greenwood, Chris Hewitt, Mick Middles, Steve Shy and Francis Taylor.

Thanks also to the following for their involvement and inspiration at various times: Chris Bailey, Una Baines, Ed Banger, Kay Bateman, Howard Bates, Dave Bentley, Bernard, Richard Boon, Graham Brooks, Ann Burke, Knox Carnochan, Richard Chang, Hugh Cornwell, Jayne County, Peter Crookes, Christine Crowther, Kevin Cummins, Steve Cundall, Garth Davies, Juliet deVee, Howard Devoto, Steve Diggle, Paul Doyle, M J Drone, John (Eddie) Edwards, John Ellis, Vini Faal, Philip Fletcher, Gus Gangrene, Rob Gretton, Ivor Hay, Peter Howells, Jon the Postman, Ed Keupper, John Maher, Paul Morley, Jeff Noon, Vini Reilly, Denise Shaw, Pete Shelley, Chris Sievey, Mark Smith, Chris Staines, Steve Strange, Adrian Thrills, Gary Tibbs, Toby Toman, Traci, Geoff Travis, Maur Vanian, Venom Vindictive, John Webster and Woody.

The following publications have provided stimulation or empowerment: *Buzzcocks the Complete History* by Tony McGartland, *England's Dreaming* by Jon Savage, *Factory: the Story of the Record Label* by Mick Middles, *I Swear I Was There* by David Nolan, *Imprinting the Sticks* by Robert Dickinson, *Joy Division: Piece by Piece* by Paul Morley, *Looking For the Light Through the Pouring Rain* by Kevin Cummins, *Not Abba* by Dave Haslam, *48 Thrills*, *City Fun*, *Girl Trouble*, *God is a Newt*, *Gun Rubber*, *New Manchester Review*, *New Pose*, *NME*, *Noisy People*, *Out There*, *Plaything*, *Shy Talk*, *Situation 3*, *Sniffin' Glue*, *Sounds*, *White Stuff* and *Zigzag*.

Finally a huge thank you to Manchester City Library for their complete collection of *New Manchester Reviews* from the period and to all those who supply so much valuable information on the world wide web, in particular Manchester Digital Music Archive and its many contributors without whom etc.

appendix I

ghast up - issue one

MARTIN'S PAGE

I was beginning to think that this mag was gonna stay just another of my crackpot ideas, like the one I had when I was about fifteen of building a recording studio in a tree house. There's a guy called Tim in Oldham who advertised in Manchester's Virgin shop that he was trying to start a fanzine. Sorry Tim, but we lost your address. If you'd like to get in touch though, we would like to meet you, even if you've got a mag together now.

As for this issue, we've got an interview with The Buzzcocks. One of the few groups who have fitted naturally into this new wave, just by being themselves. I do hope they carry on writing great songs, even though Howard Devoto has left, and they continue to be themselves.

I've also reviewed two bands at the Circus, AC/DC and Ultravox. The latter was a surprise on the night. You see a band called The Enid were supposed to play but for some reason didn't, so instead we got Ultravox. It's a shame really cos it could've been a great night, if half the audience hadn't gone to see The Enid, and subsequently been disappointed, while Ultravox fans stayed in or went to the pub. Still I'm not gonna knock the Circus, I'm sure it's a lot of hassle to get hold of these bands, and the Circus have layed on a pretty good schedule for the near future. I just hope there's no aggro at any of the gigs (no heckling either you hippies), cos if there is we all know what'll happen. We just won't be seeing 'em again in Manchester. Any band that's got anything to do with new wave'll just be too hot to handle. But to look on the bright side (y'know no aggro, just bloody good gigs, like The Heartbreakers at the Oaks), then I reckon things could really happen here in Manchester. Sorry to go on about all this, I mean our audience on the Anarchy tour were pretty good, I think. Oh you know what I mean, let's make the London bands wanna play Manchester. The Damned should've regained their confidence hear anyway after the tour with T.Rex.

I was gonna put a review in of the Iggy Pop concert at the Apollo, written by a guy called Big Bad Brinner. He's just a kid in the audience who really digged our Ig. It's a shame that never came off really. If we've got space I'm definitely gonna do something like it in the next issue. Talking of Iggy, which we were a minute ago, if you wanna know quite a few facts on the guy, score a copy of the mag PENETRATION No 10. It's got a good feature for those who haven't know him for too long. Like the two guys who were stood next to me and Mick Middles in Neild and Hardy's shop in Stockport, saying "eh they've got both THE STOOGES and FUNHOUSE, don't faint.", and equally stupid remarks. I wouldn't mind but they were old enough to have got 'em first time around. Enough about boring gets anyway, they'll probably make similar noises when they see this mag on the counter at their local newsagent.

Oh yeh if any fanzines wanna free ad. Let us have the details. In fact if you want, you could send us a copy (cheeky), and if we like 'em we'll say nice things about 'em.

MARTIN

AC/DC live at The Circus

The crowd were a good bunch to start with. Sorry if I go on about crowds, but they are the most important part of the gig anyway. But most of this audience, with the exception of a few

hecklers at the back, were right behind the band. The deejay at the Circus did a fair bit towards helping the atmosphere, by playing a good cross-section of stuff, including "Anarchy", "Neat Neat Neat" and the incredible "Boredom" by The Buzzcocks.

Anyway on to the band, and what a band. The opener "Live Wire" one of their tried and tested numbers, really got the crowd moving. It's hard not to move to these Scottish-Aussie rockers, the band are so stimulating. Yeah that's the word to describe Angus' guitar work and spastic-like movements. On their last gig, I found Bon Scott's stance, a bit too much like Alex

Harvey. Okay I'll not go into that, it's history now anyway. This time he had a great personality on stage, and handled the crowd almost immaculately. He was good at being himself. They played a few numbers off a forthcoming album, but even these received as much crowd reaction as their standard numbers. The set, naturally included the classic "High Voltage" and the perverts anthem "She's Got The Jack" (V.D. to you).

As I've already said there were some hecklers at the back, but Bon Scott chose to ignore them, rather than shout them down (I'm sure he could have). I don't think they bothered the band who had too much going for them tonight. Towards the end as Angus prepared for his traditional piggy back on Bon's shoulders, Bon had to clear a few fans from the edge of the stage,

but nothing nasty, everyone co-operated, even the hippies. After his venture into the crowd Angus finally fell over on the stage, in what looked like an epileptic fit, but he seemed to recover quickly.

And that was it; no encore, which probably would have been "Baby Please Don't Go" accompanied by Angus diving into the crowd, and the roadies panicking with the wires. However that spectacle was denied to this crowd. Still it was an exciting set, this band have got guts, and despite having two albums released, haven't yet joined the realms of the elite. They're still very much a people's band, raw and exciting. Terrific stuff.

THE VIBRATORS AT THE APOLLO

Considering the fact that most of the audience were only there to see DAVID BOWIE, the VIBRATORS did bloody well. It was miraculous that they survived at all under enormous pressures. Pressures like the size of the place. They should stick to playing small clubs, pub cellars etc. not dirty great concert halls like the Apollo.

The crowd should be up on it's feet not politely clapping, like a bleedin' bunch of morons. It could end up in a Led Zep at Earls Court type of crap. If it does then I'm afraid we are wasting our time. That point is the reason for writing this review so long after the event. Anyway they played WE VIBRATE, I WANNA BE YOUR NAZI and a great version of WHIPS AND FURS. The latter sounding so much better than on the dreary single. They were monotonous in parts, I cannot deny that, but I'll havta see em in the proper surroundings before I can tell how good or bad they really are.

THE VIBRATORS play the electric circus on April 9th.
Mick.

MICK'S PAGE

THE Ed. has let me loose on this page to write a few things that are bugging me. Firstly I've a confession to make. I've never seen the SEX PISTOLS. Martin has and it gets me bloody annoyed. There must be hundreds of kids like me who are waiting patiently for a chance to see em. What right have councillors etc. got to stop the PISTOLS from touring. It's more than just annoying it's, oh never mind you know the rest. We are gonna try and interview em sometime there are loads of points that us northerners would like to know.

My head's still buzzing from the HEARTBREAKERS gig last night. It was terrific. (See Martin's review). Talking of Martin's reviews havya read his review of AC/DC. I think that they are a great live band but on record they are shit. The lyrics are pathetic and seemed all cleaned up. In fact the two albums have no balls. (As Bon would say).

Remember the DAMNED gig at the Electric Circus, well I've just got to write about the hippy majority that gave them a simply charming chorus of SHIT, SHIT, SHIT. (Good title for a song that innit.) I thought the DAMNED were pretty good and the few kids who agreed with me were continually stopped from enjoying themselves by the bouncers. (I think they were bouncers anyway). They seemed to think that the kids had no right to like the band. What made this all the more ridiculous is that these same hippies were leaping about like nutters to records like 'PARANOID' ten minutes later. I don't think that these songs are all that far removed from the DAMNED'S music do you?

The scene has improved slightly since then, I think.

Some good bands coming our way soon. Don't miss The RAMONES or CHERRY VANILLA.

I hope you are not too critical of our first issue. We are still ironing out a few problems, if you don't like it then start your own. If you do then the next issue will be brilliant. (HONEST). We will have a decent camera for a start.

If you have any questions or nasty remarks to tell us, don't hesitate to write. We will answer all letters and if the ed. likes them we may print a few.

I would like to dedicate this piece to all the kids who live in small villages way out in the country and rarely get a chance to see any new wave bands. I know coz I lived in one for a year and it was really frustrating. All I can suggest is that you start a band, behave like nice little boys, score a gig at the church hall and suddenly blast the vicar through the windows with a rendition of ANARCHY. More seriously take your records to the local disco and DEMAND to hear them. Or make a few trips to town, see the bands and start a fanzine. DO SOMETHING TO MAKE YOURSELF HEARD.

MICK MIDDLES

THE BUZZCOCKS

An interview

Somehow we managed to find a fairly quiet pub in the centre of Manchester, and that aint easy. The landlady hated us from the moment we entered. Anyway we ignored her and got this great interview with STEVE DIGGLE, JOHN MAHER, GARTH and the new addition to Manchester's homeless PETE SHELLEY.

US (That's me and Martin). "Do you play all your own material?"

PETE "Yes; well what happens with a lot of bands at the moment is, that they just recycle other people's songs. That's just like playing records on a Juke Box. Also a lot of bands get up on stage, dress up a bit and become PUNK, which is a dirty word with us."

US "And us."

PETE "Yeah well they sing a few extremely banal songs, a couple of Velvet's numbers, and worse still Slaughter and the Dogs, who don't stop at that, they do things like 'Jumping Jack Flash'."

US "So you don't like Slaughter and the Dogs?"

PETE "Oh they are OK, I mean they are good musicians, but they are not progressive. Sorry that's a terrible word innit. Anyway, unless you play all your own stuff you are just recycling other people's ideas."

US "What equipment have you got?"

PETE "Oh I've got my Starway guitar, which I got for £18 with the case. I once threw it on the floor and it smashed in half."

US "So what do ya use now?"

PETE "I still use it."

GARTH "Gibson have got nothing on it."

PETE "We've got an Audition back-up guitar which Garth uses."

STEVE "I've got a £17 bass. The Audition has a set of strings that has been passed down from generation to generation. We can't afford a set."

JOHN "I've got a bin lid as a cymbal."

GARTH "Yeah he has, that's true."

JOHN "These three were practising songs in Salford, and I joined in and started banging a bin lid. So I keep it now."

Somehow the conversation turns to Johnny Thunders and the Heartbreakers.

PETE "They are nice guys, they'll talk to you y'know (make a note of that). On the first gig we played with 'em, I talked to their manager, the famous Leee Black Childers, who did the inside sleeve for "Diamond Dogs" ("My God fame at last." Someone chirps in.) And he said that Johnny Thunders liked my guitar so much that he was going to saw off half of his, to make it look like mine."

STEVE "Except that you can't do that with a Gibson can ya?"

US "Bloody rich these Yanks. What was the idea with the New Hormones label?"

PETE "We just wanted to be in control; not have anyone tell us what to do. We can release whatever suits us."

US "Can we expect more songs soon?"

<u>PETE</u> "Yeah we've written loads."

<u>US</u> "How about an album?"

<u>PETE</u> "We'll only do an album if we have twelve or so songs, that are as good as each other. Not like most bands, who make two singles, and then fill the rest of the album with anything."

<u>STEVE</u> "Just look at the Damned album."

<u>US</u> "What was it like down at the Harlesden Roxy?"

<u>PETE</u> "It's not the Roxy, it's the Coliseum."

<u>US</u> "Oh did you read the N.M.E. report on that?"

<u>PETE</u> "Yeah Nick Kent. He's just cheesed off, because before the Damned became the Damned, Kent used to sing for them, but they kicked him out and got Dave Vanian – or so rumour has it."

<u>US</u> "Were Subway Sect any good?"

<u>PETE</u> "No." (They all agreed) "<u>We</u> didn't think too much of them anyway. The Slits were really good though."

We showed them the review of "Spiral Scratch" in "Ripped and Torn"

<u>US</u> "Who is Martin Zero?"

<u>GARTH</u> "It was the first and last time he produced the Buzzcocks."

<u>US</u> "Careful it's all going down in print y'know."

<u>GARTH</u> "Hello Martin."

<u>STEVE</u> "The reason for the razor blade thing is that the kids thought society was abusing them, so they abused themselves."

<u>JOHN</u> "What's he talking about?"

<u>GARTH</u> "Lying sod."

<u>US</u> "The Stranglers' review isn't as good as yours in 'Ripped and Torn'."

<u>JOHN</u> "Not much competition for us."

<u>STEVE</u> "Their money is better than ours."

<u>US</u> "They've reviewed Mud down here."

GARTH "'Tiger Feet', it's great 'Tiger Feet'."

STEVE "I had Athletes Foot, that was bad enough."

The actual interview would have probably filled an entire magazine, so it's been edited slightly.

The Buzzcocks have been together since about last June. The group were then Howard Devoto-Vocals, Pete Shelley-Guitar, Steve Diggle-Bass and John Maher-Drums. Howard left the band and about a month ago Garth (just Garth) joined the band. As most of you know, they formed their own label, "New Hormones" and released an E.P. or as they put it a mini L.P., in that they dropped the concept of a single being an A side, with just anything on the B side. "Spiral Scratch" is four tracks "Breakdown/Times Up/Boredom/Friends Of Mine", all of which are well worth the £1 it'll cost ya. It's not that easy to get hold of, but you should be able to get it in Manchester without too much messin'; that is of course, if you've not got it already. If your friendly neighbourhood record dealer says they can't get it, tell 'em to get in touch with New Hormones, 182 Oxford Road, Manchester M13 9GP, who of course supply it.

You can also catch them live at The Band On The Wall, Swan Street, Manchester on April 11th, but get there early cos it's quite a small place and liable to get packed. Not too early though, I mean we wanna get in......

MICK MIDDLES

L.P. REVIEWS

TELEVISION-MARQUEE MOON

It's so easy to be hailed "genius" just by writing lyrics that nobody understands. Yet everyone pretends to understand, because it's cool to like TELEVISION. Tom Verlaine is not a genius, he just writes good songs. Why make him out to be more than he is? The *NME/Sounds* mob try to make out this album's a classic, it's not. That's a shame coz it so easily could have been. Three songs, "Venus", "Prove It" and "Friction" are so original it's uncanny; they are something special. If only the rest of the songs matched these three, this album would have some relevance, but they don't. They're just boring. Even "Marquee Moon" has no guts (it's far too long as well). I'd even admit to being bias coz I prefer Dumb music to all this genius crap. It's better to beat on the brat, than to blind him with science. The message gets across better. Tom Verlaine does have a good voice, and who knows the next L.P. might be something to shout about, but by then the N.M.E. will have found another genius no doubt.

RAMONES-LEAVE HOME

No point in reviewing this album in depth as it's already been reviewed by just about everybody, but as I've only just been able to get it at a reasonable price (featuring "Carbona Not Glue"), this is the first time I've heard it. Anyway I agree with 'em all, this album is so likeable, no one could dislike it. It's all about fun. They are not serious, no one's really gonna grab a tube of Araldite, sorry Carbona cleaning fluid, after hearing this. It's just a laugh. Anyway this album is every bit as good as the first, and even funnier. Best cuts here are "Pinhead", "Carbona Not Glue" (glad I got this one) and "California Sun". They're all good though, go and get a copy quick, before the pinheads cut "Carbona" out.

STOOGES-STOOGES

Although this is a reissue, there are probably none of our readers who heard it first time round, which is a shame cos listening to it now it seems to have little relevance to what Iggy, or anyone else is doing nowadays. That isn't to say this album's bad. Far from it, it contains some of the great Iggy's best ever tracks. I'm talking of course about "No Fun" and "Real Cool Time". Certainly not the absolutely dreary "We Will Fall". Now that could have been a good bridging track, if it had been restricted to two minutes and slipped in between "1969" and "I Wanna Be Your Dog", but to take up a half side, I dunno, it just seems a gross waste of Iggy Pop's talents. Anyway this L.P.'s worthwhile if you want to build up a collection of Iggy's material, in which case you'll probably have to fork out over four quid for "Raw Power". I suggest you just get "The Idiot". I've not reviewed that because I haven't got a copy yet, but what I have heard in Virgin Records, and on Radio Piccadilly sounds pretty good. In fact "Sister Midnight" sounds pretty incredible (even more so when he sang it at the Apollo).

EH LISTEN!

How many rats have you seen in your town, or tramps asked you for money for a cup o'tea?

How many people have you seen having sex in shop doorways or equally inconspicuous places? How about starving dogs attacking young children, perhaps even rooting through dustbins (well I mean, they've got to eat.)

Please let us know, as we are in the process of compiling a top ten chart of revolting things. On second thoughts don't bother, it was a daft idea anyway. If you like though you could send in your fave single, album track, whatever, so we can compile a sort of chart. Don't be influenced by our tastes, if you send in a suggestion what either of us doesn't like we'll just not print it. No doubt none of you will bother to write in anyhow, but who cares, it's a good way to fill up a page, when you've run out of L.P.'s to review.

Seriously though, perhaps some above average intelligence deejay, might decide to be influenced by it when he's deciding what to play. We won't object. I'll have to confess I'm just rabbiting on now to fill up this page, to fill up this page, to fill up this page, to fill up this page.

TELEVISION & RAMONES reviews by Mick.

STOOGES review by Martin.

REVIEWS & NEWS

CLASH – WHITE RIOT/1977

This is already being hailed as the most important event of the year. I hope that this is only the first of many, and we can expect more goodies like it. However this is a great single, it overspills with chaos. One snag though, the words are almost impossible to decipher. O.K. so maybe that was deliberate, but for us Clash fans outside London, who don't see them as often and don't know the word, your best bet is to get hold of "London's Burning", Clash's own mag. and read along with it. The B side 1977 is just as good, in fact better. This has to sum it all up. Look, this record explains what is happening, much better than I can. Get it now, as it's not likely to be on their L.P., either "Riot" or "77". What Clash say is truth, they are totally dedicated. If you don't believe it, then you should stick to one of the National pop papers, because we are not writing this review for you.

EATER – OUTSIDE VIEW

Now this is a complete waste of a single release. The actual song is good enough, in fact commercial enough to be a hit single (in the national charts that is), but the way this single has been put together is just awful. Yes, I'm afraid it's crap. I just hope they withdraw it soon, and release a new version, better played and better produced. Now that could really be something. I know a few kids who do like it, so perhaps I'm in the minority, but anyway I was very disappointed with this one.

T.REX – SOUL OF MY SUIT

No, I haven't put this in because Marc and his new gang have been touring with The Damned. Nor do I claim to have always been a secret admirer of T.Rex. I saw them about five years ago at Belle Vue, and I thought they were pretty bad. However this is a good single, it's got far more boogie, than anything he's done for ages. You may have heard it anyway, but I think it's great.

ELVIS COSTELLO - LESS THAN ZERO

Now this time I admit, the only reason this got a review is coz it's on STIFF. It's not too bad actually, but it certainly doesn't grab you. It's basically a straight pop tune, not bad, but certainly not brilliant. If you wanna hear it, it's getting' quite a bit of airplay on "independent local radio."

TALKING HEADS - LOVE TURNS...

This one's O.K. I suppose, but it sadly lacks the fun and excitement we've come to expect from New York bands. Mind you it does get better with a few plays. Interesting one anyway.

EDDIE & THE HOT RODS - I MIGHT BE LYING

I've only heard this once, as it doesn't seem to be in the shops up Norf. Sounds pretty good an' all. Much better than "Teenage Depression". Still very much The Hot Rods. I can't remember much else about it. I think it's fairly fast, but not quite as fast as "Get Out Of Denver". I can't remember what it's about. I suppose it'll either be another love song, or a cry from the heart of pissed-off-with-life youth. I think the kids'll like it anyway.

AC/DC - DIRTY DEEDS DONE DIRT CHEAP/ BIG BALLS/THE JACK

This maxi single has been out for a while, and probably hasn't sold many copies. The reason being it's just pure nothingness. The title track off their last L.P. is the absolute weakest of the lot. It's just, I dunno pathetic. It just aint rock'n'roll. I really believe in AC/DC, and I think they really deserve to make it, but not with crap like this. Seeing as the Hot Rods and AC/DC used to take turns at selling out the Marquee, perhaps AC/DC should release a live E.P. Yeh that would be great. How about "Live Wire", "High Voltage", "Jailbreak" and "Problem Child". Sounds too good to be true dunnit. In the meantime I'll stick to seein' 'em live. Although "High Voltage" wasn't a bad L.P. for their first one (or was it their second?)

STOP PRESS

Slaughter and the Dogs also have a single in the pipeline, which I believe is on their own Rabied label. It might even be out, but it wasn't in the shops at time of going to press. Also The Drones another Manchester band, should have an E.P. out soon, also on their own label. The Drones are also set to play the Electric Circus on April 13th. (not listed.)

CLASH & HOTRODS reviews by Mick.
The rest by Martin

HEARTBREAKERS & ULTRAVOX

JOHNNY THUNDERS & THE HEARTBREAKERS AT THE OAKS

Having heard reports of the Heartbreakers' gig at the Marquee the night before, I came expecting a knockout set. The only thing that got my back up a bit was the American expressions. OK I'm sorry, they can't help it, but it did seem a bit overdone.

Anyway onto the music. CHINESE ROCK was first away, not their best number (or the Ramones!) but it's got plenty of lift to open the set.

"What's the matter wi' you guys, aint ya got any rythurrrm, don't ya daaance." Sorry Johnny but this aint Max Kansas y'know. You don't play here every week, we wanna see ya. OK and bop to ya, but not dance around like pillocks in discos.

Anyway enough bitching. They played this number called, I think GET OFF THE FOOD. My favourite of the night was "One for all the poseurs" ALL BY MYSELF. A terrific number, with an almost bluesy chorus. If CHINESE ROCK's gonna be the first single then I hope this's the B side.

It's dirty time now, and CAN'T KEEP MY COCK IN YOU. Mmm nice number, that conjures up some images of violent sexual passion, unless you're a prude. Then there was simply I LOVE YOU. Yeh they do sing about jus' plain love.

BORN TO LOSE or BORN TOO LOOSE as they call it,

has to be my second favourite. Even the kids hanging from the birdcage type set, are bopping away.

Billy Rath was absolutely amazing, skipping about with his bass; what a showman, in fact what a pair, him and Johnny Thunders. Another dirty track ONE TRACK MIND, well suggestive anyway.

The set ended, the lights went out, but the band never left the stage. The chants for "more" were too strong already. So off they went again with their version of DO YOU LOVE ME. This might be recycling, but who cares? This is a great new version of a pop classic (or soul classic, well it was written by the head of Tamla Motown.) It certainly left us all in a great mood.

On second thoughts, perhaps the accent wasn't so bad. This band certainly don't try to be any better than the crowd watching 'em. Or maybe it's just that I realise now, how good the best New York acts can be. These are undoubtedly a fun-time band. If this is the New York scene, then roll on May when the cream of N.Y.'s current offerings are coming to Manchester.

ULTRAVOX AT THE CIRCUS

I must admit I never wanted to like Ultravox, ever since I saw their L.P. cover, which I found too much to take, without hearing a track. Tonight however turned up minus most of the tinsel and glitter, and played some good stuff. They are a visually striking band (an odd looking bunch in other words). John Foxx, is certainly a character to see, as is Warren Cann the drummer.

The music here was completely new to me, so I couldn't sing along like most of the crowd, including (gasp) the hippies. With John Foxx singing and staring, the band set up a good, consistent rhythm.

The third number WIDE BOYS was where it really started to happen. With SAT'DAY NIGHT, the single DANGEROUS RHYTHM, and the incredible I WANNA BE A MACHINE with John Foxx picking up the guitar, the audience really started to warm up.

There were two amazing numbers namely THE CITY DOESN'T CARE and THE WILD, THE BEAUTIFUL AND

THE DAAAAMNED. The first was an almost frightening number, and the latter had the most amazing ending. There was a slow bit, you almost thought he'd started another song, but then he dived back into the chorus.

As they tried to make their way to the dressing room, everyone wanted to pat them, y'know well done chaps'n all that. Mind you they acknowledged everyone; part of the image maybe, who knows. Either way it's better than having bottles thrown at you or being heckled, mind you there were some at back (again). This time it was "Where's Timothy Leary" and "Where's Paul Morley" (fame in Stockport at last).

The crowd must've shouted louder that the AC/DC lot, cos back came the boys to do an encore of YOUNG SAVAGE followed by a really good version of The Velvet's FEAR IN THE WESTERN WORLD. Although I've never heard the original, so this was the first time I've heard this number.

It's been done before, and I'm not totally convinced by them, but they were entertaining. I think I'd see 'em again.

ghast up issue two

MANCHESTER ROCKS/MANCHESTER ROCKS
MANCHESTERROCKS / MANCHESTER ROCKS

Sorry you've had to wait so long for Ghast Up 2. It'll definitely be out regularly from now on.

Despite the fact that the Oaks has moved the stage so everyone can see, the attendances have been getting thinner. Why? There have been great gigs lately from The Vibrators, Adverts, Siouxsie & the Banshees and The Drones. There are usually a band on Tuesday and Thursday, (see Manchester Evening News for details on the night) so let's see some support, otherwise Manchester could lose out on a lot of these bands if the Oaks is forced to close to live bands, due to lack of support.

Speaking of The Adverts I've only seen 'em twice and I'm fucking mad about 'em. I can't wait to see an L.P. out 'cos there's so many good songs, and T.V.'s got such an original voice, I think they're one of the best bands I've seen for ages., shame I had no room to review 'em.

This issue's dedicated to Maur Vanian from Newcastle who soon hopes to have a band together, could be an all girl band, nice!

MORE SINGLES REVIEWZZZZZZZZ .....

SEX PISTOLS - GOD SAVE THE QUEEN: this has of course been banned off daytime radio, just to make sure that nobody gets it right. All Johnny and the lads are trying to say is that H.R.H. is the biggest victim of overkill ever, that she can't even take her dogs for a walk in peace. It's great, buy it nowwww!

VIBRATORS - BABY BABY/INTO THE FUTURE: Pure pop music when done so well is appealing to everyone, and I mean everyone. I really doubt if anyone could dislike this mid-speed poppy offering. The clumsy guitar sound is good, and the chorus hits you so much you find you're singing along after a few lines. It reminds me of days spent walking behind girls in tight jeans.

The B-side is faster, less commercial but still good. If you like The Flaming Groovies you'll like this.

CHELSEA - RIGHT TO WORK: What a disappointment this is. It's just a fast dirge with Gene October shouting about the right to work along with one or two other puritanical sentiments.

HEARTBREAKERS - CHINESE ROCKS: This is great 'Born To Lose' is a bit disappointing compared to the live version, but still very good and 'Chinese Rocks' is really good. These lads are gonna be big no messin'.

GHAST UP ARE:- MARTIN: Editor, layout, this & that; MICK MIDDLES: Writer, blah blah; Thanks to Modest Young for contributing.

DRONES PICS SUPPLIED BY KEVIN CUMMINS PHOTOGRAPHY. TEL. 061-737-8369

THE DRONES

THE DRONES are: Mike J.Drone (lead vocals), Steve Cundall (bass), Gus Gangrene (guitar) and Peter Howells (drums). Mike, Steve, Gus and Modest Young their manager, were here for the interview, but Pete we were told was jamming with Bad Company; or was it Led Zeppelin?

MARTIN: How long have you been playing?

MODEST Y.: Oh clichés!

STEVE: No we've been together about – just under a year now. We've been playing new-wave for about eight months, since the beginning of last summer.

MARTIN: So where've you played more or less throughout the country?

STEVE: Well we've played The Roxy about six times now.

GUS: With the occasional heavy metal gig at The Houldsworth

Hall.

MIKE: Actually we've played in a lot of places that new-wave really hasn't hit at the moment. Like we did a five date tour of Carlisle, we've done a couple of dates in Doncaster, a couple of dates in Workington. Sheffield, we were the first band to go up to Sheffield – we've got a really good following in Sheffield. Naturally Manchester gigs, but we're hoping to go to a lot of places like Morecambe, and obscure towns like that; like Lancaster, places that are not provincial towns, but where a lot of the kids are getting into new-wave music.

MODEST: What I was thinking about playing places like Morecambe and all that crap, big overkill in the cities, people are getting fed up. Like May every other night there's a fucking new wave gig, people can only do so much right? Morecambe, Carlisle they never see it. Drones'll play that 'cos they're not bothered about fashion or front. If they can make their names in Liverpool, Carlisle, Morecambe, Doncaster, Workington, it's good, they'll be the first. A lot of kids don't realise what's happening.

MIKE: Yeh, like I was saying before we were the first to bang up in Sheffield right?

MODEST: Thus you're the best new wave band in Sheffield, what people are gonna see, I mean you got 500 at that gig.

GUS: We found out, that guy, on Wednesday nights doesn't charge to get in and he normally gets something like 250-300 in. We played, he charged about ten bob to get in and he got nearly 600 in.

MIKE: Actually Gus you've got the figures wrong, he usually got about 100 in on a Wednesday night for nothing, and he put an ad' in the paper saying that The Drones would play and he got over the 500 mark which I think's great. A great turnout to see us.

MODEST: And Sheffield's a fucking apathetic city so that's good going.

GUS: It fucking isn't for new wave, I don't think it is.

MODEST: Well no. But how much new wave do they get y'know, who bothers to go? It's an unfashionable place. The only fashionable places are Manchester and London basically, we're lucky in Manchester to get what we get, as is proved by the fact that no provincial new wave bands have been signed up by a major record label.

STEVE: The thing is about "the smoke", the bands in London that are playing now, this is Clash/Pistols besides, the rest of 'em, they're just into the fashion sort of thing.

MODEST: Not all.

STEVE: They are, course they are.

MODEST: No 60%.

STEVE: There's a lot of 'em.

MODEST: And a lot are good fun.

STEVE: We're getting bands in Manchester that are doing it know.

GUS: When we played Pips half of 'em don't know what the fucking hell's going on, I don't think. It's just another thing to follow, last year they could look like David Bowie, the year before that they could look like Bryan Ferry, now they can look like Johnny Rotten. I'm not saying it's a bad thing but I'm saying it's a bad thing when the bands do it.

MODEST: The Roxy's worst for bands though, bands like Smack. Y'know like er – Smack!

STEVE: Shit. I'll tell you who's another one of them, The Models.

MIKE: They're fucking crap, they really are.

STEVE: They're into sort of, ripping fashion off.

GUS: Or there again all the punters in the Roxy are aren't they? They're not interested in the bands really, they just want to be seen there.

MODEST: At least they're making an effort, they're doing something, which is a lot better than a year ago when everyone was going around out-apathetic-ing the next person.

MIKE: You know our chat on Saturday, you asked me whether The Drones get any money out of what we do and I said, when you meet the lads you ask 'em the last time they can remember having anything out of playing, cos we don't. All our money goes into The Drones cos we care about The Drones.

MICK: What do you live on then?

MIKE: I live on the dole, like we all do.

MICK: But you want to make enough money to live?

MIKE: Oh yeh right, but we happen to own a really good van and we own really good equipment. We don't hire because we care about our sound and that's one of the things that Modest first noticed about The Drones, wasn't it?

MODEST: Yeh it was sincerity. Like to say they're on the dole is no fashion kick, I mean they're on the DOLE, but they've never proffered that they're a dole queue rock band.

MICK: Say The Drones make it big ….?

MODEST: That's what it's all a–fucking-bout, they wanna get on telly, be stars interviewed by Russell Harty, it's traditional.

MIKE: Like we said on Piccadilly we want to make it, any big company'll do. Any honest.

MICK: Well that's honest innit?

MIKE: We're being honest we're in it to get The Drones to the top.

MODEST: It's not honesty it's fact.

STEVE: It's like Rotten, he sings about anarchy, but really he'd like a nice big house in the country.

MODEST: All anarchy is to him is self-will.

STEVE: It's pop music, they wanna be successful or else they wouldn't make records.

MIKE: That was a great term summed up by Modest Young. "It's '77 pop" is what it's all about. A great example if you caught the Circus gig is, it was so good to see people going berserk. It was a great feeling to see 20 or 30 on the stage and off the stage all going mad, even geeks with long hair going mad. It was great.

STEVE: We believe we are playing '77 pop like the Dogs are playing '55 pop. I mean to say that band could be Chuck Berry's backing band. That's not a knock at 'em it's true.

MARTIN: Which bands do you reckon are really serious and really doing something?

MIKE: Which bands do I admire? Honestly I find it very hard, not being selfish, to get into a lot of these bands, because some play a lot slower that The Drones play, some are a bit more sophisticated and some are unmore sophisticated, if that's the word. I've seen nearly all the bands and a band I enjoyed, I liked The Vibrators when we played with them in London, and I thought The Only Ones they had a bad gig, they had to follow us at The Roxy Club and they didn't do it, they couldn't pull it off even though they were headlining. I thought they had like a Velvet Underground-type image which was O.K.

GUS: The Rats, I thought they were pretty genuine.

STEVE: What I'd like to see is a few more bands like The Damned, getting into the custard pie type rock that they do, a lot of them are doing the political thing that Clash are doing and there's too many doing it.

MIKE: I think The Clash L.P.'s a bit more poppy.

MODEST: No I don't think so, it's too heavy to be pop. I mean other '77 pop bands I think Generation X, The Boys and The Vibrators are a good example, whereas someone like The Clash, Buzzcocks, they're into the heavier areas, they're saying something, and Chelsea they're the old heavy rock under the new wave thing. There's a load of sub-labels and it's really good, it's branching out.

You remember when Johnny Rotten said that he'd like to see loads and loads of bands like the Sex Pistols? Well in a way that idea's been perverted and you're getting the twits that Steve was talking about that are just doing it for the sake of it, the fashion, but in another way it's really good that there are bands like The Drones, The Boys, The Vibrators, who are taking that Johnny Rotten statement at face value, and whereas a year ago you'd go to a pub' and see a 3-piece trio playing various

Lynyrd Skynyrd, Thin Lizzy, Deep Purple out-takes, now you go into a pub' and you see a really good '77 pop group playing really good music that you can dance to. That's locally as well, I mean whereas a year ago you'd go to the Phoenix, now you can go to the Oaks, see The Drones, Buzzcocks, anyone like that and it's really good, and it's what Johnny Rotten wanted, and although he's got caught up in the sideshow effects of it, his best contribution to this whole crap was saying that he wanted to see lots and lots of bands. He's a poet Johnny Rotten, nobody knows that though.

MIKE: Vini at the Oaks wanted to put a Manchester night on at London, what's happening now there's gonna be a Manchester night with The Buzzcocks and the Drones.

MICK: What about Slaughter?

MIKE: I don't like Slaughter.

MODEST: I like Slaughter and the Dogs, but they're not a new wave band, they're traditional in their approach, but it aint new wave. They're a good R'n'B band.

GUS: They do a few zany stunts like Wayne going on stage at The Roxy and shouting "United", things like that. It's not gonna do 'em any good is it?

MIKE: that was the most unprofessional, unspontaneous stunt I've ever seen, when The Dogs played the Electric Circus, and that guy got on and Wayne started cutting his T-shirt up with a 2 bob knife. I don't think The Drones could ever have a stage act because everything is too spontaneous, and that's how it's gotta be with us.

THE CLASH

LIVE & ALBUM

THE CLASH - THE CLASH: This album just has to be one of the most essential statements ever made. To call it brilliant is just taking a short cut. This is _real_ music in that it's heart felt. Music born of frustration.

"THE CLASH" is a pop album right? The trouble with most intellectual (or so called) musicians is that they try to pretend you've got to be a genius to understand where they are at. Not The Clash, they speak everyone's language, your language! This album needs no analysis, it's so straight up. The rip-offs are good. The Gary Glitter type into to POLICE AND THIEVES, better still the AUTOBAHN bit at the end of CHEAT. You've gotta cheat to survive, even in rock'n'roll. If nothing else it proves that Clash can play.

WHITE RIOT is here unfortunately for them who bought the single. It's slightly better though, the words are clearer; I think it's faster even. I just hope people listen and act now. Everything they sing is last resorts, when all else fails. There's a lot of irony too. It's a warning of what might happen O.K. This L.P. rools O.K.

THE SLITS/SUBWAY SECT/THE CLASH LIVE!

First on were The Slits, who really astounded. They really are the first _real_ all girl group. They play what they can play, without trying to be too butch. They're as honest as any male band, but they're still women. Definitely something different here. Loved every minute of it.

Subway Sect. Again something different. Most people dismiss them as amateurish, but they had an immediacy and directness which I really liked. Vic Godard had a good couldn't-care-less stance. I think Pail Myers and Robert Miller should have moved a bit more or something. I don't know I just feel they let Vic down in stage presence. I still think there's something there, Subway Sect could become an important band if they try to expand within their own limits.

Now the moment we've all been waiting for. The packed Electric Circus crowd all surged forward. On the way in a lot of the kids from the Collyhurst flats had been hanging around beneath the yellow lights, watching all them punkies arrive, excitement huh, you guessed it, "Manchester's burning with boredom."

Look at them kiddies go, everyone, bar no one's up there dancing. Just a mo' this is The Clash, are you supposed to dance to these, who cares? CAPITAL RADIO, BORED WITH THE U.S.A. they played 'em all.

"This song's written by a ★★★," silence "If you don't like ★★★s you know where the back door is!" POLICE AND THIEVES and what an arrangement they played tonight. Junior Murvin woulda been real proud.

During REMOTE CONTROL I just had to get nearer the front line (heh). The most amazing thing about The Clash live, is that they're just there, no theatrics you just wanna touch them. To be truthful I moved nearer the front to be nearer the W.C. but how? How can you leave the sight of Clash on stage, jump about and hope the urge'll go away, jump around to JANIE JONES, CAREER OPPORTUNITIES, WHITE RIOT and that was it, the ultimate. Those scattered around the edges just dived into the hopping pile. It was like a rubber ball, you couldn't hold it down. Two minutes of pure rock'n'roll magic. It must have been recorded forever on the minds of all present. Wanna riot of my own.

The Clash later gave us an encore of GARAGELAND and a bonus 1977, and that was that, or was it? The crowd drifting out were, how you say, spellbound! Was Beatlemania ever like this? Will Manchester ever forget The Clash, will The Clash ever forget Manchester?

Look out Who and Stones this up and coming band are gonna grab your crown. Up and coming, they've fucking come!

BUZZCOCKS AT THE BAND ON THE WALL.
MAY 2ⁿᵈ 1977 Part 2

The second set commenced with SIXTEEN which is a rock'n'roll classic. It gives us Pete Shelley where the recovered simplicity of BREAKDOWN/BOREDOM excerpts gave us Howard Devoto. SIXTEEN is open '77 romance and Shelley's persistent intense inquiries and available statements are a soft nasty naivity, a startling astute revelation about much contemporary folk consciousness. Pete Shelley would like to be Peter Pan. Devoto aimed for specific historic unity and fucking George Buckner. Where Howard would quote "Every man's a chasm. It makes you dizzy when you look down in." Pete would quote "D'ya wanna be in my gang." And who doesn't. SIXTEEN's steady systematic rhythm intensity owes much to Bolero and Bowie, tainted, it is a chant, a march. The flexible temporary matureness of the untogether bridge emphasises nothing so much as its existence. At the end of the song Shelley recovers his senses and angrily voices the feelings of many. "And I hate modern music, disco boogie and pop, it just goes on and on and on and on" he threatens to extend to infinity. The people out front looked on, danced and things, pushed and sung. Jon the Postman beserked. WHAT DO I GET is a joyous mid-sixties absolute monster pop song that expounds and expands the difference between the Devoto quartet and the naturalist pop group that is Buzzcocks. Can you imagine Devoto forcing out a song that owes more to the Searchers than Coltrane's horn at 78 r.p.m.? Coleman's at 12?

Fast cars, who does like them? It needs plugging, let's not forget the little things of life. They played LOVE BATTERY again. Shelley's quirky teen sex ball play. Shelley's totally imaginary. Out front on look the audience, stunned, Buzzcocks finished. And then? And then? And then. Forty years old? Elvis on stage! Thirty years old The Beatles reformed! Twenty years old? Howard Devoto (you think I'm exaggerating – ya shoulda bin there!) sneaks on stage, a snake swallowing rabbit. The song played is the old Troggs tune I CAN'T CONTROL MYSELF which a lot symbolises Devoto's reason for lung-jamming. The reaction is phenomenal. People laugh and push each other over in glee. I LOVE YOU BIG DUMMY penetrates thickly through astonished flesh. It was, um an occasion and destined for, er legend. "Just dusting the hat" said Howard, he goddamn polished it shiny.

"Feeling the itch were you" I asked later. "Oh you do it's inevitable; there's somethings you miss, somethings you don't. I was just scratching." Will the itch inflame people wondered I, or will sheer Devoto projects such as Beckettian tackling soothe the itch? No matter, this night the urges roamed. Afterwards, outside in what's called life, everything had crashed. No truth was possible.

Modest Young

On The Fringes of New Wave, by Modest Young.

On the fringe of new wave!!! (huh?)

Three Dog Night: that one that begins 'jeremiah was a bullfrog, was a good friend of mine' is sheer speculative fabulation at its excessively nostalgic utmost and for a few silver seconds it's a clear winner, one of the golden greats but RAPID degeneration comes cleanly and it fades one of the worst all-american alas polished singles of all time. Shame. Mentioned 'cos b + g records stockport have copies at 1.35 a time. Unfortunately the first fifteen seconds are only worth 74 pennies. Pain.

Judas Priest: on the new J.P album they play nazareth playing joni by playing bazz's diamonds and rust and despite tedious heavy metal faggots crusting non rippling folkie-cabaret tune it comes out at least seven tenths talking head, five ninths pere ubu and it'll only take drastic self criticism in months to come for J.P. to be two eighths good.

Voice on the Ogun label: in fact more new wave than even a doncaster royal procession using purely the sound of the human voice it embraces all emotions, makes me laugh, makes me cry, makes me want to join in, puts me in heat. Demands attention concentration but if you love television as much as abba as much as patti as much as metal machine music then it is for you and well worth loving.

Low by Brian Eno: anything by eno has speculation covering constipation smothering static motivation with more motives than even patti for rearing on the defense in the face of ugly cynics. Low is an astonishing piece of music because it exists and because it's the perfect follow on to another green world which was the perfect follow on to taking tiger mountain which was the perfect follow on to here come the warm jets which was the perfect follow on to you really got me which was the perfect follow on.

Gary Glitter's Golden Greats: really it only requires ponderance that glitters baby please don't go is definitive that his songs are anthems and his anthems are romantic like jim morrisons and then take it from there of course he is to the ramones what arthur lee, artonin artaud and jimi hendrix is to tom verlaine and what peter noone, brian eno and maurice ravel is to pete shelley.

Roadrunner by Jonathan Richman, All For The Love of Rock'n'Roll by the Tuff Darts take the cosy way out with late fifty eight ice cream grinning whereas shelleys '16' [most written on a Kit-Kat wrapper] strains with realism:

> *"I hate modern music – disco boogie pop,*
> *it just goes on and on and on and on"*

And as per usual he threatens to extend to infinity. And if you think that Shelley don't like nothing not even french kissing then i hate you big dummy you're just like the tories who take the Boys 'I don't like rock'n'roll' stand at 1 dimensional face value. Think!

Ultravox: The City Doesn't Care. Confusion as an epidemic about this entertaining quartet of plasticine poseurs. 'The City Doesn't Care' was taught to the audience at the Electric amsterdam sixty eight Circus gig and most everyone missed it's unrelated dirge-divorced beatles connections – beatles as in love me do and that's pre-mccartney anti-blues beatles! 'The City Doesn't Care' is in the same league as even Shelleys 'What Do I Get' as '64 pop literally rammed into '78 – and that's okay, right? Must must must be a single.

Talking about fringe of new wave – what the fucks that mean – can it be long before someone really does dub rock music? Then we'll see things. Obviously Eno's a prime target, but Verlaine's splintered antics would chop\overlay\undecut\fuss\buzz\fret\bleep neatly, and the Rollers have always left hollow gaps just aching to be echoed. Other candidates must be Iggy, Love, Henry Cow, Hendrix, Jarrets solo piano, Duke Ellington, James Brown, Beefheart, Velvet Underground, Bohannon, Plastic Ono Band, Lol Coxhill, Beethoven, Burt Bacharach, Patti Smith, Black Sabbath, Small Faces, Miles Davis.

RATTUS NORVEGICUS: THE STRANGLERS

This album is very predictable, it's very much an attempt at getting away from the new-wave dub by trying to adopt just about any other image. Yeh I really like it but it does threaten? It threatens that the next 12 inch Stranglers' offering is gonna have longer, drawn out tracks and less of them, or even a concept.

The Stranglers write some good stuff of which PEACHES, the new single and the one everyone's raving over, is just about my least favourite. Best cuts are HANGING AROUND, LONDON LADY (sigh), GOODBYE TOULOUSE, and (GET A) GRIP (ON YOURSELF).

I don't think this album's psychedelic at all, I think it's more sleazy-French-nightlife-type imagery. I can just imagine Hugh Cornwell strolling down The Pigalle telling all the prostitutes to fuck off. The psychedelia bit probably started with the track UGLY. Wasn't psych... whatever, the period when everyone and everything was made of love, peace and beauty, or at least the surreal imagery surrounding it, and not images of Acne greatly exaggerated by the influences of (whisper) L.S.D. Or has the truth behind the hippy movement been uncovered at last; another Stranglers first. DOWN IN THE SEWER is the most sensational track, 'cos it's strange. I don't fancy living in a sewer, it's bad enough up here.

The Stranglers have got an original sound, difficult to define. Dave Greenfield's organ playing, although overemphasized, does add that vital spark to the overall effect. It's commercial but not overtly. It grows on you, like Peaches!

THE IT'S BEEN DONE BEFORE COLUMN.

This column is very predictable, it's very much an attempt at getting away from being different than every other fanzine.

TOP TWENTY TRACKS

The votes were a bit sparse, but what can you expect from the first issue. If D.J.s are interested, all the votes were from in and around Manchester.

1. WHITE RIOT Clash
2. BOREDOM Buzzcocks
3. ONE CHORD WONDERS Adverts
4. ANARCHY IN THE U.K. Sex Pistols
5. DENY Clash ★
6. IN THE CITY The Jam
7. I DON'T CARE The Boys
8. LONDON LADY The Stranglers
9. FAN CLUB The Damned ★
10. LOVE HER MADLY The Doors
11. NEAT NEAT NEAT The Damned
12. GLORIA Patti Smith
13. EROTIC NEUROTIC The Saints
14. SHAKE SOME ACTION The Flamin' Groovies
15. CAREER OPPORTUNITIES Clash ★
16. JANIE JONES Clash ★
17. BLITZKRIEG BOP The Ramones
18. I'M SO BORED WITH THE U.S.A. Clash ★
19. HANGING AROUND The Stranglers ★
20. NEW ROSE The Damned

 ★ *Album Tracks. (As if you didn't know.)*

REVIEWS

THE JAM - IN THE CITY: Ready Steady Go, dinner dinner dinner dinner Batmaaan, dinner dinner dinner dinner Batmaaan, Maximum R'n'B Tuesdays at the Marquee.

I hated this album when I first heard it, I thought who wants a collection of early Who proxy statements in '77. So I've played it continually for the past 4 hours and found that behind the conventional greyness lies a good album, not a great one though.

ART SCHOOL with it's do what you wanna do-type lyrics is about the best cut. NON STOP DANCING, AWAY FROM THE NUMBERS, BRICKS AND MORTAR and of course IN THE CITY are the other goodies that make this L.P. listenable, but BATMAN? That is taking The 'oo thing a bit too far innit? Oh shit they're gonna be successful anyway, but I think it's a highly overrated and very ordinary album.

SLAUGHTER & THE DOGS - CRANKED UP REALLY HIGH/THE BITCH: Hey remember when singles use to begin with an instrumental version of the chorus, and that bit used to stimulate everyone into dancing, foot-tapping whatever. Well this "bring back the spark" offering from The Dogs is just that crossed with a Slade workout. This track was the highpoint of The Dogs' recent gig at the Oaks, but unfortunately was the opener, and they couldn't quite lift the crowd to the same level again. This is however a good single in straight pop terms, the na-na-na-naaa towards the end is the best part, which reminds me even more vividly of Slade when they were at their peak, almost surrealistic. THE BITCH is O.K. with it's piercing vocals. The whole thing is a Criminal Production, truly.

RAMONES - SHEENA IS A PUNK ROCKER: On first listening this one seemed little more_than the dumb style of the first The Ramones' first L.P. combined with the slightly more sophisticated lyrics of LEAVE HOME. On following the lyrics however, there's definitely a strong message here. It's the first time I've heard the phrase "Punk Rocker" used with any real definition. Sheena's bored with the glamorous West Coast existence, she wants to go to downtown New York with the real people, and that really is what it's all about. It's simple but it's there, it applies to England and America. People are getting bored with the commercialised plastic existence that we're all forced to live in.

<u>THE DRONES – TEMPTATIONS OF A WHITE COLLAR WORKER E.P. (S Label):Lookalikes/Corgi Crap/Hard On Me/You'll Lose</u>: If you live in Manchester you've gotta start and finance your own label if you ever wanna get a record out; sad so sad, but it doesn't stop these Mancunians.

An E.P. so there's no crappy fill-in tracks, just CORGI CRAP, the best one here. An incredible arrangement with a change in pace for the chorus; a masterstroke. It's all about the Royal farce. Monarchy for you!

LOOKALIKES is probably The Drones own anthem, sung with as much provocation as CITY DRONES it attacks all you poseurs who think it's hip to dress up like your idol and stand looking bored. Be yourself for fucks sake, then M.J. won't be verbally assaulting you.

HARD ON ME gallops along at just the right pace. Slight shades of the Pistols here but very subtlely done. The fastest one here just about.

YOU'LL LOSE is to me the track here with the most impact. It's fast yet restraint, the message is clear, if you don't fight you'll lose. The perfect finale.

This E.P. really works, it's got it's own excitement, different than their live energy, and with CORGI CRAP there's clear signs that they're heading somewhere. Up. It's '77 pop, what else?

Available soon 99p plus 15p p.p. from:

GOODMIX, 19 TOOTAL ROAD, SALFORD

Slaughter & the Dogs' single is out now from Virgin or H.M.V.Shops or 85p from:

RABID RECORDS, 178 WATERLOO PLACE, OXFORD RD. MANCHESTER 13.

DAMNED LIVE!

The Captain was wearing his silly dress, Dave lurched around glaring at us, Rat sat behind the drums his arms extended in a V shape and Brian was blasting out the opening chords to I FEEL ALRIGHT. Then it exploded, that incredible guitar riff, Rat beating fuck out of skins, Dave leaping and spitting out the lyrics and the Cap. was clearly enjoying himself punching the bass lines out.

The atmosphere – electric, the crowd right behind the band from the start. Most of the album flashed passed us. They played great versions of NEAT NEAT NEAT, FAN CLUB, STAB YOUR BACK, a lousy HELP (joke over lads).

This is a much tighter band than the one that played the Electric Circus in January, which I think's good 'cos no energy's been lost yet. There is perhaps a danger of The Damned becoming too professional and lose the original rawness, but there again rehearsed rawness is as bad as rehearsed professionalism.

Then there was spitting, non stop from the crowd, showers of bleeding gob.

"No spitting, naughty" the Captain joked, then hid behind a speaker stack. Rat rushed to the front of the stage, took a swig of beer and spat it up the middle of the crowd soaking 'em. All good fun? No, you could tell it wore on the band's nerves (well who the fuck wants to be gobbed at continually). Okay joke over, Brian invited the next spitter onto the stage for some damned aggro. Who started this spitting anyway? A shame 'cos it was the only flaw in a crowd who were magnificent otherwise, and lifted the band to provide a memorable night for all concerned.

MOAN/MOAN/MOAN/MOAN/MOAN

The other Saturday (or was it the other) we went to see The Drones at the Roxy, and spent enough to make a Howard Hughes blank cheque bounce! What with admission at £1.50, canned beer, or draught if you're rich enough to buy it at over fifty pence a pint. Pity 'cos it's the ideal venue, small sweaty atmosphere, everyone can see. Long live the Electric Circus. see ya MICK

WAYNE COUNTY

Poor Wayne, pulled in instead of Cherry Vanilla, (whom we aint seen yet in Manchester) he had to try and entertain a crowd who just wanted to hear Ritchie Blackmore's Rainbow, instead of listening to what the band had to offer.

To those of us who enjoyed Wayne's act this was clearly a very competent band who played real tight, and Wayne, who's got one of the best voices I've heard for a long time is a genuine rock'n'roller with a good stage act.

From the moment he hit the stage I knew I was gonna like what he does, no more dressing up in women's clothing, just a bit of make-up and a scar with stitches drawn on his neck. Sheer maniacal excitement.

Wayne also has some great songs like CREAM IN MY JEANS, MAX KANSAS, and ROCK'N'ROLL RESURRECTION, sick lyrics maybe but really grabbing. I doubt if the majority of the crowd noticed the lyrics anyway, they were just there to shout "Shit" and "off", they've obviously read somewhere that Wayne County has something to do with new wave; did I even hear someone remark "New wave rubbish".

As the set progressed the crowd got more and more resentful, but Wayne, the perfect host, told the band who were playing the opening chords of the next number to "shut the fuck up" while he addressed the audience, and what more could they do? As they chanted "off" Wayne said it was great, I can't describe his excellent handling of a crowd who clearly don't like rock'n'roll,

what other reason could they have?

Then the climax IF YOU DON'T WANNA FUCK ME, FUCK OFF with Wayne screaming "Fuck off, fuck off, fuck off." The perfect theme for the occasion. Then exit the band, Wayne still smiling to show he really doesn't give a fuck.

Back stage after and Wayne had his woolly hat on by now. I gave him a wad of GHAST Ups to take back to New York which he promised he would. GHAST UP in C.B.G.B.S huh! We also had an interesting chat with one of his road men. When a bird asked Wayne what "Punk Rock" was about he replied "I dunno I just play Rock'n'roll" Right on….

ghast up summer '77

JUST A TOUCH OF GOOD CLEAN FUN BLOSSOMED IN THE SUMMER OF HATE AND WAR !!!!!!!!

Ghast Up 3 is here, late as usual, with our traditional poor printing quality.

Things could get pretty bad in Manchester. Fortunately Rafters has given an alternative venue to the Oaks which has stopped putting live groups on temporarily (we hope), but it looks as if the Electric Circus could be in trouble 'cos there aren't enough fire exits, therefore attendances must be limited to 300. I wonder if they'd have had this trouble if they'd have refused to stage new wave bands just like the council-run halls try to. We'll see what happens anyway, perhaps they'll find another venue in Manchester, it did say in *Melody Maker* that they were looking for one.

It was good to see Brass Tacks on BBC2 showing Manchester's best known punks who, aided and abetted by John Peel, succeeded in making the city councillors look completely stubborn and pompous. It was great to see John Peel arguing with the Glasgow councillor, I wish John had been given more time to speak his views, in fact the whole debate should have been extended so that a definite conclusion could have been reached. Perhaps then these over-reactive newspapers'd be put in their place. Still you've got to make the best of the situation.

The Nosebleeds, formerly Ed Banger and The Nosebleeds, have a single out on Rabid Records which sounds okay. I couldn't review it 'cos I couldn't get hold of a copy in Stockport but good old John Peel played it on his show the night after his trip to Manchester for Brass Tacks. There was to be a feature on The Nosebleeds in this issue it should definitely be in number 4.

Martin

THE GOOD TIME MUSIC OF THE SEX PISTOLS

Naturally I played this album for the first time with child-like anticipation, well I mean the track listing is impressive enough just look; Outa My Head/Pushing And Shoving/I'm a Lazy Sod/Stepping Stone/Unknown (that's not the name of the song)/Whatcha Gonna Do About It/Substitute/Pretty Vacant/Problems/No Fun.

The main drawback with such a poor quality bootleg is that you can't leave it playing, you have to give it undivided attention and even then it's hard to appreciate it.

The first number OUTA MY HEAD (DID YOU NO WRONG) is a waste of time really because the same song appeared more audibly on the B–side of GOD SAVE THE QUEEN.

PUSHING AND SHOVING is alright as a songbut here it's far too fuzzy as is I'M A LAZY SOD which you can hardly hear the first verse of.

STEPPING STONE is about the best track on the L.P. mainly because it doesn't matter whether you can hear the words of this one or not. The beat says everything.

PRETTY VACANT is surprisingly similar in arrangement to the current single, although Glen Matlock's backing vocals don't sound very sorely missed, at least not on this recording.

All in all this L.P. is a poor substitute for a real Pistols' L.P. although it must be the only record of those peaceful days of tranquillity so far removed from these days of Pistol bashing.

Saints in Manchester – review and interview

THE SAINTS have always fascinated me, more for the image which I've always attached to 'em, rather than their musical achievements. I've always imagined a typical day in the life of an Australian band to be: up at 1:00 p.m., just a cup o' coffee for Breakfast, and into the estate car with all the gear, and off through the desert with all it's wildlife, supping endless cans of lukewarm beer. Later as evening approaches pulling up at Alice Springs or some "town like Alice" to play a gig to a handful of locals to whom The Saints are probably the best group in the world and worthy of about four encores. After the show they'd sit in the bar supping more beer until dawn breaks or someone crashes out, whichever comes first. Then back to the guest house to sleep it off till 1.00 the next day and so it goes. Sunday the third of July 1977 at the Electric Circus however, showed us the truth behind the myth as The Saints suddenly became real human beings.

Visually The Saints are very casual, very relaxing; the myth could well be true. That's visually! Musically they rip through most numbers as if there's a time limit on the set and, I suppose they live up to their "Twice as fast as The Ramones" image. The playlist includes standard numbers like C'MON EVERYBODY (pretty monotonous) and RUNAWAY (pretty good, more emphasis on arrangement than speed). Twice they played numbers which to me sounded like "Teenager In Love" type arrangements, but substituting different choruses each time.

Having established that they do, to English audiences at least, lack some originality they did play good versions of I'M STRANDED (classic single), THIS PERFECT DAY (even better) and EROTIC NEUROTIC (for those who like that sort of thing). The usual pogoing crowd were there to greet The Saints and they did get an encore but the spark wasn't quite there yet. At least not for me …

SAINTS INTERVIEW AND CONCLUSION

PRESENT WERE: (A) GHAST UP, (B) NEW POSE, (C) JOHN THE POSTMAN, (D) PAUL AND (E) THE SAINTS. TAKE IT AWAY G.P.O. JOHN.

JOHN: What's it like for scoring in Australia?

IVOR HAY (Saints' drummer): What, you mean drugs?

JOHN: No not drugs, cannabis.

IVOR: Oh we don't touch drugs, we're clean living. If you want them over there they're easy to get, 'cos they grow up the east coast.

PAUL: What did you think of the crowd tonight?

CHRIS BAILEY (Saints' singer): Oh pretty good, they moved around a lot.

MICK: Which are the best gigs you've played so far in England?

ED KUEPPER (Saints' guitarist): The Nashville was O.K., tonight was pretty good, there was some trouble at the Hope and Anchor. This kid kept grabbing hold of Chris' tie, and heckling us. It was alright at first but it got a bit much so Chris jumped on him and beat shit out of him. A few kids joined in on Chris' side and a few on the kid's side.

JOHN: What's all this in the music papers about shouting things off the stage?

CHRIS: Oh that's just the papers.

JOHN: It said you shouted posing pommie bastards or something.

CHRIS: Look at me – d'ya think I'd say a stupid thing like that?

JOHN: No that was good, putting down the poseurs.

MICK: What do you think of the British new wave bands you've heard?

IVOR: Oh yeah The Clash, Damned, Pistols. I like the usual lot; actually The Buzzcocks' "Spiral Scratch" was one of the first

British new wave records we heard. A friend of ours sent it down to us, they're from round here aren't they?

ANSWER (Can't remember who): Yeh Salford!

MICK: What are the crowds like in Australia?

SAINT'S ROAD MAN: What do you mean crowds? Just a few kids at the bar who don't really know what's going on, they're just stood with their mouths open like goldfish.

MICK: What are you talking about Australia in general?

SAINT'S R.M.: Well mainly Brisbane, that's the worst.

MICK: Yeh but surely if you kept going back there they'd come round eventually?

SAINT'S R.M.: Yeh maybe!

JOHN: It said in one paper that Manchester reminds you of home, is that right?

ED: Where, you mean London?

MARTIN: So you're over here permanently now are you?

ED: There's a good chance.

Maybe the Saints over here isn't so bad after all. They've been playing long enough to not get dragged into the heavy political scene which is looming over the British new wave scene at the moment, nothing wrong with that I know but we all need some light relief and The Saints are a relaxing band in that way. Perhaps they kicked off too high in Britain after all the kids over here are if anything over-reactionary. With luck the criticism which the British pop papers are levelling at them might make that difference, 'cos basically The Saints want the same things as many of our new wave bands and certainly the American bands, which, once again brings them in line with The Ramones.

The Saints are not so much a new wave band as "sort of new wave"; indeed they could play to most kinds of audience with reasonable response. The Saints would surely be good fun in the colleges and universities with their primitive fun-time pop music, and their cover versions which even the hippies could never call "punk", although I wouldn't bet on that. Just give 'em three months' trial.

GENERATION X LIVE AT RAFTERS

Generation X could only happen during this golden age of rock'n'roll a.k.a. Punk Rock a.k.a. The New Wave. This is our generation, Generation X are part of the triumph of youth. Rock'n'roll lives.

Billy Idol looks to have lost about five years by merely changing his hair colour, he looks almost ready to start again. This band are about sound, speed and keeping fit. The heavy smokers and drinkers wouldn't last through half the set. Me, I made about three quarters and gave up.

Whatever politics are present in their lyrics are scraped along the sides by the sheer driving force of this band, more of a pop band than a threat to society. YOUR GENERATION is, I'm told, a parody of MY GENERATION. None of this matters, just let 'em play. Let Billy Idol mop his brow as often as he likes.

Billy even commented on hearing reggae played up north, unlike the clubs in London. I hope nobody tells him we nicked the idea from London. Didn't we?

The numbers have, on first hearing at least, little melody or commercialism, that's why I got knackered so quickly. That's not to say they're bad, far from it; just a little too much to take in one go. All that surplus energy never seemed to let up, not even during their "contribution to Reggae."

Now that the band have signed to Chrysalis perhaps they'll give us something to hold and familiarise ourselves with. Then when all the papers are bored with shocking us with scandal and sensationalism, perhaps Generation X'll still be sitting up there smiling to the world, but as I've said they would never have been born in any other age. Freedom of speech is a luxury. EVEN NOW!!!!!

The Roxy, London WC2 (Jan-April '77).

As the album title suggests, THE ROXY is more of an illustrative album than a musical statement. With the use of gossip, heckling and breaking glass it does, I suppose, recreate some of the atmosphere of a night at The Roxy, although having never  been a Roxy regular I dunno, perhaps it holds more fascination for those out of town kids who've never been there, or like me have only made the odd fleeting visit.

The musical content is a good cross-section in as much as it includes the varied aspects of bands that are playing at the moment, although whether it's worth paying three quid just to hear how bad a band is, is debatable.

Side one opens with Slaughter And The Dogs, who may sound like broad Northerners but musically they shine through as one of the best on the album. RUNAWAY is the strongest number, which despite attempts at making them fit in with the rest of the album, is pure rehearsed efficiency as is BOSTON BABIES which is probably more The Dogs' live act than The Dogs on record.

The Unwanted seem to strum a few basic chords on a guitar while the singer desperately tries to make some tuneless vocals fit. Raw it may be but so what? Presumably this was the best number of the night unless they all sounded the same. Either way this track doesn't say much for The Unwanted.

Wire, who play two tracks sound like something and nothing really. More nothing at the moment but full marks for managing to sound different than most of the smaller bands who are around at present. 1.2.X.U. is quite an original lyrical composition, perhaps the future'll bring success of sorts to Wire but not just yet.

The Adverts are one of the best bands around at the moment

and BORED TEENAGERS is one of their strongest tunes; despite the fact that the backing in general is just a thud thud rhythm and Gaye Advert has to struggle to keep up with Laurie on drums it could well be the best track on the album. An album by The Adverts must definitely be in the pipeline, in the meantime this is a sampler of what could well become a pop classic given a sharp production.

Johnny Moped opens side two and somehow they've manged to catch an occasion when you can decipher every word he says, which is good 'cos he really is a scream. "Are you gonna pogo to this number, basically it's called HARD LOVIN' MAN" You'd have to see him about ten times to catch as much of his conversation as this album does.

I find it difficult to take Eater very seriously. Perhaps I'm in the wrong age group, but to me they're just another band who don't play particularly well and have no striking originality, except for perhaps their ages; a novelty which only holds for so long.

X-Ray Spex is the naughty track which even John Peel won't risk playing. OH BONDAGE UP YOURS! It's a scream, now read on!

The fact that the entire album has been recorded at such a level that all the bands sound similar tends to illustrate the strengths and weaknesses of the better bands like The Buzzcocks. BREAKDOWN is very typically their live set, vocally and instrumentally. LOVE BATTERY could equally well be the best track on the album 'cos this is very much a Shelley song which shows how The Buzzcocks are gonna make it.

First to hit the stage was "the elusive" Johnny Moped whom I've seen twice in five days, no matter 'cos he's something else really! "A living legend", "One hundred percent insane", call him what you like but he is it. I mean who else would sing LITTLE QUEENIE in a crazed high pitch voice, who else'd even dream of doing NEW ROSE as an encore. The also legendary Slimey Toad, who is of course responsible for INCENDIARY DEVICE, looked just about the maddest person to ever hit the stage. It was great, I love mad people so long as they're funny.

Despite being totally crazy, somehow the likes of Slimey Toad, Fred Burke and Dave Burke manage to produce a strong and highly tolerable sound to back the looney visual antics of Mr. Moped.

X-Ray Spex were a sensation.

"Little girls should be seen and not heard OH BONDAGE UP YOURS!" and away we go into the song everyone knows.

Polly Styrene danced and sang her way through the numbers, eyes grinning while Laura Logic huffed and puffed at the sax' and in between blasts just stared into space looking pretty, pretty vacant!

I CAN'T DO ANYTHING (I think) sung to the tune of TEENAGER IN LOVE was an incredible updating which gave X-Ray Spex a touch of insanity, just a touch.

"It's been said before, but it has to be said again, OH BONDAGE UP YOURS!" and that was just about the most deserved encore of the night. X-Ray Spex are a sensation, they should be on "Rock Follies".

(See page 11 for more X-Ray Spex)

Eater had it tough, for a start I don't think many of the audience were familiar with their set, and despite having two singles released and two tracks on the "Roxy" album they showed a distinct lack of confidence here in Manchester.

The band moved around quite a bit although by now the audience were warmed up and some of them mildly pissed so a few plastic glasses were thrown albeit out of fun, but the band were discouraged by this and the spitting, at one point Andy Blade remarked "Would you mind not spitting please, I know it's hip and all that."

OUTSIDE VIEW sounded slightly worse than the single, while THINKING OF THE U.S.A., which is a fair single, just sounded like all the rest. The overall musical standard was I suppose as good as some of the older groups and even more ambitious than some, but Eater don't have any spark of originality except the will to get up and play which is everything.

No doubt Eater sound better on home territory, and in any case they'd have had to be good to follow the two previous bands.

Slaughter And The Dogs came on stage and amidst a cloud of talcum powder, free singles and free "Roxy Albums" they charged into their single CRANKED UP REALLY HIGH followed closely by THE BITCH.

Call The Dogs "bandwaggoners" if you like but who draws the crowd and plays so loud.

YOU'RE A BORE is or could be a top five single. Mike Rossi's guitar work gives the perfect framework for the song, while each verse provides an adequate build up to the "What ya doin' to me, what ya sayin' to me," chorus. The whole song is so simple it's amazing.

WHITE LIGHT, WHITE HEAT, MYSTERY GIRLS and WAITING FOR THE MAN are the three non-originals of which WAITING FOR THE MAN is the only number that is usually requested by the crowd. Their own numbers are beginning to form the main strength of their act, tonight I noticed that more than ever, and although there's still a long way to go, songwriting wise, the potential's beginning to show and they're moving in the right direction.

WHERE HAVE ALL THE BOOT BOYS GONE is a song lamenting the demise of the skinheads in Wythenshawe, while WE DON'T CARE was tonight dedicated to the kids that hang about The Civic Centre.

If The Dogs become too much visually just picture the many faces and images which they've attached to themselves since they evolved in February '76, while Bowie was up to STATION TO STATION and Ferry was working on becoming a fashion leader. The Dogs have a surrealistic image that relies on the vivid imagination of the spectator. "Manchester Rains" should have tried to capture that sort of image, still they are young, I mean musically young as opposed to what's on their birth certificates (see *Manchester Rains*), there's time for that to come from the band. Lots of effort from both band and audience made tonight worthwhile, and the support bands (sorry there was no support it was a package tour) not to mention the dollies in the disco, well who'd regret paying £1.25 for all that and more.

OH NO! NOT THE BUZZCOCKS AGAIN SURELY?

Yes but first The Fall who supported The Buzzcocks on the opening night of the new Vortex Club. The crowd reaction was relatively pale and people were still coming into the club during most of the set, but this band are something different. The crowd could be excused for not taking notice 'cos neither did I when I first saw them at The Squat Club. It was the second time that it hit me, The Fall are worth watching.

As The Buzzcocks have already replied to the N.M.E. I'll just say that they were booked as the main act surely, and although I can sympathise with The Heartbreakers who wanted to thank the British audiences on maybe their last night in Britain, one must surely understand the position of The Buzzcocks after sweating out a really superb set marred only by the breaking of a string, which didn't really take that long to repair, they were told that The Heartbreakers were to come on in twenty minutes to "jam", and subsequently "Sounds" and "N.M.E." loosely dismissed The Buzzcocks as a supporting band, which makes it all seem a waste of time and effort. Why bother? None of this need've happened if it hadn't been for the Home Office.

The Worst were O.K. the other week supporting The Drones at The Circus. It kills me watching 'em sometimes, especially when Allan, the singer starts improvising the words and usually says "fucking" every other word. Once you realise that they're not too serious it's easy to appreciate what they're trying to do. They're also rehearsing a lot these days, one of these days they'll be playing like Pink Floyd or Yes. I doubt it not the worst.

MR. WELLER'S ELECTRIC PUPPET SHOW.

THE JAM LIVE.

Seventy five per cent of the audience loved it. They loved Bruce Foxton's lightning movements and thrilling bass lines, Rick Buckler's continual hammering of the drums and Paul Weller's completion of the double Townsend image.

They opened with ART SCHOOL which was pretty good. Played their way through most of the album plus Foxton's CARNABY STREET and (I think) ALL AROUND THE WORLD. Most disappointing was IN THE CITY, probably the most danceable song in years, yet it failed completely to capture the excitement found on the single. However the kids loved 'em and brought them back for an encore of that classic (hmmm yeah well!) BATMAN, so that's all that matters OR IS IT?

I was unfortunately one of the "miserable sod" 25% who were turned cold by the suits, the haircuts, the nice shiny Rickenbacker, it's all been said and answered before I know but I felt like fodder. I hate that feeling and unless Mr. Weller loosens some of the strings I won't be seen at a Jam gig again.

Mick

Okay, okay, it's easy to criticise, let's try and be constructive. The strong number played here was SOUNDS FROM THE STREET. The L.P. version sounds like a straight rip-off from the B-side of The Who's SUBSTITUTE, in other words it uses the more modest side of Pete Townsend, the side which he swept under the carpet. Tonight the song was heavy, more danceable The Jam created a sound of their own which partly repays their debt to the 'oo.

Twice they tried IN THE CITY, twice they failed, failed to even make it crystal clear what they were playing to those who have only heard the single a handful of times.

As for the suits, well who cares, manafactured imagery has

always been a part of pop music so why stop now when the going's good, although did they really all decide to take their jackets off at the same time to avoid any one looking different. The Jam are basically using all the old tricks of the sixties, trying to recapture it, trouble is a movement like "The Mods" has to happen. Is there any point singing about Carnaby Street, when all Carnaby Street is today is just one of London's shopping streets with another branch of Ravel, Topper, in other words Carnaby Street doesn't exist, and London girls are just like any girls from the city, or "In the city".

Let's see some real happenings, The Jam have the capabilities. It's all around ya!

Martin

REVIEWS

<u>NEW WAVE – VARIOUS.</u>

Ramones – Judy Is A Punk/Dead Boys – Sonic Reducer/ Patti Smith – Piss Factory/New York Dolls – Personality Crisis/Runaways – Hollywood/Skyhooks – Horror Movie/ Richard Hell – Love Comes In Spurts/Little Bob Story – All Or Nothing/Boomtown Rats – Looking After No.1/Talking Heads – Love Goes To Building On Fire/The Damned – New Rose/Ramones – Suzy Is A Headbanger/Dead Boys – All This And More/Flamin' Groovies – Shake Some Action/Runaways – Cherry Bomb/New York Dolls – Who Are The Mystery Girls.

Phew quite a few there and only £2.45, seems a waste of time reviewing it.

PISS FACTORY is perhaps better know as a collector's item, well here it is on an album that costs little more than the single's market value. It's ok I s'pose but nothing special, I prefer everything else Patti's done to this..

Both tracks from The New York Dolls are good but we already knew that didn't we?

HORROR MOVIE by the Skyhooks is pretty ordinary, as

are The Dead Boys' SONIC REDUCER and ALL THIS AND MORE.

My favourite track is LOVE COMES IN SPURTS by the one and only Richard Hell and the Void-Oids. Richard Hell's voice is rather like Tom Verlaine's but whereas I find Verlaine's voice too sickly for words, Hell has a more neutral, less strained screech.

HOLLYWOOD is a good number if you like The Runaways, while CHERRY BOMB is good if you like Suzi Quatro. I don't like Suzi Quatro but quite like CHERRY BOMB!

Little Bob Story's ALL OR NOTHING sounds like Rod Stewart and what is worse than Rod Stewart cover versions?

The Boomtown Rats, I am reliably informed are "really chronic for the first twenty-five minutes", LOOKIN' AFTER NO. 1 sounds like a cross between several tracks off The Vibrators' album, although I'm not certain which. This again is just alright. Second thoughts it's good.

LOVE GOES TO BUILDING ON FIRE is that single that wasn't worth £1.50 as an import, wasn't really worth 70p either, but is nice enough to have as a bonus so here it is, like it or not. Listening to it now I really can't imagine how everyone at The Circus was jumping around wildly while Talking Heads gently strummed this and other slowies. Perhaps they were getting warm for The Ramones.

You surely know the rest of this platter.

FREEZE/MAN OF THE YEAR – THE MODELS.

This is excellent stuff, the best release from Step Forward so far. MAN OF THE YEAR is slightly better, but both sides are good. I've never seen The Models but if this debut single is typical they must be recommended.

DO ANYTHING YOU WANNA DO – EDDIE AND THE HOT RODS.

If this is The Hot Rods country style then it's o.k. by me. I first heard this in Rough Trade off a John Peel show, and promptly bought it when I had saved up 70p. the sound is quite strong compared to previous offerings, Graham Douglas is obviously being used to good effect in their line up, he also co-wrote both sides. This new member evidently arrived at the right time when The Rods were threatening to churn out the same tunes again and again with little progression.

The words are painful in parts, perhaps that's why they didn't print them on the 12" sleeve.

"Don't need no politician, tell me things I shouldn't be, Neither no optician, tell me what I oughta see."

It does drag on a bit, but it's well worth buying. Oh yeh it's just The Rods now. Dunno why.

ALL AROUND THE WORLD – THE JAM

The Jam are quite capable of producing singles of just the right length that they don't become boring. This is very r'n'b and although not as good as IN THE CITY, is already making more of an impact on the national charts. Nostalgia's an incredible thing in 1977.

X-RAY SPEX

X-Ray Spex: a name straight out of whoopee! Many marks on the merit board. They're a typically recent sprout new wave job if only because a hefty 1-2-3-4 propels all their nugget – songs into charted territory, but they're above average 'cos their lead singer is a quantish quainty in jersey-sack mini pointed stillettos and her 1-2-3-4's are screeched a few octaves higher than everyone elses; and, because she wears an army helmet that balances precariously, her movements are restricted and wimpily erotic. The song – nuggets are obvious lethal drone bass-drum-guitar execution jobs with minimum research curiosity BUT there's a warm syrupy sax' clogging it all, pouring through all the clichés and hinting at groovy exploratory and tension conversations for a REAL BRIGHT FUTURE. Laura Logic is the sax. HER deadpan sexuality is irresistible to those who have lost faith in humanity. Outside in the Wimpy Bar I ask whose her favourite player. "Charlie Parker" she says, staring straight into my eyes, yearning for her father. A real bright future X-Ray Spex.

SEVERN UPP

SLITS

The Slits; it takes time to go up to allow the cortical stimulation to spread out and reinforce itself by positive feedback. Early recognition of this fact may have underlain the prolongation of ragas in concert performances, and it was almost certainly the basis of prolonged instrumental breaks in much of the more advanced rock. Forty minutes of increasingly far out improvisation is not too much, even on record. Even granting that to date there has not been a single piece of music produced which will be a turn on for anyone, still we be not too many years away from the discovery of techniques which will enable musicians to evoke psychedelic effects at will in even the straightest audiences. Cool themes. Mind conditioning. Was she a good lay? God only knows.

SEVERN UPP

A NEGATIVE REACTION:- The Negatives are, Modest Young – Lead guitar (well the only guitar) Steve Shy – Bass, Kevin Snap – Percussion (drums) and Dave Bent – vocals. The first gig they ever played was at the Oaks supporting The Drones (once again). Not much to say about that gig really, some people liked it, some didn't! The best laugh was when they played The Squat Club, all the crowd who were mostly students expected something professional or something, and after a few minutes the organisers threatened to close the bar if they didn't leave the stage. So they didn't until the atmosphere got so mean that a riot was probably brewing. No smoking, no exit, no fun ……

The Negatives did release an E.P. entitled BRINGING FICTION BACK INTO MUSIC on their own label although very few copies were actually sold.

THE VIBRATORS (L-R): KNOX, PAT COLLIER (NOW REPLACED BY GARY TIBBS), JOHN ELLIS, JOHN EDWARDS.

The Drones, Penetration, and The Vibrators live!

THE BRIGHT LIGHTS were due to a B.B.C. film crew being present made the Circus look more like the Top Of The Pops studio (or is that what they were there for?). The Drones were the first band who, unaccustomed as they are to being T.V. stars, played their usual strong set which consists of all original material with the exception of Iggy's SEARCH AND DESTROY and MY GENERATION (Patti style). The sound wasn't particularly well mixed on certain numbers notably MY GENERATION where the Guitar and bass were much too quiet, still there's not much chance of that one being shown at any length on T.V. "Why don't you all fuck off, Don't try to dig what the city drones say." Despite the bad mixing which is hardly The Drones' fault, they still survived in front of cameras (dunno if they were actually filming). Visually they were exciting as ever including a spectacular leap into the crowd by Mike Drone, with Whispa and Gus giving visual and musical support.

Penetration are, for the record, from Co. Durham and consist of Pauline on vocals, Gary Grant on lead guitar, R on bass and Gary Smallman on drums. They play all their own songs which include titles like DESTROY, MONEY TALKS, HATE STATE, FIRING SQUAD, I DON'T CARE (I'M NOBODY) and tonight they played the Electric Circus in Manchester. Penetration are very very good and Pauline, who could almost have learnt her art from the Wayne County of late, gave the audience plenty to gloat over as she stared into the crowd with her "T.V. Eyes" and sliced through a heavy set. Penetration, like The Adverts, like The Buzzcocks, are different because they don't come straight out of our crazed capital. Go and see 'em if you haven't already done so, 'cos you'll like 'em. If Warm Records are reading this, yes we would like to hear a cassette-tape, that's if we qualify as a "ZINE".

The crowd were suitably warmed up from the two previous bands when The Vibrators joined us for the grand finale. Lights, action, sound. O.K. roll 'em, all those who wanna become T.V. stars to the front and POGO. Get yourself real high if you want those cameramen to see ya.

Knox is still the main man but only just. John Ellis' eyes bulge as he pulls mock-sneering faces at the forever leaping, occasionally gobbing crowd. (You saw them the other night on telly). Knox sounds every bit a pop group singer with style but John Ellis adds variety which ensures The Vibrators never get dull, his jokey remarks belong on The Goodies.

SWEET SWEET HEART is one of those songs that has that extra catchy other verse which is something very special. Other contenders include GOIN' HOME by The Osmonds, Go BUDDY GO by The Stranglers. You know what I mean "I remember when we were young, Things used to be so pretty. But now we're getting old, things are so bad and that's a pity".

By contrast KEAP IT CLEAN about the pleasures of NOT taking drugs is very seventy-ish tongue-in-cheek type thing. While The Vibrators insist that they mean every word, John Ellis tries to convince us it's all good fun and if you do smoke dope so what, enjoy the gig.

STIFF LITTLE FINGERS is a remnant from the vaults, it's that one about dead people that they actually announced whilst on tour with Iggy Pop. It's a shame that they used to rip through their set express train style, if John Ellis had addressed the audience more often it could well have brought the band closer to the kids in those BIG halls, then again perhaps not, perhaps they were only intended to keep the kids warm till Iggy hit the stage.

BABY BABY as ever the pop number that makes you grin whilst giving you three minutes to recover from pogoing. In the same vein WHIPS AND FURS, a classic stage number is very poppy but whereas BABY BABY builds up to a climax, WHIPS AND FURS keeps on changing then suddenly STOPS!

JUMPING JACK FLASH has been added alongside NO FUN. File under high speed cover versions that rely on words per second where the originals relied on hip dancing.

LONDON GIRLS who sure take some knox these days are we're told the reason The Vibrators ventured northward.

To summarise, the band were heavy with new bassist Gary Tibbs, John Edwards is a remarkably good drummer considering he's only been drumming as long as The Vibrators have been vibrating more or less, which reminds me that WE VIBRATE has now been omitted. If they'd seen the sudden renaissance of that single in Manchester recently perhaps that move would have been re-thought.

The Vibrators could no doubt have made it to a lesser extent in any year, particularly if Mickie Most had modelled them into a pop group and made full use of their ability to write catchy little toons which are the main part of their album. The album may not be the best album ever produced but it does help familiarise everyone with their songs so we can sing-a-long and pogo in time. Why do I keep going on about fucking pogoing.

TALKING TO THE VIBRATORS

<u>MICK</u>: Which bands do you like?

<u>GARY TIBBS</u>: The Vibrators.

<u>JOHN ELLIS</u>: D'you mean just new wave?

<u>MICK</u>: No not really.

<u>JOHN ELLIS</u>: Barbara Streisand. I like The Pistols' <u>singles</u>, they're very clever, but they're more of a business enterprise than a group.

<u>GARY TIBBS</u>: I don't like many of the new wave bands, The Clash, The Jam are rubbish.

<u>KNOX</u>: The Damned had better do something quick or they'll just disappear, which is a shame 'cos I like their attitude, they're a lot of fun. Anyway enough about other bands, let's talk about The Vibrators. Have you heard the album?

<u>MARTIN</u>: Hmmm yeh.

<u>JOHN ELLIS</u>: What don't you like about it?

<u>MARTIN</u>: I like it but …..

<u>MICK</u>: The production's a bit weak.

<u>KNOX</u>: Yeh, perhaps it should have been produced louder, I don't know though, I mean look at RAW POWER, Iggy Pop, that's my favourite album.

<u>MICK</u>: Have you got a lot of material for another album?

<u>JOHN ELLIS</u>: We may be doing a live album which should be good.

<u>KNOX</u>: I'd like to do an album of half live stuff, half studio stuff. We've got some new numbers that we played tonight. FEEL ALRIGHT, not the Stooges, HE'S A PSYCHO and FLYING DUCK THEORY.

<u>JOHN EDWARDS</u>: Dying Fuck Theory.

<u>JOHN ELLIS</u>: No it should be really good, I know you always think that.

<u>KNOX</u>: We've been called to Berlin, we're going in the middle of August, so we might lay down some tracks over there.

MICK: What are the kids like over there?

JOHN EDWARDS: Pretty good crowd, really good in fact, very responsive. Have you seen our fanzine (shows 1977 London Offensive).

KNOX: A German guy did it for us.

MICK: What do you think of all this spitting?

KNOX: I personally don't mind it that much, we don't seem to attract that much. There's a group of kids from The Nashville who follow us round that always spit, but I don't mind if people want to spit, then we'll just spit back.

MARTIN: It's got nasty at Damned gigs lately.

KNOX: Yeh but they attract violence to an extent, for some reason.

JOHN EDWARDS: Yeh and their music's sort of doomy.

KNOX: Do you get any trouble with kids round here?

MARTIN: Not at the circus, they're a good crowd round here, pretty friendly. It's getting a bit heavy in town, Sunday papers' fault mainly if you ask me.

Vibrators interview and live review!

JOHN EDWARDS: Yeh they're very irresponsible the people that write them articles.

KNOX: I mean the Ted's are okay. I know Ted's who are great guys, you probably do.

MICK: They want the same thing really anyway.

GARY TIBBS: Oh yeh we're all on the same side.

MICK: Does it bother you all this fighting that seems to take place in some parts?

KNOX: I never, or rather I try not to think about it, I mean one of these nights we might walk outside and get jumped on by some big blokes who'll attack us with crowbars.

JOHN EDWARDS: It's the young kids that I worry about, I mean what chance has a fifteen year old kid got against a bloke of thirty or forty? We had a lot of trouble like that at the West Runton gig.

KNOX: Yeh I was really fucked off with that place.

JOHN EDWARDS: All these older blokes were waiting outside beating the kids up on the way home.

KNOX: All the dates apart from that one have been really good though, on this tour.

The main reason The Vibrators have suddenly found greater popularity with provincial audiences is probably the strength of their songs in general. They have the ability to assess a crowd and keep them satisfied, an art which most of the younger groups don't have and therefore rely more on chance. Also I suppose as the old wave of the new wave i.e. Pistols, Damned, Clash etc. become more competent and professional (it has to happen), it surely becomes futile to keep knocking any bands that can play. The first new wave is completing their full cycle.

Two weeks later I saw The Vibrators again at Stafford, the day before they played Crackers in Wardour Street to the C.B.S. people. That gig could well earn them a trip to America if it was as good as Stafford the night before, 'cos they played hard and got two encores despite the fact that a lot of people were sat at the table drinking, completely oblivious that there was even a group on stage. Yeh that was weird, Stafford I mean, we were just coming back from London, pulled off the motorway to find a pub' (cos' it was 9:00) and who should walk through the lounge but The Vibrators themselves, who I then found out were playing that very night, and were staying in that very hotel.

SAVE THE CIRCUS

As most of you probably know the Circus looks almost certain to close at the end of September. This would of course leave Manchester without a proper rock venue, as the only alternatives would be Rafters, which only opens to groups on Thursday nights and is anyway, too small for some of the bigger bands, or the big halls like the Free Trade Hall and the Apollo.

The closure of The Circus would also threaten the future of Manchester as a music centre, The Circus was, after all the venue which "pioneered 'new wave'" in Manchester.

"Save The Circus" is a campaign which has been started by the local groups and such; for this to have any chance of success in keeping the Circus open we need plenty of support. If you are interested in helping in anyway, e.g. distributing leaflets, posters or financially, or anyway you can think of, please give us a ring at 0161-494-XXXX between six and seven o'clock on Tuesday or Thursday evenings, ask for Martin.

Sorry the Patti Smith piece didn't appear in this issue but it got lost in the post, somewhere in the region of Stockport. Cry not it will appear in a future issue. Promise.

<u>WHAT?</u> A POEM BY MICK MIDDLES.

None happenings don't happen,
Nobody wanders in alone,
Nobody is sitting'
Nobody is rotting,
Nobody is saying "So what?"
(Who cares?)
Doing is the way,
Doing nothing is hate,
Doing nothing is war,
Doing nothing is victory,
Over nothing.
Doing something is VICTORY,
Over doing nothing.
No chance to say "Don't",
No chance to say "We are",

Or "We aren't" because we will,
And we will if we try.
And you do laugh,
And you do ignore.
And you wont laugh,
And you wont ignore when we do.
And we will.
(So) just sit and rot,
And watch us do.
'Cause we will.
Then again we might NOT!

YET MORE SINGLES REVIEWS * YET MORE SINGLES REVIEWS * YET MORE SINGLES

AINT BIN TO NO MUSIC SCHOOL / FASCIST PIGS – THE NOSEBLEEDS : The Nosebleeds are: Ed Banger-lead vocals, Vincent Riley-Guitar, Pete Crookes-Bass/vocals and Toby-Drums. The first time I ever saw them they were supporting The Dogs at Wythenshawe Forum and were then called Wild Ram. They made quite an impact on the audience and were only denied an encore because time was so tight. As Ed Banger and the Nosebleeds their live show has been variable but nevertheless has steadily improved.

This single, the second release from Rabid Records, is probably the most catchy and certainly the best production yet from a Manchester band. The chorus of MUSIC SCHOOL is the bit that sticks in your mind, although the whole track is really powerful and very interesting.

FASCIST PIGS is not as commercial but too good to be classed as a B-side.

If you want this single and can't get it write to:

RABID RECORDS, 178 WATERLOO PLACE,
OXFORD ROAD, MANCHESTER 13.

GARY GILMORE'S EYES – THE ADVERTS : I've waited a long time to get my paws on this tasteless bit of plastic. It's better live but the songs cleverness makes it an essential buy. T.V. Smith's ability to produce a hook must ensure a bright future for the band. The flip side is the very wonderful BORED TEENAGERS. I prefer it on the Roxy album actually but again you can't keep a good song down. The screeming finish of 'bored out of our MIIINDS' captures the desperation that is the essence of rock'n'roll. On the whole it is one of the best releases this year. MICK

appendix II

gigography - 1976-78

1976

April

Thu 1st
Buzzcocks .... Bolton Institute of Technology
Flywait .... Commercial Hotel, Stalybridge
On the Rocks .... Farmers Arms, Cheadle Heath
SFW .... Phoenix
Fri 2nd
Leo .... Commercial Hotel, Stalybridge
Glance .... Mersey Tavern, Stockport
Abreast .... Surrey Arms, Glossop
Sat 3rd
Slack Alice .... Commercial Hotel, Stalybridge
Menace .... Mersey Tavern, Stockport
Shazam .... Midland Hotel, Didsbury
Sun 4th
Menace .... Commercial Hotel, Stalybridge
Thu 8th
Slack Alice .... Commercial Hotel, Stalybridge
Spiderjive .... Farmers Arms, Cheadle Heath
Dennis Delight .... Phoenix
Fri 9th
Nirvana .... Commercial Hotel, Stalybridge
Leo .... Mersey Tavern, Stockport
Sat 10th
Leo .... Commercial Hotel, Stalybridge
On the Rocks .... Mersey Tavern, Stockport
Slack Alice .... Streetbridge Inn, Hollinwood
Sun 11th
Menace .... Commercial Hotel, Stalybridge
Tue 13th
Orphan .... Mersey Tavern, Stockport
Wed 14th
Shakin' Stevens and the Sunsets
.... Midland Hotel, Didsbury
Thu 15th
Nirvana .... Commercial Hotel, Stalybridge
Harpoon .... Farmers Arms, Cheadle Heath
Hot Property .... Phoenix
Sat 17th
Menace .... Commercial Hotel, Stalybridge
Sun 18th
Pachuco .... Commercial Hotel, Stalybridge
Thu 22nd
Leo .... Commercial Hotel, Stalybridge
Spiderjive .... Farmers Arms, Cheadle Heath
Menace .... Phoenix
Fri 23rd
Menace .... Commercial Hotel, Stalybridge
Jevutshta .... Mersey Tavern, Stockport
Sat 24th
Nirvana .... Commercial Hotel, Stalybridge
Memory Lane .... Streetbridge Inn, Hollinwood
Sun 25th
Plasma .... Commercial Hotel, Stalybridge
Thu 29th
Slack Alice .... Commercial Hotel, Stalybridge
Harpoon .... Farmers Arms, Cheadle Heath
Leo .... Phoenix

Fri 30th
Nirvana .... Commercial Hotel, Stalybridge
Torque .... Mersey Tavern, Stockport
May
Sat 1st
Menace .... Commercial Hotel, Stalybridge
Memory Lane .... Streetbridge Inn, Hollinwood
Sun 2nd
Leo .... Commercial Hotel, Stalybridge
Thu 6th
Rainbow Bridge .... Farmers Arms, Cheadle Heath
Fri 7th
Menace .... Commercial Hotel, Stalybridge
SFW .... Cavalcade, Didsbury
Sat 8th
Leo .... Commercial Hotel, Stalybridge
Southern Comfort .... Streetbridge Inn, Hollinwood
Sun 9th
Slack Alice .... Commercial Hotel, Stalybridge
Wed 12t
Aaron .... Commercial Hotel, Stalybridge
Thu 13th
SFW .... Commercial Hotel, Stalybridge
Spiderjive .... Farmers Arms, Cheadle Heath
Kiss/Stray .... Free Trade Hall
Fri 14th
Nirvana .... Commercial Hotel, Stalybridge
Sat 15th
Nirvana .... Commercial Hotel, Stalybridge
Namesakes .... Midland Hotel, Didsbury
Slack Alice .... Streetbridge Inn, Hollinwood
Sun 16th
Menace .... Commercial Hotel, Stalybridge
Thu 20th
SFW .... Commercial Hotel, Stalybridge
Harpoon .... Farmers Arms, Cheadle Heath
Fri 21st
Menace .... Commercial Hotel, Stalybridge
Alberto Y Lost Trios Paranoias
.... Palace Theatre
Sat 22nd
Slack Alice .... Commercial Hotel, Stalybridge
Nirvana .... Streetbridge Inn, Hollinwood
Sun 23rd
Sting .... Commercial Hotel, Stalybridge
Thu 27th
Azel .... Commercial Hotel, Stalybridge
Spiderjive .... Farmers Arms, Cheadle Heath
Fri 28th
Slack Alice .... Commercial Hotel, Stalybridge
Sat 29th
Menace .... Commercial Hotel, Stalybridge
Slack Alice .... Streetbridge Inn, Hollinwood
Sun 30th
Mudanzas .... Commercial Hotel, Stalybridge

June

Thu 3rd
Dirty Work .... Commercial Hotel, Stalybridge

Caterpillas Don't Believe In Butterflies
......................................Farmers Arms, Cheadle Heath
Fri 4th
Menace ....Commercial Hotel, Stalybridge
Sex Pistols/Solstice ....Lesser Free Trade Hall
Sat 5th
Aftermath......................Commercial Hotel, Stalybridge
Slack Alice ....Streetbridge Inn, Hollinwood
Sun 6th
Slack Alice ....Commercial Hotel, Stalybridge
Tue 8th
Nirvana...........................Cavalcade, Didsbury
Sat 12th
Ready Steady Go...........Midland Hotel, Didsbury
Nirvana...........................Streetbridge Inn, Hollinwood
Mon 14th
Dr Feelgood...................Free Trade Hall
Thu 17th
Train ....Phoenix
Fri 18th
Aftermath......................Commercial Hotel, Stalybridge
Sat 19th
Sting...............................Commercial Hotel, Stalybridge
Slack Alice ....Streetbridge Inn, Hollinwood
Sun 20th
Menace..........................Commercial Hotel, Stalybridge
Thu 24th
Menace..........................Commercial Hotel, Stalybridge
Plasma...........................Phoenix
Fri 25th
Dirty Work ....Commercial Hotel, Stalybridge
Sat 26th
Mudanzas......................Commercial Hotel, Stalybridge
Sting...............................Streetbridge Inn, Hollinwood
Sun 27th
Slack Alice ....Commercial Hotel, Stalybridge
Bob Marley and the Wailers
......................................Kings Hall, Belle Vue

July

Thu 1st
Mudanzas......................Commercial Hotel, Stalybridge
Nirvana...........................Phoenix
Fri 2nd
Mudanzas......................Commercial Hotel, Stalybridge
Eclipse............................St George's Hall, Poynton
Sat 3rd
Mudanzas......................Commercial Hotel, Stalybridge
Sun 4th
Menace..........................Commercial Hotel, Stalybridge
Thu 8th
SFW................................Phoenix
Sat 10th
Johnny and the Jailbirds Midland Hotel, Didsbury
Thu 15th
Azel ....Phoenix
Tue 20th
Sex Pistols/Slaughter and the Dogs/Buzzcocks
......................................Lesser Free Trade Hall
Wed 21st
 Buzzcocks ....St Boniface Youth Club,
Salford
Thu 22nd
Dead Fingers Talk...........Phoenix
Sat 24th
Eclipse...........................Squat Club

Thu 29th
Aaron..............................Phoenix

August

Sun 1st
Slack Alice ....Commercial Hotel, Stalybridge
Thu 5th
Slack Alice ....Commercial Hotel, Stalybridge
Caterpillas Don't Believe In Butterflies
......................................Phoenix
Fri 6th
Vardis ....Commercial Hotel, Stalybridge
Sat 7th
Vardis ....Commercial Hotel, Stalybridge
Ready Steady Go...........
......................................Midland Hotel, Didsbury
Slack Alice ....Streetbridge Inn, Hollinwood
Sun 8th
Slack Alice ....Commercial Hotel, Stalybridge
Thu 12th
Rudy and the Zipps.......Phoenix
Buzzcocks ....Ranch
Sat 14th
Vardis ....Commercial Hotel, Stalybridge
Slack Alice ....Streetbridge Inn, Hollinwood
Sun 15th
Slack Alice ....Commercial Hotel, Stalybridge
Thu 19th
Leo.................................Phoenix
Buzzcocks (cancelled) Ranch
Fri 20th
Slack Alice ....Commercial Hotel, Stalybridge
Sat 21st
Slack Alice ....Streetbridge Inn, Hollinwood
Thu 26th
Swede Larsen ....Phoenix
Fri 27th
Menace..........................Commercial Hotel, Stalybridge
Sat 28th
Buzzcocks ....Commercial Hotel, Stalybridge
Heavy Metal Kids...........Middleton Civic Hall
Memory Lane.................Streetbridge Inn, Hollinwood
Sun 29th
Menace..........................Commercial Hotel, Stalybridge

September

Wed 1st
Son of a Bitch ....El Patio, Stretford
Thu 2nd
Mudanzas......................Commercial Hotel, Stalybridge
Central Christian.............Phoenix
Fri 3rd
Orchiss ....Commercial Hotel, Stalybridge
Sat 4th
Spacers..........................Commercial Hotel, Stalybridge
Hellraisers ....Midland Hotel, Didsbury
Sting...............................Streetbridge Inn, Hollinwood
Sun 5th
Wild Ram ....Commercial Hotel, Stalybridge
Wed 8th
Azel ....El Patio, Stretford
Thu 9th
Sundog..........................Commercial Hotel, Stalybridge
Spacers..........................Phoenix
Fri 10th

Orchiss ....Commercial Hotel, Stalybridge
Slaughter and the Dogs/Mudanzas/Wild Ram
....Forum Theatre. Wythenshawe
Sat 11th
Menace..........................Commercial Hotel, Stalybridge
Uncle Sam ....Streetbridge Inn, Hollinwood
Sun 12th
Vardis ....Commercial Hotel, Stalybridge
Wed 15th
Solstice ....El Patio, Stretford
Thu 16th
Leo.................................Commercial Hotel, Stalybridge
Solstice ....Phoenix
Fri 17th
Deja Vue ....Commercial Hotel, Stalybridge
Sat 18th
Dirty Dog........................Commercial Hotel, Stalybridge
Cadillac..........................Midland Hotel, Didsbury
Hawkwind ....Palace Theatre
Sting...............................Streetbridge Inn, Hollinwood
Sun 19th
Caterpillas Don't Believe In Butterflies
....Commercial Hotel, Stalybridge
Mon 20th
Eater/Buzzcocks ....Houldsworth Hall
Wed 22nd
Ladykiller........................El Patio, Stretford
Thu 23rd
Eskimo Blue ....Commercial Hotel, Stalybridge
Nirvana/S.F.W (Benefit for RNIB) (Cancelled)
....Phoenix
Fri 24th
Leo.................................Commercial Hotel, Stalybridge
Sat 25th
Mudanzas.......................Commercial Hotel, Stalybridge
Slack Alice.....................Streetbridge Inn, Hollinwood
Sun 26th
Spacers..........................Commercial Hotel, Stalybridge
Mon 27th
Spacers..........................Victoria Hotel, Heywood
Thu 30th
Dwarf.............................Commercial Hotel, Stalybridge
Son of a Bitch ....Phoenix

October

Fri 1st
Caterpillas Don't Believe In Butterflies
....Commercial Hotel, Stalybridge
Sex Pistols (Cancelled)
....Didsbury College
Sat 2nd
Menace..........................Commercial Hotel, Stalybridge
Crazy Cavan and the Rhythm Rockers
....Midland Hotel, Didsbury
Septimus ....Streetbridge Inn, Hollinwood
Sun 3rd
Sloth ....Commercial Hotel, Stalybridge
Mon 4th
Captain Zap ....Victoria Hotel, Heywood
Wed 6th
Spacers..........................El Patio, Stretford
Thu 7th
Uncle Sam ....Commercial Hotel, Stalybridge
Captain Zap ....Phoenix
Bicycle Thieves ....White Lion, Withington
Fri 8th

Spacers..........................Commercial Hotel, Stalybridge
Supercharge ....Electric Circus
Buzzcocks ....St Boniface Youth Club,
Salford
Sat 9th
Caterpillas Don't Believe In Butterflies
....Commercial Hotel, Stalybridge
Phoenix..........................Electric Circus
Barclay James Harvest ... Free Trade Hall
Slack Alice.....................Streetbridge Inn, Hollinwood
Sun 10th
Mudanzas.......................Commercial Hotel, Stalybridge
Wed 13th
Fresh Air.........................El Patio, Stretford
Thu 14th
Outside Stuff ....Commercial Hotel, Stalybridge
Upp ....Electric Circus
Grendel ....Phoenix
Bicycle Thieves ....White Lion, Withington
Fri 15th
Caterpillas Don't Believe In Butterflies
....Commercial Hotel, Stalybridge
Loving Awareness
....Electric Circus
Sat 16th
Menace..........................Commercial Hotel, Stalybridge
Riot Rockers ....Midland Hotel, Didsbury
Septimus ....Streetbridge Inn, Hollinwood
Sun 17th
Menace..........................Commercial Hotel, Stalybridge
Thu 21st
Mudanzas.......................Commercial Hotel, Stalybridge
Tiger...............................Electric Circus
Caterpillas Don't Believe In Butterflies
....Phoenix
Fri 22nd
Menace..........................Commercial Hotel, Stalybridge
Babe Ruth ....Electric Circus
Sat 23rd
Orchis.............................Commercial Hotel, Stalybridge
Slack Alice.....................Streetbridge Inn, Hollinwood
Sun 24th
Leo.................................Commercial Hotel, Stalybridge
Mon 25th
Azel ....Victoria Hotel, Heywood
Wed 27th
Captain Zap ....El Patio, Stretford
Thu 28th
Caterpillas Don't Believe In Butterflies
....Commercial Hotel, Stalybridge
Doctors of Madness........ Electric Circus
Patti Smith/Stranglers .....Free Trade Hall
Azel ....Phoenix
Fri 29th
Mudanzas.......................Commercial Hotel, Stalybridge
Enid ....Electric Circus
Sat 30th
Biggleswartime Band.....Commercial Hotel, Stalybridge
Graham Parker and the Rumour
....Manchester University
Flying Saucers ....Midland Hotel, Didsbury
Uncle Sam ....Streetbridge Inn, Hollinwood
Sun 31st
Menace..........................Commercial Hotel, Stalybridge

November

Mon 1st
Caterpillas Don't Believe In Butterflies
....Victoria Hotel, Heywood
Wed 3rd
Leo.................................El Patio, Stretford
AC/DC.............................Manchester University
Thu 4th
Leo.................................Commercial Hotel, Stalybridge
Frankie Miller.................Electric Circus
Captain Zap...................Phoenix
Fri 5th
Spacers..........................Commercial Hotel, Stalybridge
String Driven Thing.........Electric Circus
Sat 6th
Menace..........................Commercial Hotel, Stalybridge
Motorhead.....................Electric Circus
Roogalator/Cado Belle...Manchester University
Dirty Dog........................Streetbridge Inn, Hollinwood
Sun 7th
Orciss ....Commercial Hotel, Stalybridge
Mon 8th
Buzzcocks/Bob Williamson/Tom McMaster and the
Phantom Band/CP Lee/John Cooper Clarke
....Band on the Wall
Jevutshta........................Victoria Hotel, Heywood
Wed 10th
Buzzcocks/Chelsea........Electric Circus
Jobe St Day ....El Patio, Stretford
Thu 11th
Eskimo Blue ....Commercial Hotel, Stalybridge
Scorpions ....Electric Circus
Swede Larsen................Phoenix
Fri 12th
Spacers..........................Commercial Hotel, Stalybridge
Steve Gibbons Band .....Electric Circus
Motorhead.....................Wigan Casino
Sat 13th
Menace..........................Commercial Hotel, Stalybridge
Stretch ....Electric Circus
Leo.................................Streetbridge Inn, Hollinwood
Sun 14th
Caterpillas Don't Believe In Butterflies
....Commercial Hotel, Stalybridge
Mon 15th
SFW................................Victoria Hotel, Heywood
Wed 17th
Caterpillas Don't Believe In Butterflies
....El Patio, Stretford
Thu 18th
Dirty Dog........................Commercial Hotel, Stalybridge
Pat Travers Band.............Electric Circus
Rudy and the Zipps.......Phoenix
Motorhead.....................Salford University
Fri 19th
Orciss ....Commercial Hotel, Stalybridge
Sassafras ....Electric Circus
Sat 20th
Leo.................................Commercial Hotel, Stalybridge
Moon ....Electric Circus
Kursaal Flyers/Burlesque Manchester University
Slack Alice.....................Streetbridge Inn, Hollinwood
Sun 21st
Menace..........................Commercial Hotel, Stalybridge
Mon 22nd
Mud ....Davenport Theatre, Stockport

Eclipse...........................Victoria Hotel, Heywood
Wed 24th
Hinkley's Heroes ....Electric Circus
Swede Larsen................El Patio, Stretford
Thu 25th
Eskimo Blue ....Commercial Hotel, Stalybridge
Jevutshta........................Phoenix
Fri 26th
Caterpillas Don't Believe In Butterflies
....Commercial Hotel, Stalybridge
Sat 27th
Menace..........................Commercial Hotel, Stalybridge
Slack Alice.....................Streetbridge Inn, Hollinwood
Sun 28th
Sloth ....Commercial Hotel, Stalybridge
Buzzcocks/Slaughter and the Dogs
....Electric Circus
Mon 29th
Tractor...........................Victoria Hotel, Heywood

December

Wed 1st
Automatic Fine Tuning...Electric Circus
Jevutshta........................El Patio, Stretford
Thu 2nd
Jobe St Day ....Phoenix
Fri 3rd
Leo.................................Commercial Hotel, Stalybridge
Trapeze...........................Electric Circus
Sat 4th
Slack Alice.....................Commercial Hotel, Stalybridge
Charlie............................Electric Circus
Sun 5th
Dirty Dog........................Commercial Hotel, Stalybridge
Mon 6th
Leo.................................Victoria Hotel, Heywood
Tue 7th
Eddie and the Hot Rods/Aswad
....Free Trade Hall
Wed 8th
SFW................................El Patio, Stretford
Motorhead.....................Bolton Institute of Technology
Thu 9th
After The Fire ....Commercial Hotel, Stalybridge
Sex Pistols/Johnny Thunders and the Heartbreakers/
Clash/Buzzcocks (Anarchy Tour) Electric Circus
Stash (?) ....Phoenix
Fri 10th
Partisan...........................Commercial Hotel, Stalybridge
Tiger................................Electric Circus
Sat 11th
Menace..........................Commercial Hotel, Stalybridge
Jenny Haan's Lion ...... Electric Circus
Slack Alice.....................Victoria Hotel, Heywood

Sun 12th
Caterpillas Don't Believe In Butterflies
....Commercial Hotel, Stalybridge
Mon 13th
Sonny Richard's Band ....Victoria Hotel, Heywood
Wed 15th
Sonny Richard's Band ....El Patio, Stretford
Thu 16th
Orciss ....Commercial Hotel, Stalybridge
Flamin' Groovies............Electric Circus
Sonny Richard's Band .... Phoenix

Fri 17th
Snapper........................Commercial Hotel, Stalybridge
Shanghai ....Electric Circus
Drones/Generation X .....Houldsworth Hall
Sat 18th
Uncle Sam ....Commercial Hotel, Stalybridge
Sam Apple Pie..............Electric Circus
Boss Evil........................Streetbridge Inn, Hollinwood
Sun 19th
Menace..........................Commercial Hotel, Stalybridge
Sex Pistols/Johnny Thunders and the Heartbreakers/
Clash (Anarchy Tour) .....Electric Circus
Wed 22nd
Sun Dog........................El Patio, Stretford
Thu 23rd
Vardis ....Commercial Hotel, Stalybridge
SFW................................Phoenix
Fri 24th
Slack Alice....................Streetbridge Inn, Hollinwood
Sad Café ....Electric Circus
Sun 26th
Sarke ....Commercial Hotel, Stalybridge
Ray Phillips Woman........Electric Circus
Mon 27th
Menace..........................Commercial Hotel, Stalybridge
Wed 29th
Solstice ....El Patio, Stretford
Thu 30th
Orciss ....Commercial Hotel, Stalybridge
Leo................................Phoenix
Fri 31st
Menace..........................Commercial Hotel, Stalybridge
Son of a Bitch ....Electric Circus

1977

January

Sat 1st
Click..............................Commercial Hotel, Stalybridge
Foster Brothers..............Electric Circus
Sun 2nd
Sun Dog........................Commercial Hotel, Stalybridge
Mon 3rd
Jack the Ripper.............Commercial Hotel, Stalybridge
Wed 5th
Hazzard........................El Patio, Stretford
Thu 6th
Hazzard........................Phoenix
Sat 8th
Cado Belle ....Electric Circus
Thu 13th
Solstice ....Phoenix
Fri 21st
Damned.......................Electric Circus
Fri 28th
Charlie...........................Electric Circus
Sat 29th
Snapper........................Commercial Hotel, Stalybridge
Mr Big ....Electric Circus
Mon 31st
SFW................................El Patio, Stretford

February

Thu 3rd
Tractor...........................Phoenix

Fri 4th
Jenny Haan's Lion ....Electric Circus
Sat 5th
Strife ....Electric Circus
Mon 7th
Son of a Bitch ....El Patio, Stretford
Tue 8th
Sensational Alex Harvey Band Without Alex
....Electric Circus
Thu 10th
Azel ....Phoenix
Fri 11th
Prescence ....Commercial Hotel, Stalybridge
Dirty Tricks ....Electric Circus
Sat 12th
Kukulklan.......................Commercial Hotel, Stalybridge
George Hatcher Band
....Electric Circus
Little Bob Story ....Manchester Polytechnic
Sun 13th
Magnum Opus ....Commercial Hotel, Stalybridge
Wed 16th
Azel ....El Patio, Stretford
Thu 17th
On the Rocks ....Commercial Hotel, Stalybridge
Pat Travers/Doctors of Madness
....Middleton Civic Hall
Chaser............................Phoenix
Fri 18th
Dirty Dog.......................Commercial Hotel, Stalybridge
Sat 19th
Jack the Ripper.............Commercial Hotel, Stalybridge
Sun 20th
Snapper........................Commercial Hotel, Stalybridge
Tue 22nd
Slaughter and the Dogs .Oaks Hotel, Chorlton
Suzie Quatro/Supercharge/Ultravoxl/Gags
....Salford University
Wed 23rd
Jevutshta.......................El Patio, Stretford
Drones ....Flanagans
Thu 24th
Prescence ....Commercial Hotel, Stalybridge
Bicycle Thieves ....Midland Hotel, Didsbury
Gags...............................Phoenix
Fri 25th
Kukulklan.......................Commercial Hotel, Stalybridge
Meal Ticket....................Electric Circus
Sat 26th
Mr Distorted ....Commercial Hotel, Stalybridge
Lovin' Awareness...........Electric Circus
Leo................................Streetbridge Inn, Hollinwood
Sun 27th
Snapper........................Commercial Hotel, Stalybridge
Mon 28th
Quench ....El Patio, Stretford

March

Tue 1st
Sad Café ....Oaks Hotel, Chorlton
Wed 2nd
Snooky...........................Midland Hotel, Didsbury
Thu 3rd
Iggy Pop/Vibrators.........Apollo Theatre
Leo................................Commercial Hotel, Stalybridge
SFW................................Phoenix

Fri 4th
Prescence ....Commercial Hotel, Stalybridge
Little Bob Story ....Electric Circus
Sat 5th
Dirty Dog.......................Commercial Hotel, Stalybridge
Stranglers ....Electric Circus
Snapper.........................Streetbridge Inn, Hollinwood
Sun 6th
Gags...............................Commercial Hotel, Stalybridge
Mon 7th
Legend...........................El Patio, Stretford
Wed 9th
Snooky...........................Midland Hotel, Didsbury
Thu 10th
Snapper.........................Commercial Hotel, Stalybridge
Fri 11th
T Rex/Damned ....Apollo Theatre
Prescence ....Commercial Hotel, Stalybridge
Gorillas (cancelled).......Electric Circus
Sat 12th
Prescence ....Commercial Hotel, Stalybridge
Charlie............................Electric Circus
Somebody Else.............Streetbridge Inn, Hollinwood
Sun 13th
A La Carte ....Commercial Hotel, Stalybridge
Mon 14th
Gags/Come in Big Thick/John Cooper Clarke
....Band On The Wall
Wed 16th Leo.................Electric Circus
Thu 17th
American Autumn ....Commercial Hotel, Stalybridge
AC/DC...........................Electric Circus
Fri 18th
City Boy.........................Electric Circus
Sat 19th
Nasty Pop ....Electric Circus
Gags...............................Streetbridge Inn, Hollinwood
Sun 20th
Tractor...........................Electric Circus
Wed 23rd
Zeth ....Electric Circus
Fri 25th
Burlesque.......................Electric Circus
Sat 26th
Kulkulkan.......................Commercial Hotel, Stalybridge
Ultravox!........................Electric Circus
Gags...............................Streetbridge Inn, Hollinwood
Sun 27th
Against the Grain ....Commercial Hotel, Stalybridge
Mon 28th
Cobra.............................Commercial Hotel, Stalybridge
Tue 29th
Johnny Thunders and the Heartbreakers
....Oaks Hotel, Chorlton
Wed 30th
Gags...............................Electric Circus
Thu 31st
Mudanzas.......................Commercial Hotel, Stalybridge
Gags...............................Phoenix

April

Fri 1st
Bicycle Thieves..............Commercial Hotel, Stalybridge
Ray Phillips Woman........Electric Circus
Sat 2nd
Leo..................................Commercial Hotel, Stalybridge

Radiator ....Electric Circus
Crazy Cavan and the Rhythm Rockers
....Midland Hotel, Didsbury
Sun 3rd
Prescence ....Commercial Hotel, Stalybridge
Graham Parker and the Rumour/Southside Johnny and
the Asbury Dukes ....Palace Theatre
Mon 4th
B Bush ....Commercial Hotel, Stalybridge
Thu 7th
Against the Grain ....Commercial Hotel, Stalybridge
Fri 8th
Slipstream......................Commercial Hotel, Stalybridge
Hungry Horse ....Electric Circus
Sat 9th
Magnum Opus ....Commercial Hotel, Stalybridge
Grind ....Electric Circus
Sun 10th
Frogbox ....Commercial Hotel, Stalybridge
Mon 11th
Snapper.........................Commercial Hotel, Stalybridge
Tue 12th
Buzzcocks ....Oaks Hotel, Chorlton
Wed 13th
Drones/Ed Banger and the Nosebleeds
....Electric Circus
Thu 14th
Corndog ....Commercial Hotel, Stalybridge
Fri 15th
Mudanzas.......................Commercial Hotel, Stalybridge
SALT..............................Electric Circus
Sat 16th Leo ....Commercial Hotel, Stalybridge
Casino............................Electric Circus
Sun Session ....Midland Hotel, Didsbury
Sun 17th
Kulkulkan.......................Commercial Hotel, Stalybridge
Thu 21st
Mutants..........................Oaks Hotel, Chorlton
Fri 22nd
Magnum Opus ....Commercial Hotel, Stalybridge
The Scorpions ....Electric Circus
John Cale/Boys/Count Bishops
....Free Trade Hall
Sat 23rd
Mr Distorted ....Commercial Hotel, Stalybridge
Roogalator ....Electric Circus
Snapper.........................Streetbridge Inn, Hollinwood
Sun 24th
A La Carte ....Commercial Hotel, Stalybridge
Cobra.............................Spread Eagle Hotel, Ashton-
Under-Lyne
Mon 25th
Hottentot ....Commercial Hotel, Stalybridge
Tues 26th
Slaughter and the Dogs/ Ed Banger and the
Nosebleeds..
Oaks Hotel, Chorlton
Wed 27th
Cobra.............................El Patio, Stretford
Thu 28th
Snapper.........................Commercial Hotel, Stalybridge
Slits ....Oaks Hotel, Chorlton
Fri 29th
Kulkulkan.......................Commercial Hotel, Stalybridge
Flying Aces ....Electric Circus
Sat 30th
Boxus ....Commercial Hotel, Stalybridge

Strider ....Electric Circus
Flying Saucers ....Midland Hotel, Didsbury
Slipstream.....................Streetbridge Inn, Hollinwood

May

Sun 1ˢᵗ
Leo ....Commercial Hotel, Stalybridge
Wayne County and the Electric Chairs (Cancelled)
......................................Electric Circus
Mon 2ⁿᵈ
Buzzcocks/John Cooper Clarke
......................................Band On The Wall
Tues 3ʳᵈ
Little Bob Story ....Oaks Hotel, Chorlton
Thu 5ᵗʰ
A La Carte ....Commercial Hotel, Stalybridge
Jam (Cancelled) ....Oaks Hotel, Chorlton
Fri 6ᵗʰ
Bethnal...........................Electric Circus
Sat 7ᵗʰ
Cado Belle ....Electric Circus
Sun 8ᵗʰ
Clash/Subway Sect/Slits Electric Circus
Tue 10ᵗʰ
Vibrators ....Oaks Hotel, Chorlton
Fri 13ᵗʰ
Wayne County and the Electric Chairs
......................................Electric Circus
Johnny Thunders and the Heartbreakers/Buzzcocks/
Slaughter and the Dogs/Spitfire Boys
......................................Parr Hall, Warrington
Sat 14ᵗʰ
Krakatoa ....Electric Circus
Damned/Adverts ....Middleton Civic Hall
Sun 15ᵗʰ
Cyanide ....Electric Circus
Tue 17ᵗʰ
Siouxsie and the Banshees
......................................Oaks Hotel, Chorlton
Cry Wold........................St Georges Hall, Poynton
Thu 19ᵗʰ
Adverts...........................Oaks Hotel, Chorlton
Fri 20ᵗʰ
Fabulous Poodles ....Electric Circus
Sat 21ˢᵗ
AFT..................................Electric Circus
Baxus ....Streetbridge Inn, Hollinwood
Sun 22ⁿᵈ
Ramones/Talking Heads. Electric Circus
Mon 23ʳᵈ
Fall ....North West Arts Basement
Tue 24ᵗʰ
Drones/Ed Banger and the Nosebleeds/Negatives
......................................Oaks Hotel, Chorlton
Wed 25ᵗʰ
Alberto Y Lost Trios Paranoias
......................................Manchester Univesity Theatre
Thu 26ᵗʰ
Television/Blondie ....Free Trade Hall
Fri 27ᵗʰ
Nutz................................Electric Circus
Blondie ....Salford University
Sat 28ᵗʰ
Jenny Haan's Lion ....Electric Circus
Insizor............................Streetbridge Inn, Hollinwood
Sun 29ᵗ

Buzzcocks/Penetration/Warsaw/John Cooper/Jon the
Postman ....Electric Circus
Mon 30ᵗʰ
Rockin'One Per Cent/Teddy Boy Lewis/John Cooper
Clarke.............................Band On The Wall
Tue 31ˢᵗ
Johnny Thunders and the Heartbreakers/Warsaw
......................................Rafters

June

Fri 3ʳᵈ
Eddie and the Hot RodsApollo Theatre
Hungry Horse ....Electric Circus
Drones/Negatives/Fall/Warsaw
......................................Squat Club
Sat 4ᵗʰ
Dragons ....Electric Circus
Stranglers/London ....Wigan Casino
Sun 5ᵗʰ
Stranglers/London ....Electric Circus
Wed 8ᵗʰ
Ian Hunter's Overnight Angels/Vibrators
......................................Free Trade Hall
Thu 9ᵗʰ
Heavy Metal Kids
......................................Free Trade Hall
Slaughter and the Dogs Rafters
Fri 10ᵗʰ
Flying Aces ....Electric Circus
Sat 11ᵗʰ
Sassafras ....Electric Circus
Sun 12ᵗʰ
Only Ones ....Electric Circus
Tom Petty and the Heartbreakers/Boomtown Rats
(cancelled)....................Free Trade Hall
Thu 16ᵗʰ
Harpoon/Gags/Bicycle Thieves/Split Beans/Warsaw
......................................Squat Club
Fri 17ᵗʰ
Quartz ....Electric Circus
Sat 18ᵗʰ
Jenny Haan's Lion ....Electric Circus
GJB Band ....Streetbridge Inn, Hollinwood
Sun 19ᵗʰ
Jam ....Electric Circus
Thu 23ʳᵈ
Aswad ....Rafters
Fri 24ᵗʰ
Shanghai ....Electric Circus
Sat 25ᵗʰ
'O' Band ....Electric Circus
Local Reggae Band (Exodus?)/Warsaw/Worst
......................................Squat Club
Snapper (Slack Alice renamed)
......................................Streetbridge Inn, Hollinwood
Damned/Adverts (cancelled)
......................................Wigan Casino
Sun 26ᵗʰ
Damned/Adverts/Prefects...Electric Circus
Mon 27ᵗʰ
Spider Mike King ....Band On The Wall
Thu 30ᵗʰ
Generation X/Warsaw/Worst
......................................Rafters

July

Fri 1st
Heron..............................Electric Circus
Sat 2nd
Pete Brown's Back to Front ....Electric Circus
Jam ....Middleton Civic Hall
Cadillac..........................Midland Hotel, Didsbury
Gags...............................Streetbridge Inn, Hollinwood
Sun 3rd
Saints/Berlin ....Electric Circus
Mon 4th
Bicycle Thieves..............Band On The Wall
Thu 7th
Ultravox!........................Rafters
Fri 8th
George Hatcher Band....Electric Circus
Sat 9th
Stray................................Electric Circus
Slaughter and the Dogs/Eater/X-Ray Spex/Johnny
Moped
....Elizabethan Ballroom, Belle
Vue
Snapper.........................Streetbridge Inn, Hollinwood
Sun 10th
Vibrators/ Penetration/ Drones
....Electric Circus
Mon 11th
Sneakers.........................Band On The Wall
Thu 14th
Gaffer.............................Midland Hotel, Didsbury
Pablo Moses.................Rafters
Fri 15th
Raymond Froggatt..........Electric Circus
Sat 16th
Downliners Sect ....Electric Circus
Cobra.............................Streetbridge Inn, Hollinwood
Sun 17th
Drones/Worst ....Electric Circus
Mon 18th
Bicycle Thieves..............Band On The Wall
Thu 21st
Somebody Else.............Midland Hotel, Didsbury
Elvis Costello/ Spitfire Boys
....Rafters
Fri 22nd
Snapper.........................Electric Circus
Buzzcocks/Fall ....Hulme Labour Club, Hulme
Sat 23rd
Enid ....Electric Circus
Cruisers ....Midland Hotel, Didsbury
Sun 24th
Wayne County and the Electric Chairs
....Electric Circus
Mon 25th
Rockin' One Per Cent
....Band On The Wall
Thu 28th
Alberto Y Lost Trios Paranoias/John Cooper Clarke
....Rafters
Fri 29th
Nail 'Em Down...............Boundary Inn, Oldham
Eclipse..........................Commercial Hotel, Stalybridge
Killer...............................Electric Circus
Sat 30th
Liar ....Boundary Inn, Oldham
Menace..........................Commercial Hotel, Stalybridge

ALT.................................Electric Circus
Sun 31st
Snapper.........................Boundary Inn, Oldham
Gags...............................Commercial Hotel, Stalybridge
Only Ones ....Electric Circus

August

Mon 1st
Harpoon ....Band On The Wall
Thu 4th
Leo.................................Boundary Inn, Oldham
Fri 5th
SFW................................Boundary Inn, Oldham
Corn Dog ....Commercial Hotel, Stalybridge
Motorhead/Count Bishops
....Electric Circus
Sat 6th
Shy Tot...........................Boundary Inn, Oldham
Leo.................................Commercial Hotel, Stalybridge
Ray Phillips Woman
....Electric Circus
Sun 7th
Child's Play....................Boundary Inn, Oldham
Chelsea/Cortinas ....Electric Circus
Mon 8th
No Mystery ....Band On The Wall
Thu 11th
Gags...............................Boundary Inn, Oldham
VSM Moonband.............Commercial Hotel, Stalybridge
XTC/Table......................Rafters
Fri 12th
Snapper.........................Boundary Inn, Oldham
Swakara.........................Commercial Hotel, Stalybridge
Heavy Metal Kids...........Electric Circus
Sat 13th
Revelation ....Boundary Inn, Oldham
Menace..........................Commercial Hotel, Stalybridge
Dozy ....Electric Circus
Leo.................................Oval, Macclesfield
Sun 14th
Survivors ....Boundary Inn, Oldham
Doctors of Madness ......Electric Circus
Tue 16th
Jam/Buzzcocks/Penetration/Jon the Postman
....Electric Circus
Thu 18th
Fall ....St Georges Community
Centre*
Fri 19th
SFW................................Boundary Inn, Oldham
Alvin Lee/Zhain..............Electric Circus
Sat 20th
Dirty Dogs......................Boundary Inn, Oldham
Bethnal...........................Electric Circus
Sun 21st
Free Ride........................Boundary Inn, Oldham
Eater/Fall ....Electric Circus
Mon 22nd
Child's Play....................Boundary Inn, Oldham
Thu 25th
Gags...............................Boundary Inn, Oldham
Nosebleeds...................Rafters
Fri 26th
Crazy Face ....Boundary Inn, Oldham
Eclipse..........................Commercial Hotel, Stalybridge
Jenny Darren Band.........Electric Circus

Slaughter and the Dogs/Drones
....Middleton Civic Hall
Sat 27th
Tennessee Belle Band....Boundary Inn, Oldham
Rodent Enterprises ....Commercial Hotel, Stalybridge
Tractor............................Electric Circus
Sun 28th
Snapper........................Boundary Inn, Oldham
Vardis ....Commercial Hotel, Stalybridge
Adverts/999/Distractions/Slugs
....Electric Circus
Mon 29th
Exodus/John Cooper Clarke
....Band On The Wall

September

Thu 1st
Child's Play....................Boundary Inn, Oldham
Admiral Wold...............Commercial Hotel, Stalybridge
Buzzcocks/Prefects/Distractions
....Rafters
Fri 2nd
Corn Dog ....Commercial Hotel, Stalybridge
Radio Stars....................Electric Circus
Sat 3rd
SFW................................Boundary Inn, Oldham
Vardis ....Commercial Hotel, Stalybridge
Drones/Slaughter and the Dogs
....Electric Circus
Drones/Nosebleeds/Exodus/China Street
....Wigan Casino
Sun 4th
Frogbox ....Boundary Inn, Oldham
Boys ....Electric Circus
Mon 5th
Distractions...................Ranch
Thu 8th
Survivors ....Boundary Inn, Oldham
Rejects ....Commercial Hotel, Stalybridge
Fri 9th
Tractor..........................Boundary Inn, Oldham
Strife ....Electric Circus
Sat 10th
Munro ....Commercial Hotel, Stalybridge
Surburban Studs/Snatch
....Electric Circus
Sun 11th
Tennessee Belle Band
....Boundary Inn, Oldham
Models/Stiletto..............Electric Circus
Tue 13th
Crazy Cavan and the Rhythm Rockers
....Midland Hotel, Didsbury
Thu 15th
Spoonful........................Commercial Hotel, Stalybridge
Jonathan Richman and the Modern Lovers/Andy
Dunkley The Living Jukebox
....Free Trade Hall
Fri 16th
TNK...............................Commercial Hotel, Stalybridge
Pirates ....Electric Circus
Hawkwind.....................Palace Theatre
Sat 17th
Alan Revell....................Commercial Hotel, Stalybridge
Alternative TV ....Electric Circus
Sun 18th

Shy Tots ....Boundary Inn, Oldham
Motors/Skrewdriver
....Electric Circus
Mon 19th
Amazorblades...............Band On The Wall
Tue 20th
Flints..............................Midland Hotel, Didsbury
Wed 21st
Subway Sect/Worst/Killjoys
....Electric Circus
Thu 22nd
SHW Band ....Commercial Hotel, Stalybridge
Fri 23rd
SFW...............................Boundary Inn, Oldham
Shy Tots ....Commercial Hotel, Stalybridge
Killer/American Autumn
....Electric Circus
Generation X.................Rafters
Sat 24th
Changes ....Boundary Inn, Oldham
Corn Dog ....Commercial Hotel, Stalybridge
Rezillos/Warsaw.............Electric Circus
Riot Rockers ....Midland Hotel, Didsbury
Sun 25th
Iggy Pop/Adverts...........Apollo Theatre
Stormtrooper.................Commercial Hotel, Stalybridge
Slits/Prefects/Worst ....Electric Circus
Mon 26th
Gags/Cry Wolf ....Band On The Wall
Thu 29th
Ichthus..........................Commercial Hotel, Stalybridge
Slaughter and the Dogs .Rafters
Fri 30th
Cry Wolf........................Commercial Hotel, Stalybridge
Jenny Haan's Lion ....Electric Circus

October

Sat 1st
Swakara ....Commercial Hotel, Stalybridge
Drones/Distractions/Panik/Manicured Noise/Rip-Off/
Steel Pulse ....Electric Circus
Sun 2nd
Liar ....Boundary Inn, Oldham
Buzzcocks/John Cooper Clarke/Magazine/FallPrefects/
Negatives/Warsaw ....Electric Circus
Mon 3rd
Mudanzas......................Boundary Inn, Oldham
Tue 4th
Adrian Henri/Carol Ann Duffy/John Cooper Clarke
....Band On The Wall
Wed 5th
Tom Robinson Band/Mink DeVille/XTC
....Middleton Civic Hall
Thu 6th
Dr Feelgood/Mink DeVille
....Free Trade Hall
Cherry Vanilla/Berlin.....Rafters
Fri 7th
Plasma...........................Boundary Inn, Oldham
Overlode.......................Commercial Hotel, Stalybridge
Gags...............................Rafters
Slaughter and the Dogs/Drones/V2/Fastbreeder/
Warsaw ....
Salford College of Technology
Sat 8th
SFW...............................Boundary Inn, Oldham

Grogbox ....Commercial Hotel, Stalybridge
Big Youth/Dennis Brown Kings Hall, Belle Vue
Warsaw/Worst/Slugs ......Manchester Polytechnic
Boomtown Rats ....Salford University
Sun 9th
Shy Tots ....Boundary Inn, Oldham
Mon 10th
Rockin' One Per Cent.....Band On The Wall
Dirty Dogs ....Boundary Inn, Oldham
Tue 11th
Snookie and Friends......Boundary Inn, Oldham
Young Street ....Cavalcade, Didsbury
Wed 12th
John Cooper Clarke/Streetwreckers
....Sale Hotel
Thu 13th
Stranglers/Drones...........Apollo Theatre
Oasis..............................Boundary Inn, Oldham
Yachts/Warsaw...............Rafters
Fri 14th
Andromeda...................Boundary Inn, Oldham
Leviathan........................Commercial Hotel, Stalybridge
Tom Robinson Band/Harpoon
....Rafters
Jon the Postman's Puerile
....Squat Club
Sat 15th
American Autumn
....Commercial Hotel, Stalybridge
Johnny Thunders and the Heartbreakers/Models
....Manchester University
Bob Seger and the Silver Bullet Band
....Palace Theatre
Tue 18th
Snookie and Friends......Boundary Inn, Oldham
Wed 19th
Distractions/Snyde/Warsaw/Nervous Breakdown
....Pipers
Thu 20th
X-Ray Spex ....Rafters
Fri 21st
Bunch of Stiffs Tour (Elvis Costello/Ian Dury/Nick Lowe/
Dave Edmunds/Larry Wallis)
....Apollo Theatre
Free Ride........................Boundary Inn, Oldham
Hybrid ....Commercial Hotel, Stalybridge
Rezillos/Sneakers ....Rafters
Sat 22nd
Insizor............................Boundary Inn, Oldham
Rodent Enterprises ....Cavalcade, Didsbury
Corn Dog ....Commercial Hotel, Stalybridge
Gags/Rouge ....Manchester University
Sun 23rd
Liar ....Boundary Inn, Oldham
VSM Moon Band ....Commercial Hotel, Stalybridge
Mon 24th
Bicycle Thieves ....Band On The Wall
Knubber..........................Boundary Inn, Oldham
AC/DC...........................Free Trade Hall
Tue 25th
Snookie and Friends......Boundary Inn, Oldham
Thu 27th
Mudanzas.......................Boundary Inn, Oldham
Bicycle Thieves ....Cavalcade, Didsbury
Red Dog.........................Midland Hotel, Didsbury
Saints ....Rafters

Fri 28th
SFW................................Boundary Inn, Oldham
Bullett.............................Commercial Hotel, Stalybridge
Magazine/Fall.................Rafters
Sat 29th
Clash/Richard Hell and the Voidoids/Lous
....Apollo Theatre
Bullett.............................Boundary Inn, Oldham
Glass Eye ....Commercial Hotel, Stalybridge
Pirates ....Manchester University
Kursaal Flyers.................UMIST
Sun 30th
Dirty Dogs ....Boundary Inn, Oldham
Vardis ....Commercial Hotel, Stalybridge

November

Tue 1st
Snookie and Friends......Boundary Inn, Oldham
Thu 3rd
Chris Spedding Band (cancelled)
....Apollo Theatre
Bicycle Thieves ....Cavalcade, Didsbury
Young Street ....Midland Hotel, Didsbury
Distractions/Jon the Postman's Puerile
....Ranch
Fri 4th
Liquid Glass...................Boundary Inn, Oldham
American Autumn ....Cavalcade, Didsbury
Overlode........................Commercial Hotel, Stalybridge
Burning Spear/Steel Pulse
....New Century Hall
90° Inclusive ....Rafters
Sat 5th
Free Ride.........................Boundary Inn, Oldham
Bullett.............................Commercial Hotel, Stalybridge
Boys ....Elizabethan Ballroom, Belle
Vue
Sun 6th
Overlode........................Boundary Inn, Oldham
Mon 7th
Exodus/Spider Mike King
....Band On The Wall
Tubes/Wire ....Free Trade Hall
Tue 8th
Snookie and Friends......Boundary Inn, Oldham
Overlode........................Cavalcade, Didsbury
Thu 10th
Mudanzas.......................Boundary Inn, Oldham
Fast Breeder...................Cavalcade, Didsbury
Roogalator ....Rafters
Fri 11th
Hot Lanta ....Boundary Inn, Oldham
Orphan ....Commercial Hotel, Stalybridge
Amazorblades...............Rafters
Sat 12th
SFW................................Boundary Inn, Oldham
Hot Lanta ....Commercial Hotel, Stalybridge
Cherry Vanilla.................Elizabethan Ballroom, Belle
Vue
Runaways/999................Free Trade Hall
Buzzcocks/Lurkers ....Manchester Polytechnic
Sun 13th
Fall/Trevor Wishart/Pride Band On The Wall
Shy Tots ....Boundary Inn, Oldham
Plasma............................Commercial Hotel, Stalybridge
Mon 14th

Harpoon ....Band On The Wall
Magazine/Steel Pulse/John Cooper Clarke
....Elizabethan Ballroom, Belle Vue
Graham Parker and the Rumour
....Palace Theatre
Tue 15th
Snookie and Friends......Boundary Inn, Oldham
Fast Breeder...................Cavalcade, Didsbury
Clash/Siouxsie and the Banshees/Subway Sect
....Elizabethan Ballroom, Belle Vue
Thu 17th
Circus.............................Boundary Inn, Oldham
Rodent Enterprises ....Midland Hotel, Didsbury
Tyla Gang ....Rafters
Buzzcocks (cancelled)...Wigan Casino
Fri 18th
Tennessee Belle Band....Boundary Inn, Oldham
Prescence ....Commercial Hotel, Stalybridge
Third World...................Rafters
Motorhead.....................Salford University
Sat 19th
Nirvana...........................Boundary Inn, Oldham
Insizor...........................Commercial Hotel, Stalybridge
Sun 20th
Cry Tough......................Boundary Inn, Oldham
Shy Tots ....Commercial Hotel, Stalybridge
Damned/Dead Boys ......Elizabethan Ballroom, Belle Vue
Rodent Enterprises ....Seven Stars, Heywood
Tue 22nd
Snookie and Friends......Boundary Inn, Oldham
Wed 23rd
Steel Pulse ....New Electric Circus
Thu 24th
Wayne County and Electric Chairs/Alternative TV
....Manchester Polytechnic
Rodent Enterprises .....Midland Hotel, Didsbury
Warsaw/Accelerators/Fast Breeder
....Rafters
Fri 25th
SFW................................Boundary Inn, Oldham
Rodent Enterprises
....Commercial Hotel, Stalybridge
Tom Robinson Band
....Salford University
Vardis ....Seven Stars, Heywood
Sat 26th
Rejects ....Boundary Inn, Oldham
Jevutshta.......................Commercial Hotel, Stalybridge
Mick Farren and the Deviants
....Manchester Polytechnic
Sun 27th
Free Ride.......................Boundary Inn, Oldham
Tunes ....Commercial Hotel, Stalybridge
Nirvana...........................Seven Stars, Heywood
Tue 29th
Jam ....Apollo Theatre
Snookie and Friends......Boundary Inn, Oldham
Wed 30th
Eater................................Rowntrees

December

Thu 1st
Belair...............................Boundary Inn, Oldham

Drones/Distractions ....Carlton Club, Warrington
Fri 2nd
Bullett.............................Boundary Inn, Oldham
Cry Wolf ....Cavalcade, Didsbury
Circus.............................Commercial Hotel, Stalybridge
Orchids ....Spread Eagle Hotel, Ashton-Under-Lyne
Sat 3rd
Orphan ....Boundary Inn, Oldham
Odin Story.....................Commercial Hotel, Stalybridge
Boomtown Rats ....Elizabethan Ballroom, Belle Vue
Darts...............................Manchester Polytechnic
Orchids ....Spread Eagle Hotel, Ashton
Sun 4th
Insizor............................Boundary Inn, Oldham
Stainless Steel Rat....Commercial Hotel, Stalybridge
SFW................................Seven Stars, Heywood
Mon 5th
Liquid Glass...................Band On The Wall
Tue 6th
XTC/Fast Breeder............Elizabethan Ballroom, Belle Vue
Thu 8th
Rodent Enterprises ....Boundary Inn, Oldham
Overlode ....Cavalcade, Didsbury
Orphan ....Midland Hotel, Didsbury
White Fire.......................Oaks Hotel, Chorlton
Penetration.....................Rafters
Pete Farrow Band...........Sale Hotel
Fri 9th
SFW................................Boundary Inn, Oldham
Prescence ....Commercial Hotel, Stalybridge
Steel Pulse ....Rafters
Ian Dury and the Blockheads
....Salford University
Glass Eye ....Seven Stars, Heywood
Sat 10th
Liquid Glass...................Boundary Inn, Oldham
Sun 11th
Merlin.............................Boundary Inn, Oldham
American Autumn ....Commercial Hotel, Stalybridge
White Fire.......................Seven Stars, Heywood
Orchids ....Spread Eagle Hotel, Ashton
Mon 12th
Swift ....Band On The Wall
Tue 13th
Pirates/Septimis/Slugs...Elizabethan Ballroom, Belle Vue
Rodent Enterprises ....Oaks Hotel, Chorlton
Wed 14th
Gags...............................Midland Hotel, Didsbury
Thu 15th
Overlode ....Midland Hotel, Didsbury
Gammer..........................Oaks Hotel, Chorlton
Chris Spedding Band/Reactions
....Rafters
Pete Farrow Band..........Sale Hotel
Fri 16th
Cry Tough......................Boundary Inn, Oldham
Pork Dukes ....Rafters
Fall/Manicured Noise/Elite
....St John's College
Bulletts ....Seven Stars, Heywood
Orchids ....Spread Eagle Hotel, Ashton-Under-Lyne
Fly ....White Lion, Didsbury

Sat 17th
Darts .... Bolton Institute of Technology
Free Ride .... Boundary Inn, Oldham
Fly .... Commercial Hotel, Stalybridge
Alberto Y Lost Trios Paranoias
.... Elizabethan Ballroom, Belle Vue
Rodent Enterprises
.... Mersey Tavern, Stockport
Sun 18th
Buzzcocks/Siouxsie and the Banshees/Penetration
.... Elizabethan Ballroom, Belle Vue
Mon 19th
Buzzcocks/Siouxsie and the Banshees/Penetration
.... Elizabethan Ballroom, Belle Vue
Thu 22nd
Jon the Postman's Puerile/Nervous Breakdown
.... Ranch
Fri 23rd
Prime Time Suckers/Victor Brox Blues Train/Smirks
.... Rafters
Buzzcocks/Drones/Nervous Breakdowns/Jon the
Postman .... Ranch/Fall/Worst/John Cooper Clarke
.... Stretford Civic Hall
Wed 28th
Moving Targets/Nervous Breakdown/Jon the Postman's/
Puerile .... Pips
Thu 29th
V2/Fast Breeder .... Rafters

1978

January

Sun 1st
Fly .... Boundary Inn, Oldham
Snookie and Friends ...... White Lion, Didsbury

Mon 2nd
Gags .... Cavalcade, Didsbury
Rodent Enterprises
.... Sale Hotel
Tue 3rd
Crazy Face .... Champion, Salford
Thu 5th
Old Tennis Shoes .... Midland Hotel, Didsbury
Fri 6th
Snatch Back .... Boundary Inn, Oldham
Idiot Rouge .... Commercial Hotel, Stalybridge
Sat 7th
Poseidon .... Boundary Inn, Oldham
Juggernauts .... Commercial Hotel, Stalybridge
Orchids .... Spread Eagle Hotel, Ashton-Under-Lyne
Sun 8th
Crazy Face .... Boundary Inn, Oldham
Shy Tots .... Commercial Hotel, Stalybridge
Snookie and Friends
.... White Lion, Didsbury
Mon 9th
Gags .... Cavalcade, Didsbury
Rodent Enterprises
.... Sale Hotel
Tue 10th

Crazy Face .... Champion, Salford
Gammer .... Gransmore, Gorton
Wed 11th
Tunes .... Belmont Hotel, Cheetham
Thu 12th
Merlin .... Boundary Inn, Oldham
Old Tennis Shoes .... Midland Hotel, Didsbury
Pete Farrow Band .... Sale Hotel
Fri 13th
Snatch .... Boundary Inn, Oldham
Any Trouble .... Commercial Hotel, Stalybridge
Sat 14th
Free Ride .... Boundary Inn, Oldham
Insizor .... Commercial Hotel, Stalybridge
Sun 15th
Any Trouble .... Boundary Inn, Oldham
Mistress .... Commercial Hotel, Stalybridge
Mon 16th
Smirks .... Band On The Wall
Gags .... Cavalcade, Didsbury
Bethnal/Heat .... Rafters
Rodent Enterprises .... Sale Hotel
Tue 17th
Shabby Tiger .... Boundary Inn, Oldham
Gammer .... Champion, Salford
Wed 18th
Tunes .... Belmont Hotel, Cheetham
Liquid Glass .... Sale Hotel
Thu 19th
Crossfire .... Boundary Inn, Oldham
Tunes .... Cavalcade, Didsbury
Tuxedo Junction .... Champion, Salford
Liquid Glass .... Gransmore, Gorton
Jevutscha .... Midland Hotel, Didsbury
Rodent Enterprises .... UMIST
Fri 20th
Andy Frederich and Exanthus
.... Boundary Inn, Oldham
Overlode .... Cavalcade, Didsbury
Star Banner .... Commercial Hotel, Stalybridge
Sat 21st
White Fire .... Boundary Inn, Oldham
Tunes .... Commercial Hotel, Stalybridge
Talking Heads .... Manchester University
Sun 22nd
American Autumn .... Boundary Inn, Oldham
Cry Tough .... Commercial Hotel, Stalybridge
Liquid Glass .... Grosvenor, Salford
Mon 23rd
Homegrown .... Boundary Inn, Oldham
Rodent Enterprises .... Sale Hotel
Tue 24th
Gammer .... Champion, Salford
Wed 25th
Tunes .... Belmont Hotel, Cheetham
Joy Division .... Pips
Liquid Glass .... Sale Hotel
Thu 26th
Tunes .... Cavalcade, Didsbury
Tuxedo Junction .... Champion, Salford
Insizor .... Midland Hotel, Didsbury
Magazine .... Rafters
Fri 27th
Overlode .... Boundary Inn, Oldham
Liquid Glass .... Commercial Hotel, Stalybridge
Ultravox/Doll .... Middleton Civic Hall
Radio Stars .... Rafters

Gags..............................Salford University
Sat 28th
Rodent Enterprises ....Bolton Institute of Technology
Next Band......................Boundary Inn, Oldham
Virginia Wolf ....Commercial Hotel, Stalybridge
Sun 29th
Crossfire........................Boundary Inn, Oldham
Shy Tots ....Commercial Hotel, Stalybridge
Liquid Glass ....Grosvenor, Salford
Mon 30th
Spider Mike King ....Band On The Wall
Gags..............................Cavalcade, Didsbury
Gammer.........................Gransmore, Gorton
Rodent Enterprises ....Sale Hotel
Tue 31st
Tunes ....Boundary Inn, Oldham
Smirks ....Sale Hotel

February

Wed 1st
Tunes ....Belmont Hotel, Cheetham
Liquid Glass ....Sale Hotel
Thu 2nd
Homegrown ....Boundary Inn, Oldham
Tunes ....Cavalcade, Didsbury
Liquid Glass ....Gransmore, Gorton
Rodent Enterprises ....Midland Hotel, Didsbury
Stukas/Crabbs/Why Not.Rafters
Fri 3rd
Orphan ....Boundary Inn, Oldham
Dillinger/Hortense Ellis ..Rafters
Sat 4th
Odin Storm....................Boundary Inn, Oldham
Sun 5th
American Autumn ....Boundary Inn, Oldham

Mon 6th
Gags/Change ....Band On The Wall
Gammer.........................Gransmore, Gorton
Rodent Enterprises ....Sale Hotel
Smirks ....Wilton Hotel, Prestwich
Tue 7th
No Mystery ....Boundary Inn, Oldham
Heavy Metal Kids/Out ...Rafters
Smirks ....Sale Hotel
Wed 8th
Liquid Glass ....Sale Hotel
Smirks ....Spurley Hey High School
Thu 9th
Tunes ....Cavalcade, Didsbury
Rodent Enterprises ....Midland Hotel, Didsbury
Ultravox/Doll ....Rafters
Fri 10th
Shy Tots ....Boundary Inn, Oldham
Leviathan.......................Commercial Hotel, Stalybridge
Passage ....Edgeley Methodist Church
Earthquake.....................Salford University
Sat 11th
Bethnal...........................Bolton Institute of Technology
Free Ride........................Boundary Inn, Oldham
Honest John ....Commercial Hotel, Stalybridge
Steel Pulse/China Street.Manchester Polytechnic
Gloria Mundi..................Rafters
Drones/Emergency/Slugs UMIST
Sun 12th
Merlin Plumbing ....Commercial Hotel, Stalybridge

Liquid Glass ....Grosvenor, Salford
Mon 13th
Big In Japan/Prime Time Suckers
......................................Band On The Wall
Gammer.........................Gransmore, Gorton
Shabby Tiger ....Boundary Inn, Oldham
Wed 15th
Tunes ....Belmont Hotel, Cheetham
Stance and the Beat ......Pips
Liquid Glass ....Sale Hotel
Thu 16th
Band With No Name......Boundary Inn, Oldham
Tunes ....Cavalcade, Didsbury
Slaughter and the Dogs .Forum Theatre. Wythenshawe
Liquid Glass ....Gransmore, Gorton
XTC ....Middleton Civic Hall
Sham 69/Ego Trip ....Rafters
Pete Farrow Band..........Sale Hotel
Fri 17th
Liquid Glass ....Boundary Inn, Oldham
American Autumn ....Commercial Hotel, Stalybridge
Roogalator/ Torchy and the Moonbeams
......................................Rafters
John Otway and Wild Willy Barrett
......................................Salford University
Sat 18th
Automatics ....Bolton Institute of Technology
Fly ....Boundary Inn, Oldham
Jevutshta........................Commercial Hotel, Stalybridge
Adverts ....Manchester University
Yachts ....Rafters
Sun 19th
Be Bop Deluxe...............Apollo Theatre
Mistress..........................Boundary Inn, Oldham
Overlode ....Commercial Hotel, Stalybridge
Mon 20th
Oakland Johnny Mars ....Band On The Wall
Gammer.........................Gransmore, Gorton
Gags...............................Cavalcade, Didsbury
Tue 21st
Any Trouble...................Oaks Hotel, Chorlton
Wed 22nd
Liquid Glass ....Sale Hotel
Tunes ....Belmont Hotel, Cheetham
Virginia Wolf ....Pips
Thu 23rd
Nirvana...........................Boundary Inn, Oldham
Tunes ....Cavalcade, Didsbury
Liquid Glass ....Gransmore, Gorton
Buzzcocks ....Manchester Polytechnic
Boys/Fast Breeder ....Rafters
Pete Farrow Band..........Sale Hotel
Fri 24th
Eddie and the Hot Rods/Radio Stars/Squeeze
......................................Salford University
Home Grown ....Boundary Inn, Oldham
Mistress..........................Commercial Hotel, Stalybridge
Rockin' One Per Cent.....Rafters
Sat 25th
VSM Moonband............Boundary Inn, Oldham
Negatives.......................Club Afrique, Moss Side
Jevutshta........................Arts Theatre, New Mills
Dawn Weaver ....Commercial Hotel, Stalybridge
Clayson and the Argonauts/Spud
......................................Manchester Polytechnic
Sun 26th
Gammer.........................Gransmore, Gorton

Liquid Glass ....Grosvenor, Salford
SFW..................................Boundary Inn, Oldham
Insizor.............................Commercial Hotel, Stalybridge
Mon 27th
Spider Mike King ....Band On The Wall
Gags................................Cavalcade, Didsbury
Gammer..........................Gransmore, Gorton
Pirates ....Rafters
Tue 28th
Band With No Name......Boundary Inn, Oldham
Pete Farrow Band..............Cavalcade, Didsbury
No Mystery ....Sale Hotel
Motors ....Salford College of Technology

March

Wed 1st
Tunes ....Belmont Hotel, Cheetham
Any Trouble...................Oaks Hotel, Chorlton
Emergency....................Pips
XTC ....Rafters
Thu 2nd
Sandy..............................Boundary Inn, Oldham
Tunes ....Cavalcade, Didsbury
Wire ....Rafters
Pete Farrow Band...........Sale Hotel
Fri 3rd
Funny Plumbing ....Boundary Inn, Oldham
Fly ....Commercial Hotel, Stalybridge
Wayne County and the Electric Chairs/Levi and the
Rockats/Fall ....Rafters
Blondie/Advertising.......Salford University

Sat 4th
Liquid Glass ....Boundary Inn, Oldham
VSM Moonband............Commercial Hotel, Stalybridge
Gags/Tunes ....Manchester University
Cock Sparrer ....Rafters
Sun 5th
White Fire.......................Boundary Inn, Oldham
Idiot Rouge ....Commercial Hotel, Stalybridge
Mon 6th
Charge ....Band On The Wall
Idiot Rouge ....Boundary Inn, Oldham
Gags................................Cavalcade, Didsbury
Gammer..........................Gransmore, Gorton
Motorhead....................Rafters
Tue 7th
Idiot Rouge ....Boundary Inn, Oldham
Pete Farrow Band...........Cavalcade, Didsbury
Any Trouble...................Oaks Hotel, Chorlton
No Mystery ....Sale Hotel
Wed 8th
Tunes ....Belmont Hotel, Cheetham
Oasis...............................Boundary Inn, Oldham
Reducers/Frantic Elevators
......................................Pips
Pete Farrow Band...........Sale Hotel
Thu 9th
Oasis...............................Boundary Inn, Oldham
999..................................Rafters
Fri 10th
Sad Café ....Apollo Theatre
Crazy Face ....Boundary Inn, Oldham
Any Trouble...................Commercial Hotel, Stalybridge
Subway Sect/Lous ....Mayflower, Gorton
Freshies ....Pips

Errol Holt/Eclipse/Junior Mafia Sound System
......................................Rafters
Sat 11th
Crossfire.........................Boundary Inn, Oldham
Tunes ....Commercial Hotel, Stalybridge
Alberto Y Lost Trios Paranoias/Devo/Smirks
......................................Free Trade Hall
Gags................................Manchester University
Gil Gallahad...................Midland Hotel, Didsbury
Gloria Mundi.................Rafters
Black Slate.....................UMIST
Sun 12th
Jevutshta.......................Boundary Inn, Oldham
Shy Tots ....Commercial Hotel, Stalybridge
Sham 69.........................Rafters
Mon 13th
Sneakers........................Band On The Wall
Quorum ....Birch Hotel, Ashton-Under-
Lyne
Tue 14th
Alwoodley Jets ....Boundary Inn, Oldham
Depressions...................Manchester Polytechnic
Tonight...........................Rafters
No Mystery ....Sale Hotel
Wed 15th
Tunes/Geneva ....Moston College of Further
Education
Charge/Teardrops ....Pips
Thu 16th
Magic..............................Annabels
Dirty Dog.......................Boundary Inn, Oldham
Tunes ....Cavalcade, Didsbury
999..................................Rafters
Pate Farrow Band...........Sale Hotel
Fri 17th
Hala Bandura Band ....Boundary Inn, Oldham
Overlode ....Commercial Hotel, Stalybridge
V2 ....Pips
Richard Digance ....Rafters
Sat 18th
Somebody Else..............Boundary Inn, Oldham
Silver Wing....................Commercial Hotel, Stalybridge
Rocky and the DAs ....Midland Hotel, Didsbury
Pleasers/Heat ....Rafters
Motorhead....................Wigan Casino
Sun 19th
Free Ride........................Boundary Inn, Oldham
Blue Water Junction.......Commercial Hotel, Stalybridge
Sad Café ....DavenportTheatre, Stockport
Mon 20th
Prime Time Suckers........Band On The Wall
Little Bob Story..............Rafters
Tue 21st
Whitesnake ....Rafters
No Mystery ....Sale Hotel
Wed 22nd
Nervous Breakdown/Distractions
......................................Pips
Thu 23rd
Juggernaut ....Annabels
Wire ....Rafters
Pete Farrow Band...........Sale Hotel
Fri 24th
Gags................................Rafters
Sat 25th
Maracaibo ....Jodrell Arms, Whaley Bridge
Buzzcocks/Slits/Worst/Patrick Fitzgerald

....Mayflower, Gorton
Saints/Snide...................Rafters
Sad Café ....Wigan Casino
Sun 26th
Gammer...........................Gransmore, Gorton
Buzzcocks/Slits/John Cooper Clarke
....Mayflower, Gorton
Mon 27th
Yo-Yos..............................Band On The Wall
Movies............................Rafters
Tue 28th
Truth...............................Oaks Hotel, Chorlton
Zones/Winners...............Rafters
Wed 29th
Buzzcocks/Slits..............Middleton Civic Hall
Mean Street ....Pips
Thu 30th
Vindalu ....Annabels
Tunes ....Cavalcade, Didsbury
Stepper ....Gransmore, Gorton
Sad Café ....Middleton Civic Hall
X-Ray Spex/Big In Japan
....Rafters
Pete Farrow Band...........Sale Hotel
Fri 31st
Virginia Wolf ....Commercial Hotel, Stalybridge
Nervous Breakdown......Pips
Kevin Coyne/Zoot Money Rafters

April

Sat 1st
Mistress...........................Commercial Hotel, Stalybridge
Gammer...........................Gransmore, Gorton
Shakin' Stevens and the Sunsets
....Midland Hotel, Didsbury
Wreckless Eric/Torchy and the Moonbeams
....Rafters
Sun 2nd
Bicycle Thieves ....Commercial Hotel, Stalybridge
Mon 3rd
Those Naughty Lumps
....Band On The Wall
Bethnal/Reno..................Rafters
Tue 4th
Bethnal/Bicycle Thieves .Rafters
Thu 6th
Tunes ....Cavalcade, Didsbury
Stepper ....Gransmore, Gorton
Eater................................Pips
Elvis Costello and the Attractions
....Rafters
Pete Farrow Band...........Sale Hotel
Fri 7th
Merlin..............................Boundary Inn, Oldham
Skidmarks.......................Commercial Hotel, Stalybridge
Virginia Wolf ....Pips
Elvis Costello and the Attractions
....Rafters
American Autumn
....Travellers Rest, Macclesfield
Sat 8th
Orphan ....Boundary Inn, Oldham
Clearwater Junction
....Commercial Hotel, Stalybridge
Heat................................Pips
Sun 9th

Jevutshta........................Bears Head, Macclesfield
Shy Tots ....Boundary Inn, Oldham
Munroe ....Commercial Hotel, Stalybridge
Gammer...........................Gransmore, Gorton
Mon 10th
No Mystery ....Band On The Wall
Bicycle Thieves ....Rafters
Gammer...........................Sale Hotel
Drones/Fall/Slugs/Identical Zips
....Tower Club, Oldham
Tue 11th
Crazy Face ....Bees Knees, New Mills
Stepper ....Birch Hotel, Ashton-Under-
Lyne
Sheep ....Boundary Inn, Oldham
Monroes ....Cavalcade, Didsbury
Truth...............................Oaks Hotel, Chorlton
Bicycle Thieves ....Rafters
No Mystery ....Sale Hotel
Kols.................................White Gate, Chadderton
Wed 12th
Television/Only Ones ....Apollo Theatre
Somebody Else..............Birch Hotel, Ashton-Under-
Lyne
No Mystery ....Rafters
Thu 13th
Overlode ....Boundary Inn, Oldham
Tunes ....Cavalcade, Didsbury
Stepper ....Gransmore, Gorton
Siouxsie and the Banshees/Singles
....Rafters
Fri 14th
Odinstone ....Bees Knees, New Mills
Tunes ....Boundary Inn, Oldham
Funny Plumbing ....Commercial Hotel, Stalybridge
Accelerators ....Pips
Joy Division/Negatives/Fly/Jilted John/Ed Banger/Prime
Time Suckers/Out/2.3/V2/Yo-Yos/Spider Mike King/
Tunes (Stiff Test/Chiswick Challenge)
....Rafters
Crazy Face ....Travellers Rest, Macclesfield
Sat 15th
Odinstone ....Boundary Inn, Oldham
Glass Eye ....Commercial Hotel, Stalybridge
Slaughter and the Dogs/Gyro/Jilted John/Ed Banger/
Prime Time Suckers/John Cooper Clarke
....Manchester Polytechnic
Shazam............................Midland Hotel, Didsbury
Dead Fingers Talk...........Rafters
Sun 16th
Wilf ....Bears Head, Macclesfield
White Fire.......................Boundary Inn, Oldham
Orphan ....Commercial Hotel, Stalybridge
Gammer...........................Gransmore, Gorton
Mon 17th
China Street ....Band On The Wall
Bicycle Thieves ....Rafters
Gammer...........................Sale Hotel
Tue 18th
Angel's Visit...................Bees Knees, New Mills
Sandy..............................Birch Hotel, Ashton-Under-
Lyne
Monroes ....Cavalcade, Didsbury
Bicycle Thieves ....Rafters
No Mystery ....Sale Hotel
Somebody Else.............White Gate, Chadderton
Wed 19th

Out of the Blue ....Birch Hotel, Ashton-Under-Lyne
Singles ....Pips
No Mystery ....Rafters
Thu 20ᵗʰ
Magic.............................Annabels
Fly ....Boundary Inn, Oldham
Tunes ....Cavalcade, Didsbury
Stepper ....Gransmore, Gorton
X-Ray Spex ....Middleton Civic Hall
Banned ....Rafters
Fri 21ˢᵗ
Free Ride........................Boundary Inn, Oldham
Wilf ....Commercial Hotel, Stalybridge
Stepper ....Failsworth Arms
Ports..............................Pips
Smirks/Ed Banger...........Rafters
Sat 22ⁿᵈ
Girlschool ....Bolton Institute of Technology
Next Band.......................Boundary Inn, Oldham
Virginia Wolf ....Commercial Hotel, Stalybridge
Marseilles.......................Rafters
Sun 23ʳᵈ
Manchester Mekon/Passage
......................................Band On The Wall
Overlode ....Bears Head, Macclesfield
Monroes ....Boundary Inn, Oldham
Funny Plumbing ....Commercial Hotel, Stalybridge
Gammer...........................Gransmore, Gorton
Mon 24ᵗʰ
Idiot Rouge ....Band On The Wall
Tue 25ᵗʰ
Tatum ....Bees Knees, New Mills
Crazy Face ....Birch Hotel, Ashton-Under-Lyne
Nevada ....Boundary Inn, Oldham
Enid/Bicycle Thieves......Rafters
Tunes ....White Gate, Chadderton
Wed 26ᵗʰ
Maracaibo ....Birch Hotel, Ashton-Under-Lyne
Ton Tricks ....Pips
Thu 27ᵗʰ
Thunderbolts ....Annabels
Magic.............................Boundary Inn, Oldham
Stepper ....Gransmore, Gorton
Tatum ....Krumbles, Macclesfield
Adam and the Ants.......Rafters
Fri 28ᵗʰ
Gammer...........................Boundary Inn, Oldham
Race Against Time
......................................Commercial Hotel, Stalybridge
Rebel ....Jodrell Arms, Whaley Bridge
Pere Ubu........................Rafters
Tatum ....Travellers Rest, Macclesfield
Sat 29ᵗʰ
Quad ....Boundary Inn, Oldham
Jevutshta........................Commercial Hotel, Stalybridge
Whirlwind.......................Rafters
Sun 30ᵗʰ
Fall/Mechanics/Elite ....Band On The Wall
Esylom ....Bears Head, Macclesfield
No Risk............................Boundary Inn, Oldham
Grendel ....Commercial Hotel, Stalybridge

May

Mon 1ˢᵗ
Bicycle Thieves ....Band On The Wall
Tue 2ⁿᵈ
Gammer..........................Bees Knees, New Mills
Eclipse............................Birch Hotel, Ashton-Under-Lyne
Stepper ....Boundary Inn, Oldham
Tyla Gang/Magic ....Rafters
Wed 3ʳᵈ
Inside Out......................Boundary Inn, Oldham
Smirks ....Spurley Hey High School, Gorton
Thu 4ᵗʰ#
Rocking Horse................Annabels
Poseidon ....Boundary Inn, Oldham
Maracaibo ....Krumbles, Macclesfield
Banned ....Rafters
Quorum ....Sale Hotel
Fri 5ᵗʰ
Orphan ....Bees Knees, New Mills
Bratz...............................Boundary Inn, Oldham
Dawn Weaver ....Commercial Hotel, Stalybridge
Depressions...................Pips
Aswad ....Rafters
Gammer..........................Travellers Rest, Macclesfield
Sat 6ᵗʰ
Stepper ....Boundary Inn, Oldham
Ego Trip ....Commercial Hotel, Stalybridge
AC/DC............................Free Trade Hall
Shaking Stevens and the Sunsets/Frantic Elevators
......................................Manchester Polytechnic
Flying Saucers................Midland Hotel, Didsbury
Mistress..........................Senior Citizens Hall, Macclesfield
Sun 7ᵗʰ
Toy Town Symphony Orchestra/Creation
......................................Band On The Wall
Orphan ....Bears Head, Macclesfield
Idiot Rouge ....Boundary Inn, Oldham
Fly ....Commercial Hotel, Stalybridge
Café Jacques ....Rafters
Motors ....Ritz Ballroom
Mon 8ᵗʰ
Rockin' One Per Cent.....Band On The Wall
Magazine/John Cooper Clarke
......................................Ritz Ballroom
Gammer..........................Sale Hotel
Tue 9ᵗʰ
American Autumn ....Bees Knees, New Mills
Stepper ....Birch Hotel, Ashton-Under-Lyne
Rudies.............................Boundary Inn, Oldham
Monroes ....Cavalcade, Didsbury
Geneva ....Sale Hotel
Maracaibo ....Snooty Fox, Didsbury
Gammer..........................White Gate, Chadderton
Wed 10ᵗʰ
Overlode ....Birch Hotel, Ashton-Under-Lyne
Those Naughty Lumps....Pips
Thu 11ᵗʰ
Jenny Haan's Lion....Annabels
Any Trouble...................Boundary Inn, Oldham
Tunes ....Cavalcade, Didsbury
Idiot Rouge ....Krumbles, Macclesfield
Cherry Vanilla/Margo/Zinc
......................................Rafters

Fri 12th
Idiot Rouge ....Bees Knees, New Mills
White Fire........................Boundary Inn, Oldham
Rigor Mortis...................Commercial Hotel, Stalybridge
Distractions....................Pips
Vibrators........................Rafters
Gyro/John Cooper Clarke/Ed Banger/Jilted John/Prime
Time Suckers.................Russell Club, Hulme
Stepper ....Travellers Rest, Macclesfield
Sat 13th
Juggernaut.....................Boundary Inn, Oldham
Singles ....Commercial Hotel, Stalybridge
Girlschool/Freshies ....Rafters
Sun 14th
Idiot Rouge ....Bears Head, Macclesfield
Out ....Boundary Inn, Oldham
Shy Tots ....Commercial Hotel, Stalybridge
Slaughter and the Dogs/Eater
......................................Rafters
Mon 15th Spider
Mike King ....Band On The Wall
Gammer.........................Sale Hotel
Tue 16th
Jevutshta........................Bees Knees, New Mills
Sandy.............................Birch Hotel, Ashton-Under-Lyne
Monroes ....Cavalcade, Didsbury
Maracaibo ....Snooty Fox
Jonathan Young ....White Gate, Chadderton
Wed 17th
Maracaibo ....Birch Hotel, Ashton-Under-Lyne
Thu 18th
Tubes (cancelled). ....Free Trade Hall
Dealer ....Krumbles, Macclesfield
Lurkers...........................Pips
Flamin' Groovies/Radio Birdman
......................................Rafters
Quorum ....Sale Hotel
Fri 19th
Next Band......................Bees Knees, New Mills
Funny Plumbing ....Boundary Inn, Oldham
Arlington Country...........Commercial Hotel, Stalybridge
Tubes (cancelled) ....Free Trade Hall
Stepper ....Jodrell Arms, Whaley Bridge
V2/Distractions ....Mayflower, Gorton
Flamin' Groovies/Radio Birdman
......................................Rafters
Durutti Column/Jilted John...Russell Club, Hulme
Jevutshta........................Travellers Rest, Macclesfield
Sat 20th
Any Trouble...................Birch Hotel, Ashton-Under-Lyne
Cross Fire ....Boundary Inn, Oldham
Tunes ....Commercial Hotel, Stalybridge
Joy Division ....Mayflower, Gorton
Sun 21st
Next Band......................Bears Head, Macclesfield
Prawn Crackers ....Bees Knees, New Mills
Wiffer.............................Boundary Inn, Oldham
Out ....Commercial Hotel, Stalybridge
Gammer.........................Gransmore, Gorton
Mon 22nd
Accelerators/Out...........Band On The Wall
John Otway and Wild Willy Barratt/Smirks
......................................Ritz Ballroom
Tue 23rd

Shy Tots ....Birch Hotel, Ashton-Under-Lyne
Monroes ....Cavalcade, Didsbury
Gammer.........................Champion, Salford
Pirates ....Manchester Polytechnic
Stepper ....Oaks Hotel, Chorlton
Crazy Face ....White Gate, Chadderton
Wed 24th
Stacey............................Birch Hotel, Ashton-Under-Lyne
Jevutshta........................Phoenix
Snyde/Bastille ....Pips
Thu 25th
Risk................................Boundary Inn, Oldham
Sly May ....Champion, Salford
Darts..............................Free Trade Hall
Stepper ....Gransmore, Gorton
Odinstone ....Krumbles, Macclesfield
Bernie Torme/Accelerators
......................................Rafters
Fri 26th
Jailer ....Bees Knees, New Mills
Stepper ....Boundary Inn, Oldham
Sterling...........................Commercial Hotel, Stalybridge
Rezillos/Gruppo Sportivo
......................................Rafters
Big In Japan/Manicured Noise
......................................Russell Club, Hulme
Nevada ....Travellers Rest, Macclesfield
Fall/Manchester Mekon/Nives
......................................Squat Club
Sat 27th
Jevutshta........................Boundary Inn, Oldham
Sheep ....Commercial Hotel, Stalybridge
V2/Distraction/Freshies ..Mayflower, Gorton
Little Tina/ Flight 56...Midland Hotel, Didsbury
Young Bucks/Dirty Shirts...Rafters
Sun 28th
Jailer ....Bears Head, Macclesfield
Geneva ....Boundary Inn, Oldham
Vardis ....Commercial Hotel, Stalybridge
John Cooper Clarke/Exodus/Mike Harding/Trevor Hyett/
Peggy Seeger, Ewan MacColl, Callum & Neill MacColl/
Bob Williamson ....Free Trade Hall
Gammer.........................Gransmore, Gorton
Tue 30th
Shy Tots ....Bees Knees, New Mills
Monroes ....Cavalcade, Didsbury
Gammer.........................Champion, Salford
Vardis ....White Gate, Chadderton
Wed 31st ....Ian Dury and the Blockheads/
Matumbi/Whirlwind ......Free Trade Hall
Idiot Rouge/Rudies..........Phoenix

June

Thu 1st
Cyanide ....Buxton Town Hall
Vardis ....Krumbles, Macclesfield
Alternative TV ....Rafters
Pirates ....Wigan Casino
Fri 2nd
Bullitt.............................Bees Knees, New Mills
Vesuvius ....Boundary Inn, Oldham
Gammer/Images/Quad....Hyde Town Hall
Big In Japan/DistractionsRafters
Any Trouble...................Rose and Crown, Stalybridge

Durutti Column/FC Domestos/Cabaret Voltaire ....
Russell Club, Hulme
Shy Tots ....Travellers Rest, Macclesfield
Sat 3rd
Mistress...........................Boundary Inn, Oldham
Bos..................................Commercial Hotel, Stalybridge
Johnny Cougar................Mayflower, Gorton
Free Ride/Soft Shoe ....Royal Northern College of
Music
Movies/Heat ....Rafters
Sun 4th
Bullitt...............................Bears Head, Macclesfield
Accelerators ....Boundary Inn, Oldham
Distractions....................Commercial Hotel, Stalybridge
Gammer.........................Gransmore, Gorton
Idiot Rouge ....Spread Eagle Hotel, Ashton-
Under-Lyne
Mon 5th
Gyro...............................Band On The Wall
Rudies............................Boundary Inn, Oldham
Tue 6th
Vardis ....Bees Knees, New Mills
Maracaibo ....Birch Hotel, Ashton-Under-
Lyne
Sly..................................Boundary Inn, Oldham
Gammer.........................Champion, Salford
Idiot Rouge/Rudies ....Oaks Hotel, Chorlton
Warren Harry..................Rafters
Asgard ....White Gate, Chadderton
Wed 7th
Overlode ....Birch Hotel, Ashton-Under-
Lyne
Thu 8th
Magic..............................Annabels
Ego Trip ....Boundary Inn, Oldham
Idiot Rouge ....Champion, Salford
Shy Tots ....Commercial Hotel, Stalybridge
Shouter ....Krumbles, Macclesfield
Only Ones/Jab Jab ....Manchester Polytechnic
Fri 9th
Wilf ....Bees Knees, New Mills
Grendel ....Boundary Inn, Oldham
Cass Cannane Band ....Commercial Hotel, Stalybridge
Soft Boys........................Rafters
Joy Division/Tiller Boys ..Russell Club, Hulme
Sat 10th
Accelerators ....Bolton Institute of Technology
Shy Tots ....Boundary Inn, Oldham
Mistress...........................Commercial Hotel, Stalybridge
Gammer.........................Gransmore, Gorton
Amazorblades...............Manchester Polytechnic
Steel Pulse/China Street .Mayflower, Gorton
Subway Sect/Prefects....Rafters
Sun 11th
Fall/FC Domestos/Manchester Mekon
....Band On The Wall
Wilf ....Bears Head, Macclesfield
Silver Moon Band ....Boundary Inn, Oldham
A La Carte ....Commercial Hotel, Stalybridge
Subway Sect ....Rafters
Any Trouble ....Spread Eagle Hotel, Ashton
Mon 12th Guess.............Band On The Wall
Rudies............................Boundary Inn, Oldham
Gags...............................Cavalcade, Didsbury
Tue 13th
Grendel ....Bees Knees, New Mills
Idiot Rouge ....Birch Hotel, Ashton-Under-

Lyne
1feedback ....Boundary Inn, Oldham
Gammer.........................Champion, Salford
Rudies............................Oaks Hotel, Chorlton
Glasgow Express...........White Gate, Chadderton
Wed 14th
Somebody Else.............Birch Hotel, Ashton-Under-
Lyne
Freshies..........................Boundary Inn, Oldham
Sly..................................Trap, Glossop
Here and Now/Alternative TV
....UMIST
Thu 15th
Black Sabbath/Tanz Der Youth
....Apollo Theatre
Freshies..........................Boundary Inn, Oldham
Cry Tough......................Champion, Salford
Fly ....Commercial Hotel, Stalybridge
Grendel ....Krumbles, Macclesfield
Good Rats......................Rafters
Fri 16th
Gammer.........................Bees Knees, New Mills
Accelerators ....Commercial Hotel, Stalybridge
Fall/Distractions/Jon the Postman/Mechanics
....Concorde Suite, Droylsden
Jonathan Richman and the Modern Lovers
....Free Trade Hall
Boyfriends ....Rafters
Angel Visits....................Travellers Rest, Macclesfield
Sat 17th
Ego Trip ....Commercial Hotel, Stalybridge
Pleasers.........................Manchester Polytechnic
Automatics ....Rafters
Snatch Back ....White Gate, Chadderton
Sun 18th
Passage/Frantic Elevators/Creation
....Band On The Wall
Eclipse...........................Bears Head, Macclesfield
Drive From Night...........Commercial Hotel, Stalybridge
Gammer.........................Gransmore, Gorton
Somebody Else.............White Gate, Chadderton
Mon 19th
Reaction.........................Band On The Wall
Alberton Y Lost Trios Paranoias/John Dowie
....Davenport Theatre, Stockport
Tue 20th
Dealer ....Bees Knees, New Mills
Any Trouble ....Birch Hotel, Ashton-Under-
Lyne
Idiot Rouge ....White Gate, Chadderton
Wed 21st
Sly..................................Birch Hotel, Ashton-Under-
Lyne
Munroe ....Phoenix
Thu 22nd
Geneva ....Champion, Salford
Idiot Rouge ....Commercial Hotel, Stalybridge
Overlode ....Gransmore, Gorton
Dealer ....Krumbles, Macclesfield
Munroe ....White Gate, Chadderton
Fri 23rd
Odinstone ....Bees Knees, New Mills
Zanathus ....Commercial Hotel, Stalybridge
Johnny Moped/Ten Tricks
....Rafters
Dealer ....Travellers Rest, Macclesfield
Overlode ....White Gate, Chadderton

Snatchback....................Wigan Casino
Sat 24th
Cimmarons/China Street Manchester Polytechnic
Penetration.....................Rafters
Sun 25th
Fall/Spherical Objects...Band On The Wall
Fly ....Bears Head, Macclesfield
Overlode ....Commercial Hotel, Stalybridge
Gammer........................Gransmore, Gorton
Mon 26th Maracaibo ......Band On The Wall
Tue 27th
Monroes ....Bees Knees, New Mills
Shy Tot ....Birch Hotel, Ashton-Under-
Lyne
Dire Straits/Out ....Rafters
Two Plus One ....White Gate, Chadderton
Wed 28th Out.................Birch Hotel, Ashton-Under-
Lyne
Geneva ....Phoenix
Thu 29th
Overlode ....Champion, Salford
Pointed Finger...............Commercial Hotel, Stalybridge
Stacey............................Trap, Glossop
Fri 30th
Boomtown Rats ....Apollo Theatre
Somebody Else.............Bees Knees, New Mills
Nirvana..........................Boundary Inn, Oldham
Funny Plumbing ....Commercial Hotel, Stalybridge
Smirks/Ed Banger Therapy Band/Cathy La Crème
.....................................Rafters
Hybrid ....Travellers Rest, Macclesfield

July

Sat 1st
Bratz..............................Boundary Inn, Oldham
Whifter...........................Commercial Hotel, Stalybridge
Pegasus ....Rafters
Sun 2nd
Clash ....Apollo Theatre
Red Stain........................Bears Head, Macclesfield
Eddy ....Boundary Inn, Oldham
Identical Zips ....Commercial Hotel, Stalybridge
Gammer.........................Gransmore, Gorton
Mon 3rd
Pressure Shocks ....Band On The Wall
Clash/Bitch ....Rafters
Tue 4th
Quad ....Bees Knees, New Mills
Overlode II ....Birch Hotel, Ashton-Under-
Lyne
Maracaibo ....Snooty Fox, Didsbury
Wed 5th
Maracaibo ....Birch Hotel, Ashton-Under-
Lyne
Aqua..............................Phoenix
Ego Trip ....Trap, Glossop
Thu 6th
Windjammer..................Band On The Wall
Fast Cars ....Boundary Inn, Oldham
Distant Hills....................Krumbles, Macclesfield
Gloria Mundi/ Rudies/Idiot Rouge
.....................................Rafters
Fri 7th
Overlode II ....Bees Knees, New Mills
Café Astoria ....Boundary Inn, Oldham
Overlode ....Commercial Hotel, Stalybridge

Magazine ....Russell Club, Hulme
Zhain..............................Travellers Rest, Macclesfield
Sat 8th
Soft Rick and the Flexible Stems
.....................................Boundary Inn, Oldham
Cairo ....Commercial Hotel, Stalybridge
Shy Tots/Overlode II/Sapphire
.....................................Hyde Town Hall
Supercharge ....Rafters
Bullitt..............................Tower Club, Oldham
Sun 9th
No Mystery ....Bears Head, Macclesfield
Any Trouble....................Boundary Inn, Oldham
Rudies............................Commercial Hotel, Stalybridge
Gammer.........................Gransmore, Gorton
Tue 11th
Funny Plumbing ....Bees Knees, New Mills
Crazy Face ....Birch Hotel, Ashton-Under-
Lyne
Maracaibo ....Snooty Fox, Didsbury
Wed 12th
Somebody Else.............Birch Hotel, Ashton-Under-
Lyne
Rudies............................Trap, Glossop
Thu 13th
Graham Parker and the Rumour
.....................................Alexandra Park, Moss Side
Cyanide ....Krumbles, Macclesfield
Rich Kids /(cancelled) ...Tower Club, Oldham
Fri 14th
Alchemist ....Boundary Inn, Oldham
Fast Cars ....Commercial Hotel, Stalybridge
Accelerators ....Travellers Rest, Macclesfield
Rich Kids/Fall.................UMIST
Gang of Four/Emergency/Feathered Vision
.....................................Russell Club, Hulme
Sat 15th
Steel Pulse/China Street/Buzzcocks/Exodus
.....................................Alexandra Park, Moss Side
Jevutshta........................Boundary Inn, Oldham
Devil's Answer...............Commercial Hotel, Stalybridge
Matchbox ....Midland Hotel, Didsbury
Desmond Dekker ....Pembroke Hall, Walkden
Sun Jul Munroe..............Bears Head, Macclesfield
Reducers........................Boundary Inn, Oldham
Feedback........................Commercial Hotel, Stalybridge
Mon 17th Out ....Band On The Wall
Rudies............................Boundary Inn, Oldham
Gammer.........................Trap, Glossop
Tue 18th
Samson ....Bees Knees, New Mills
Sandy.............................Birch Hotel, Ashton-Under-
Lyne
Maracaibo ....Snooty Fox, Didsbury
Wed 19th Stacey............Birch Hotel, Ashton-Under-
Lyne
Thu 20th
Zanathus ....Boundary Inn, Oldham
Salem.............................Cavalcade, Didsbury
Zarathustra ....Commercial Hotel, Stalybridge
Samson ....Krumbles, Macclesfield
Siouxsie and the Banshees/Spizz Oil
.....................................RussellII Club, Hulme
Fri 21st
Out ....Boundary Inn, Oldham
Swakara ....Commercial Hotel, Stalybridge
Buzzcocks/Magazine.....Lesser Free Trade Hall

Ekos .... Old Vets Club, Farnworth
Culture/Tradition .... RussellII Club, Hulme
Samson .... Travellers Rest, Macclesfield
Sat 22nd
Samson .... Boundary Inn, Oldham
Ego Trip .... Commercial Hotel, Stalybridge
John Cooper Clarke/Exodus/Accidents
.... Manchester Polytechnic
Smirks/Ed Banger/Steroid Kiddies
.... Middleton Civic Hall
Sun 23rd
Mekons/A Certain Ratio/Toy Town Symphony
Orchestra .... Band On The Wall
Orphan .... Bears Head, Macclesfield
Captain America .... Boundary Inn, Oldham
VSM Moonband .... Commercial Hotel, Stalybridge
Mon 24th
China Street .... Band On The Wall
SFW .... Boundary Inn, Oldham
Salford Jets .... Duke of Wellington, Swinton
Tue 25th
Rudies .... Bees Knees, New Mills
Soft Rick and the Flexible Stems
.... Birch Hotel, Ashton-Under-
Lyne
Maracaibo .... Snooty Fox, Didsbury
Salford Jets .... Tonge Ward Labour Club,
Bolton
Wed 26th
Freshies .... Birch Hotel, Ashton-Under-
Lyne
Thu 27th
Shy Tots .... Boundary Inn, Oldham
Orphan .... Krumbles, Macclesfield
Fri 28th
Juggernaut .... Bees Knees, New Mills
White Fire .... Boundary Inn, Oldham
Rudies .... Commercial Hotel, Stalybridge
Suicide/Joy Division/Actors
.... RussellII Club, Hulme
Magic .... Travellers Rest, Macclesfield
Sat 29th
Whiffer .... Boundary Inn, Oldham
Andy Stark Band .... Cavalcade, Didsbury
Stance .... Commercial Hotel, Stalybridge
Spherical Objects .... Grange Arts Centre, Oldham
Rezillos (cancelled) .... Mayflower, Gorton
Krakatoa .... Tower Club, Oldham
Sun 30th
Spherical Objects .... Band On The Wall
Juggernaut .... Bears Head, Macclesfield
Red Stain .... Boundary Inn, Oldham
Shy Tots .... Commercial Hotel, Stalybridge
Gammer .... Gransmore, Gorton
Mon 31st
Salem .... Cavalcade, Didsbury

August

Tue 1st
Eclipse .... Birch Hotel, Ashton-Under-
Lyne
Wed 2nd
Crazy Face .... Birch Hotel, Ashton-Under-
Lyne
Vardis .... Trap, Glossop
Thu 3rd

Munroe .... Boundary Inn, Oldham
Overlode .... Gransmore, Gorton
Gammer .... Krumbles, Macclesfield
Fri 4th
Legend .... Boundary Inn, Oldham
Munroe .... Commercial Hotel, Stalybridge
Salford Jets .... Duke of Wellington, Swinton
Sat 5th
Quad .... Boundary Inn, Oldham
Andy Stark Band .... Cavalcade, Didsbury
Geneva .... Commercial Hotel, Stalybridge
Sun 6th
VSM Moonband .... Boundary Inn, Oldham
Orphan .... Commercial Hotel, Stalybridge
Gammer .... Gransmore, Gorton
Mon 7th
Free Ride .... Boundary Inn, Oldham
Salem .... Cavalcade, Didsbury
Salford Jets .... Duke of Wellington, Swinton
Tue 8th
Eclipse .... Bees Knees, New Mills
Dogs Body .... Birch Hotel, Ashton-Under-
Lyne
Freshies .... Boundary Inn, Oldham
Salford Jets .... Tonge Ward Labour Club,
Bolton
Wed 9th
Somebody Else .... Birch Hotel, Ashton-Under-
Lyne
Thur 10th
Freshies .... Boundary Inn, Oldham
Overlode .... Gransmore, Gorton
Monkey Wrestlers .... Krumbles, Macclesfield
Fri 11th
Captain America .... Boundary Inn, Oldham
Contraband .... Commercial Hotel, Stalybridge
Durutti Column/Feathered Version/Cabaret Voltaire
.... RussellII Club, Hulme
Sat 12th
Funny Plumbing .... Boundary Inn, Oldham
Overlode .... Commercial Hotel, Stalybridge
Sun 13th
Eclipse .... Bears Head, Macclesfield
Salem .... Boundary Inn, Oldham
Armageddon .... Commercial Hotel, Stalybridge
Gammer .... Gransmore, Gorton
Magic/Blues Train/Distractions
.... Tameside Theatre, Ashton-
Under-Lyne
Mon 14th
Tunes .... Band On The Wall
Bordello .... Cavalcade, Didsbury
Salford Jets .... Duke of Wellington, Swinton
Tues 15th
Jevutshta .... Bees Knees, New Mills
Advantage .... Birch Hotel, Ashton-Under-
Lyne
Salford Jets .... Tonge Ward Labour Club,
Bolton
Wed 16th
Sandy .... Birch Hotel, Ashton-Under-
Lyne
Overlode .... Trap, Glossop
Thur 17th
Stance .... Boundary Inn, Oldham
Salem .... Cavalcade, Didsbury
Monkey Wrestlers .... Krumbles, Macclesfield

Fri 18th
Accelerators ....Boundary Inn, Oldham
Tunes ....Commercial Hotel, Stalybridge
Giro/Ed Banger/Gordon the Moron
......................................Russellll Club, Hulme
Sat 19th
Rezillos/Fall/Squares ......Apollo Theatre
White Fire........................Boundary Inn, Oldham
Jevutshta.........................Commercial Hotel, Stalybridge
Movies ....Manchester University
Magic..............................Tower Club, Oldham
Sun 20th
Monkey Wrestlers ....Bears Head, Macclesfield
Idiot Rouge ....Boundary Inn, Oldham
Talisman ....Commercial Hotel, Stalybridge
Gammer..........................Gransmore, Gorton
Here and Now/Fall ....Salford University
Mon 21st
Mick Abrahams Band ....Band On The Wall
Gags................................Cavalcade, Didsbury
Here and Now, Fall, Wilful Damage, Alternative TV
......................................Tower Club, Oldham
Tue 22nd
Dust/Manchester Mekon/Creation
......................................Band On The Wall
Zhain...............................Bees Knees, New Mills
Dead Rox ....Birch Hotel, Ashton-Under-Lyne
Here and Now/Fall ....Tower Club, Oldham
Wed 23rd
Shy Tots ....Birch Hotel, Ashton-Under-Lyne
Thur 24th
Vardis ....Boundary Inn, Oldham
Salem..............................Cavalcade, Didsbury
Idiot Rouge ....Krumbles, Macclesfield
Fri 25th
Vesuvius ....Boundary Inn, Oldham
Funny Plumbing ....Commercial Hotel, Stalybridge
Alberto y Los Trios Paranoias
......................................Russellll Club, Hulme
Sat 26th
Shy Tots ....Boundary Inn, Oldham
Salem..............................Commercial Hotel, Stalybridge
Sun 27th
René...............................Bears Head, Macclesfield
Eddy...............................Boundary Inn, Oldham
Ryder ....Commercial Hotel, Stalybridge
Gammer..........................Gransmore, Gorton
Mon 28th
Giro................................Band On The Wall
Gags................................Cavalcade, Didsbury
Tue 29th
Joy Division ....Band On The Wall
René...............................Bees Knees, New Mills
Last Chicken in the Shop
......................................Birch Hotel, Ashton-Under-Lyne
Wed 30th
Soft Rick and the Flexible Stems
......................................Birch Hotel, Ashton-Under-Lyne
Thu 31st
Patti Smith Band/Pop Group
......................................Apollo Theatre
Salem..............................Boundary Inn, Oldham
Juggernaut.....................Krumbles, Macclesfield

Stacey.............................Trap, Glossop

September

Fri 1st
Grendel ....Boundary Inn, Oldham
Any Trouble...................Commercial Hotel, Stalybridge
Sat 2nd
Isis..................................Boundary Inn, Oldham
Red Stain........................Commercial Hotel, Stalybridge
Sun 3rd
Shy Tots ....Bears Head, Macclesfield
VSM Moonband............Boundary Inn, Oldham
Idiot Rouge ....Commercial Hotel, Stalybridge
Gammer..........................Gransmore, Gorton
Free Ride/Jackson Burns Band
......................................Middleton Civic Hall
Mon 4th
Joy Division ....Band On The Wall
Gags................................Cavalcade, Didsbury
Tue 5th
Salem..............................Bees Knees, New Mills
Alchemist ....Birch Hotel, Ashton-Under-Lyne
Wed 6th
Cry Tough.......................Birch Hotel, Ashton-Under-Lyne
Eddy ....Trap, Glossop
Thu 7th
Drones ....Russellll Club, Hulme
Fri 8th
Flying Saucers ....Old Vets Club,Farnworth
Gang of Four.................Russellll Club, Hulme
Sat 9th
JG Spoils ....Commercial Hotel, Stalybridge
Spider Jive ....Midland Hotel, Didsbury
Delroy Wilson ....Russellll Club, Hulme
Sun 10th
RBQ................................Bears Head, Macclesfield
Gammer..........................Gransmore, Gorton
Mon 11th
Spider Mike KingSpherical Objects
......................................Band On The Wall
Idiot Rouge ....Birch Hotel, Ashton-Under-Lyne
Air School......................Cavalcade, Didsbury
Tue 12th
Frantic Elevators/Not Sensibles/Unit
......................................Band On The Wall
Orphan ....Bees Knees, New Mills
Idiot Rouge ....Birch Hotel, Ashton-Under-Lyne
Gatecrasher ....Cavalcade, Didsbury
Vardis ....White Gate, Chadderton
Wed 13th
Freshies..........................Birch Hotel, Ashton-Under-Lyne
Thu 14th
Salem..............................Cavalcade, Didsbury
Blondie/Boyfriends........Free Trade Hall
Juggernaut.....................Krumbles, Macclesfield
Yachts ....Russell Club, Hulme
Vardis ....Trap, Glossop
Fri 15th
Ego Trip ....Commercial Hotel, Stalybridge
Alberto Y Lost Trios Paranoias
......................................Russell Club, Hulme

Distractions/Tunes..........Town Hall, Glossop
Sat 16th
Eddy...............................Commercial Hotel, Stalybridge
Dynamite ....Midland Hotel, Didsbury
Sun 17th
Salem.............................Bears Head, Macclesfield
Isis..................................Commercial Hotel, Stalybridge
Gammer..........................Gransmore, Gorton
Mon 18th
Magic..............................Band On The Wall
Air School.......................Cavalcade, Didsbury
Tue 19th
Crispy Ambulance.........Band On The Wall
Esylom ....Bees Knees, New Mills
Eclipse............................Birch Hotel, Ashton-Under-Lyne
Gatecrasher ....Cavalcade, Didsbury
Gammer..........................White Gate, Chadderton
Wed 20th
Last Chicken in the Shop
....Birch Hotel, Ashton-Under-Lyne
Puzzlers ....Trap, Glossop
Thu 21st
Salem..............................Cavalcade, Didsbury
Vesuvius ....Krumbles, Macclesfield
Slaughter and the Dogs (cancelled)
....Russell Club, Hulme
Fri 22nd
Snatch Back ....Bees Knees, New Mills
Hot Foot Gale ....Old Vets Club,Farnworth
Sore Throat ....Russell Club, Hulme
Idiot Rouge.....................Salford College of Technology
Sat 23rd
Sarko..............................Commercial Hotel, Stalybridge
Lurkers............................Mayflower, Gorton
Carl Terry and the Cruisers
....Midland Hotel, Didsbury
Junior Walker and the All Stars
....Russell Club, Hulme
Sun 24th
Snatch Back ....Bears Head, Macclesfield
Smack..............................Commercial Hotel, Stalybridge
Mon 25th
Distractions....................Band On The Wall
Idiot Rouge.....................Birch Hotel, Ashton-Under-Lyne
Gags...............................Cavalcade, Didsbury

Tue 26th
Any Trouble....................Birch Hotel, Ashton-Under-Lyne
Tunes ....New Mills Youth Centre
Puzzlers ....White Gate, Chadderton
Wed 27th
Stepper ....Birch Hotel, Ashton-Under-Lyne
Idiot Rouge.....................Manchester Polytechnic
Aqua...............................Phoenix
Thu 28th
Stranglers/Skids ....Apollo Theatre
Gags...............................Cavalcade, Didsbury
Bordello..........................Krumbles, Macclesfield
Radio Stars/Reaction ......Middleton Civic Hall
Neon Hearts ....Pips
Tribesmen/Exodus...Russell Club, Hulme
Shy Tots ....Trap, Glossop

Fri 29th
Idiot Rouge ....Commercial Hotel, Stalybridge
Ramones ....Free Trade Hall
Fall/Emergency ....Russell Club, Hulme
Sat 30th
Funny Plumbing ....Commercial Hotel, Stalybridge
Aqua/Crispy Ambulance/Avalon/Pete Farrow Band
....Lesser Free Trade Hall
Jab Jab ....Manchester Polytechnic
Dave Edmunds Rockpile Manchester University
John Holt.......................Russell Club, Hulme

October

Sun 1st............................Gatecrasher
....Bears Head, Macclesfield
Height.............................Commercial Hotel, Stalybridge
Mon 2nd
Last Chicken in the Shop Band On The Wall
Any Trouble....................Birch Hotel, Ashton-Under-Lyne
Joy Division ....Bolton Institute of Technology
Gags...............................Cavalcade, Didsbury
Crawler ....Russell Club, Hulme
Tue 3rd
RBQ.................................Bees Knees, New Mills
Shy Tots ....Birch Hotel, Ashton-Under-Lyne
Dr Feelgood/Bishops .....Free Trade Hall
Jab Jab ....Salford University
Flick of the Wrist ....White Gate, Chadderton
Wed 4th
Stacey..............................Birch Hotel, Ashton-Under-Lyne
Racing Cars ....Manchester University
Thu 5th
Tom Robinson Band/Stiff Little Fingers
....Apollo Theatre
Salem..............................Cavalcade, Didsbury
Vintage ....Jodrell Arms, Whaley Bridge
Fall/Distractions/Militant Frank
....Kellys
Buzzcocks/Subway Sect Middleton Civic Hall
Messagana/Jenny Darren Russell Club, Hulme
Rudies.............................Trap, Glossop
Fri 6th
Steel Pulse/China Street Apollo Theatre
Quad ....Commercial Hotel, Stalybridge
Matumbi ....Manchester Polytechnic
Cadillac...........................Old Vets Club,Farnworth
Ultravox ....Russell Club, Hulme
Any Trouble....................Spread Eagle Hotel, Ashton-Under-Lyne
Accidents........................Squat Club
Sat 7th
Hawklords/Hawkwind
....Apollo Theatre
Motorhead/Lightning Raiders
....Bolton Institute of Technology
Free Fall..........................Commercial Hotel, Stalybridge
Chalky Dusters/Flick o' the Wrist/Gutter Press/Snyde
Jevutshta.........................Hyde Town Hall
Girlschool ....Lion Hotel, Warrington
Smack..............................Midland Hotel, Didsbury
Scene Stealer.................Manchester Polytechnic
Pleasers..........................Manchester University
Black Slate......................Russell Club, Hulme

Fall/Distractions..............St John's College
Sun 8th
Spider...........................Bears Head, Macclesfield
Matchbox.....................Champagne Charlies, Beswick
Smack...........................Eccles Town Hall
Pop Group....................Russell Club, Hulme
Mon 9th
Gaffer..............................Band On The Wall
Tue 10th
Not Sensibles/Vica Versa/Manchester Mekon
....Band On The Wall
Any Trouble...................Bees Knees, New Mills
Caprice ....Birch Hotel, Ashton-Under-
Lyne
Gags...............................Cavalcade, Didsbury
Gruppo Sportivo..........Manchester Polytechnic
Pop Group/Ludus..........Russell Club, Hulme
Wliko Johnson's Solid Senders/Fischer-Z
....Salford University
Rudies............................White Gate, Chadderton
Wed 11th
Cannon ....Birch Hotel, Ashton-Under-
Lyne
Tunes ....Phoenix
Gammer.......................Trap, Glossop
Thu 12th
Smack............................Bulls Head, Walkden
Gags...............................Cavalcade, Didsbury
Joy Division/Risk ....Kellys
Idiot Rouge ....Krumbles, Macclesfield
Alien Tint ....Pips
Wayne County and the Electric Chairs/Emergency
....Russell Club, Hulme
Fri 13th
Ego Trip ....Commercial Hotel, Stalybridge
Doomed/Ivor Biggun/Straits
....Mayflower, Gorton
Matchbox ....Old Vets Club,Farnworth
Wire/Manicured Noise ..Russell Club, Hulme
Idiot Rouge ....Spread Eagle Hotel, Ashton-
Under-Lyne
Sat 14th
Pleasers ....Bolton Institute of Technology
Distractions ....Ashwood Park Hotel, Buxton
Kypo ....Commercial Hotel, Stalybridge
John Cooper Clarke/Jon the Postman
....Manchester Polytechnic
Smirks ....Manchester University
Fall/Wilful Damage ....Rochdale College
Sun 15th
Tunes ....Bears Head, Macclesfield
Smack............................Commercial Hotel, Stalybridge
Mon 16th
Ed Banger ....Band On The Wall
Idiot Rouge ....Birch Hotel, Ashton-Under-
Lyne
Smirks ....Carlton Club, Warrington
Gags...............................Cavalcade, Didsbury
Wreckless Eric/Mickey Jupp/Jona Lewie/Lene Lovich/
Rachel Sweet.................UMIST
Smack............................Waggon and Horses, Oldham
Tue 17th
Creation/Alien Tint/St Mathildas Boys
....Band On The Wall
Spider...........................Bees Knees, New Mills
Wed 18th
Flick o' the Wrist.............Birch Hotel, Ashton-Under-

Lyne
Aswad...........................Manchester University
Smack...........................Trap, Glossop
Thu 19th
Turning Point..................Band On The Wall
Eddy..............................Bees Knees, New Mills
Exodus...........................Kellys
Vibrators ....Manchester Polytechnic
Movies/Streetband........Mayflower, Gorton
Crabs ....Pips
Salford Jets/Jeff Hill Band/Fast Cars
....Russell Club, Hulme
Fri 20th
Puzzlers ....Commercial Hotel, Stalybridge
Alberto Y Lost Trios Paranoias/Phantom Captain/John
Dowie ....Manchester University Theatre
Autographs....................Mayflower, Gorton
Reddy Teddy..................Old Vets Club,Farnworth
Joy Division/Cabaret Voltaire/Tiller Boys
....Russell Club, Hulme
Radio Stars/Reaction ......Salford University
Smack ....Spread Eagle Hotel, Ashton-
Under-Lyne
Sat 21st
Racing Cars ....Bolton Institute of Technology
Swakara ....Commercial Hotel, Stalybridge
Fall/Distractions/Passage/Crass/Agony Column
....Manchester Polytechnic
XTC ....Manchester University
Alberto Y Lost Trios Paranoias/Phantom Captain/John
Dowie ....Manchester University Theatre
Dodgers........................Mayflower, Gorton
Lurkers...........................Middleton Civic Hall
Sun 22nd
Smack...........................Butchers Arms, Pendlebury
Alwoodley Jets. ....Commercial Hotel, Stalybridge
Mon 23rd
Rockin' Ricky and the Velver Collars
....Band On The Wall
Any Trouble...................Birch Hotel, Ashton-Under-
Lyne
Gags...............................Cavalcade, Didsbury
Tue 24th
Juggernaut.....................Bees Knees, New Mills
Not Sensibles ....Band On The Wall
999................................Manchester Polytechnic
Wed 25th
Distractions/Private Sector
                                        Hazel Grove Youth Club,
                                        Stockport
Only Ones/Ton Tricks ....Russell Club, Hulme
Thu 26th
Salem.............................Cavalcade, Didsbury
Frantic Elevators/Not Sensibles
....Kellys
Rudies............................Pips
Automatics ....Russell Club, Hulme
Any Trouble...................Trap, Glossop
Fri 27th
Buzzcocks/Subway Sect
....Apollo Theatre
Jackson Burns Band
....Commercial Hotel, Stalybridge
Bram Tchaikovsky's Battleaxe
....Mayflower, Gorton
Split Enz ....Russell Club, Hulme
Pirates ....Salford University

Smack .... Spread Eagle Hotel, Ashton-Under-Lyne
Skrewdriver/Fireplace .... Squat Club
Sat 28th
Ego Trip .... Commercial Hotel, Stalybridge
Lurkers/Skrewdriver .... Mayflower, Gorton
Matumbi .... Russell Club, Hulme
Rich Kids .... UMIST
Trend/Freshies .... Venue, Collyhurst
Sun 29th
Shy Tots .... Bears Head, Macclesfield
Fast Cars .... Birch Hotel, Ashton-Under-Lyne
Radio Stars/Reaction ...... Mayflower, Gorton
Distractions/Private Sector
.... Venue, Collyhurst
Mon 30th
Fall/Rodent Enterprises .. Band On The Wall
Idiot Rouge .... Birch Hotel, Ashton-Under-Lyne
Gags .... Cavalcade, Didsbury
Tue 31st
Tunes .... Bees Knees, New Mills
Shy Tots .... Birch Hotel, Ashton-Under-Lyne
Air School .... Cavalcade, Didsbury
Smack .... Grosvenor, Salford

November

Wed 1st
Virginia Wolf .... Birch Hotel, Ashton-Under-Lyne
Smack .... Midland Hotel, Didsbury
Thu 2nd
Desmond Dekker .... Blightys, Farnworth
Salem .... Cavalcade, Didsbury
Smack .... Krumbles, Macclesfield
Shots .... Pips
Pegasus/Pathetix .... Rafters
Smirks .... Russell Club, Hulme
Fri 3rd
Desmond Dekker .... Blightys, Farnworth
Shy Tots .... Commercial Hotel, Stalybridge
Motorhead/Johnny Moped
.... Free Trade Hall
Smack .... Lancashire Vaults, Oldham
Wilko Johnson's Solid Senders
.... Mayflower, Gorton
Dave Lee Sand .... Old Vets Club, Farnworth
Penetration/Crash Course Russell Club, Hulme
Jab Jab .... Venue, Collyhurst
Sat 4th
Dennis Delight .... Bees Knees, New Mills
Desmond Dekker .... Blightys, Farnworth
Rudies .... Commercial Hotel, Stalybridge
After the Fire .... Manchester Polytechnic
Siouxsie and the Banshees
.... Manchester University
Racing Cars/Straw dogs . Mayflower, Gorton
Shazam .... Middleton Civic Hall
Smack .... Trap, Glossop
Speedometers .... Venue, Collyhurst
Sun 5th
Snatch Back .... Bears Head, Macclesfield
Idiot Rouge .... Commercial Hotel, Stalybridge
Real Thing .... Mayflower, Gorton

Drones/Wilful Damage ... Venue, Collyhurst
Mon 6th
China Street .... Band On The Wall
Idiot Rouge .... Birch Hotel, Ashton-Under-Lyne
Gags .... Cavalcade, Didsbury
Wreckless Eric/Jona Lewie/Rachel Sweet/Lene Lovich/Mickey Jupp/Records.... Salford University
Smack .... Wilton Arms, Prestwich
Tue 7th
Passage/Certain Ratio/Slight Seconds
.... Band On The Wall
New Mania .... Bees Knees, New Mills
Chalky White and the Dusters
.... Birch Hotel, Ashton-Under-Lyne
Air School .... Cavalcade, Didsbury
Lee Patrick Band .... Russell Club, Hulme
Wed 8th
Stacey .... Birch Hotel, Ashton-Under-Lyne
Squeeze/Jays .... Manchester University
Smack .... Spread Eagle Hotel Ashton-Under-Lyne
Thu 9th
Gary Boyle .... Band On The Wall
Accelerators .... Bees Knees, New Mills
Smack .... Bulls Head, Walkden
Salem .... Cavalcade, Didsbury
Shy Tots .... Krumbles, Macclesfield
Ian Gillan Band .... Mayflower, Gorton
Wilful Damage .... Pips
Puzzlers .... Trap, Glossop
Drones/Jolt .... Venue, Collyhurst
Fri 10th
AC/DC/Blazer Blazer ...... Apollo Theatre
Orphan .... Commercial Hotel, Stalybridge
Skrewdriver/Bitch .... Mayflower, Gorton
Prince Far I/Creation Rebel
.... Russell Club, Hulme
Enid .... Salford University
China Street .... UMIST
Sat 11th
Gammer .... Bees Knees, New Mills
Red Stain .... Commercial Hotel, Stalybridge
Any Trouble .... Grosvenor, Salford
Shirts .... Manchester University
Gloria Mundi/One Way Subway
.... Mayflower, Gorton
Brown Sugar .... Russell Club, Hulme
Flys .... Venue, Collyhurst
Sun 12th
Buzzcocks/Subway Sect Apollo Theatre
Salem .... Bears Head, Macclesfield
Any Trouble .... Commercial Hotel, Stalybridge

Sensational Alex Harvey Band Without Alex
.... Mayflower, Gorton
Mon 13th
Jam/Patrik Fitzgerald ...... Apollo Theatre
Gags .... Band On The Wall
Any Trouble .... Birch Hotel, Ashton-Under-Lyne
Fall .... Carlton Club, Warrington
Smack .... Squat Club
Tue 14th
Frantic Elevators/Manchester Mekon/Fast Cars

......................................Band On The Wall
Salem..............................Bees Knees, New Mills
Smack.............................Birch Hotel, Ashton-Under-Lyne
Air School ....Cavalcade, Didsbury
Wed 15th
Fast Cars..........................Birch Hotel, Ashton-Under-Lyne
Slaughter and the Dogs/V2/Ed Banger
......................................Lesser Free Trade Hall
Dire Straits.....................Manchester University
Whitefire ....Phoenix
Candy ....Trap, Glossop
Thu 16th
Salem.............................Cavalcade, Didsbury
Tunes/Accelerators ....Kellys
Puzzlers ....Krumbles, Macclesfield
Spider.............................Pips
Skids/Secret Public....Russell Club, Hulme
Smack.............................Spinners, Hulme
Fri 17th
Smack.............................Commercial Hotel, Stalybridge
Pure Hell ....Mayflower, Gorton
Human League/Gang of Four/Mekons/Scars
......................................Russell Club, Hulme
Sassafras ....Venue, Collyhurst
Sat 18th
Talisman ....Commercial Hotel, Stalybridge
Smack.............................Grosvenor, Salford
Messagana/Distractions
......................................Manchester Polytechnic
Bethnal............................Manchester University
Japan ....Mayflower, Gorton
Dillinger/Fast Cars..........Russell Club, Hulme
Jolt.................................Venue, Collyhurst
Sun 19th
Jevutshta.......................Bears Head, Macclesfield
Bombers ....Commercial Hotel, Stalybridge
Merger ....Mayflower, Gorton
Bishops ....Venue, Collyhurst
Mon 20th
Zang................................Band On The Wall
Gags................................Cavalcade, Didsbury
Joy Division ....Check Inn Club, Altrincham
Tue 21st
Sham 69/ Cimmarons.....Apollo Theatre
Fall/A Certain Ratio/Grow Up
......................................Band On The Wall
Idiot Rouge ....Bees Knees, New Mills
Alchemist ....Birch Hotel, Ashton-Under-Lyne
Wed 22nd
Bombers ....Birch Hotel, Ashton-Under-Lyne
New Mania ....Phoenix
Smack.............................Spread Eagle Hotel, Ashton
Salem.............................Trap, Glossop
Thu 23th
Clash/Slits/Pressure Shocks...Apollo Theatre
Smack ....Bulls Head, Walkden
Salem.............................Cavalcade, Didsbury
Fast Cars/Sister Ray. ....Kellys
Stadium Dogs ....Mayflower, Gorton
Dawn Weaver ....Pips
Fri 24th
Tunes ....Commercial Hotel, Stalybridge
Snips................................Mayflower, Gorton

Pere Ubu/Soft Boys/Red Crayola
......................................Russell Club, Hulme
Teendreams/Out/Mekons
......................................Squat Club
Sister Ray/Cindy/Virgins .St John's College
Eric Bell Band................Venue, Collyhurst
Sat 25th
Funny Plumbing ....Commercial Hotel, Stalybridge
Magazine ....Manchester University
David Johansen Band...Mayflower, Gorton
Fall ....Prestwich Hospital Social Club
Accelerators ....Spread Eagle Hotel, Ashton
Boyfriends ....UMIST
Marseilles.......................Venue, Collyhurst
Sun 26th
Shy Tots ....Commercial Hotel, Stalybridge
Quad ....Bears Head, Macclesfield
Slade/Skrewdriver ....Mayflower, Gorton
Joy Division/Passage......Venue, Collyhurst
Mon 27th
No Mystery ....Band On The Wall
Stadium Dogs ....Carlton Club, Warrington
Gags................................Cavalcade, Didsbury
Out/Teendreams............Lesser Free Trade Hall
Generation X/Private Sector
......................................Russell Club, Hulme
Tue 28th
Moonraker ....Birch Hotel, Ashton-Under-Lyne
Wed 29th
X-Ray Spex/Sore Throat...Apollo Theatre
Sanoy.............................Birch Hotel, Ashton-Under-Lyne
Still/Holy Newts.............Hazel Grove Youth Club, Stockport
Smack............................Spinners, Hulme
Asylum............................Trap, Glossop
Thu 30th
Swift ....Band On The Wall
Salem.............................Cavalcade, Didsbury
Knives/Wilful Damage ....Kellys
Accelerators ....Krumbles, Macclesfield
Squeeze ....Mayflower, Gorton
Puzzlers ....Pips
V2/Frantic Elevators/Accidents
......................................Russell Club, Hulme

December

Fri 1st
Salem.............................Commercial Hotel, Stalybridge
Rezillos/Undertones. ......Free Trade Hall
Dave Lewis Band ....Mayflower, Gorton
Prag Vec/Normal............Russell Club, Hulme
Smack.............................Spread Eagle Hotel, Ashton
Sat 2nd
Dream Life.....................Commercial Hotel, Stalybridge
Here and Now/Fall/Anal Surgeons/Danny and the
Dressmakers...................Manchester Polytechnic
Wilko Johnson's Solid Senders
......................................Manchester University
No Dice ....Mayflower, Gorton
Fall/John Cooper Clarke
......................................Russell Club, Hulme
Sun 3rd
Peter Tosh/Matumbi.......Apollo Theatre
PaulTownsend's Heroes Bears Head, Macclesfield

Devils Answer................Commercial Hotel, Stalybridge
Wild Horses...................Mayflower, Gorton
Mon 4th
Last Chicken in the Shop Band On The Wall
Here and Now/Fall/Danny and the Dressmaker/Wilful
Damage ....Bolton Institute of Technology
Devo/Doll by Doll...Free Trade Hall
Terraplane......................Lion Hotel, Warrington
Alberto Y Lost Trios Paranoias
......................................Oldham Civic Hall
Tue 5th
Ian Matthews ....Mayflower, Gorton
Wed 6th
Shy Tots ....Birch Hotel, Ashton-Under-
Lyne
Crazy Cavan and the Rhythm Rockers
......................................Mayflower, Gorton
Smack............................Midland Hotel, Didsbury
Buzz Hawkins ....Trap, Glossop
Thu 7th
Smack............................Bulls Head, Walkden
Salem.............................Krumbles, Macclesfield
Tapper Zukie/Cygnus.....Mayflower, Gorton
AdvertsFireplace ....Russell Club, Hulme
Fri 8th
Fast Cars/Departure/I-Beats
......................................Band On The Wall
Midnight Blue ....Commercial Hotel, Stalybridge
Sister Ray......................Mayflower, Gorton
Magic.............................Venue, Collyhurst
Scritti Politti/Distractions...Russell Club, Hulme
Sat 9th
Funny Plumbing ....Commercial Hotel, Stalybridge
Streetband......................Manchester Polytechnic
Rubinoos/Spider Mike King
......................................Manchester University
Japan/Hinkley's Heroes .Mayflower, Gorton
Doomed/Penetration .....Russell Club, Hulme
Sun 10th
Accelerators ....Bears Head, Macclesfield
Idiot Rouge ....Commercial Hotel, Stalybridge
Band of Joy/Wilful Damage
......................................Venue, Collyhurst
Mon 11th
Private Sector................Band On The Wall
Gags..............................Cavalcade, Didsbury
Tue 12th
John Doe ....Birch Hotel, Ashton-Under-
Lyne
Wed 13th
Boomtown Rats ....Apollo Theatre
Freshies.........................Birch Hotel, Ashton-Under-
Lyne
Tunes ....Phoenix
Smack............................Spread Eagle Hotel, Ashton-
Under-Lyne
Gags/Distractions/Nives.Squat Club
Thu 14th
Salem.............................Cavalcade, Didsbury
Reducers........................Kellys
Juggernaut ....Krumbles, Macclesfield
Smack............................Midland Hotel, Didsbury
Scratch..........................Trap, Glossop
Human League/Manicured Noise
......................................Russell Club, Hulme
Fri 15th
Trend ....Bears Head, Macclesfield

Smack............................Commercial Hotel, Stalybridge
Generation X (cancelled)
......................................Russell Club, Hulme
Killer/Things ....Stockport College
Brent Ford and the Nylons
......................................Venue, Collyhurst
Sat 16th
JG Spoils ....Commercial Hotel, Stalybridge
Smack............................Lancashire Vaults,Oldham
Magazine/Spherical Objects
......................................Russell Club, Hulme
Blazer Blazer..................Venue, Collyhurst
Sun 17th
Freshies.........................Bears Head, Macclesfield
Jobey.............................Commercial Hotel, Stalybridge
Smack............................Jules Verne, Eccles
Bishops/Trend...............Venue, Collyhurst
Mon 18th
China Street ....Band On The Wall
Messagana ....Russell Club, Hulme
Tue 19th
Spherical Objects/Grow Up/Not Sensibles
......................................Band On The Wall
City Limit ....Birch Hotel, Ashton-Under-
Lyne
Wed 20th
Any Trouble ....Birch Hotel, Ashton-Under-
Lyne
Thu 21st
Idiot Rouge ....Krumbles, Macclesfield
Undertones....................Russell Club, Hulme
Fri 22nd
Ego Trip ....Commercial Hotel, Stalybridge
Manicured Noise/Margox/Special Guests (Pete Shelley,
Steve Garvey, Karl Burns)
......................................Russell Club, Hulme
Orphan ....Bears Head, Macclesfield
Sat 23rd
Smack............................Bulls Head, Walkden
Liar ....Commercial Hotel, Stalybridge
Gatecrasher ....Lancashire, Oldham
Tue 26th
Reducers/Addicts ....Bus-In, Bolton
Wed 27th Smack ....Spread Eagle Hotel, Ashton
Thu 28th
Zanathus ....Krumbles, Macclesfield
999................................Russell Club, Hulme
Fri 29th
Smack............................Commercial Hotel, Stalybridge
Quartz ....Venue, Collyhurst
Sat 30th
Fall ....Venue, Collyhurst
Sun 31st
Smack............................Midland Hotel, Didsbury

Printed in Great Britain
by Amazon